An Ethical and Theological Appropriation of Heidegger's Critique of Modernity

Zohar Atkins

An Ethical and Theological Appropriation of Heidegger's Critique of Modernity

Unframing Existence

palgrave
macmillan

Zohar Atkins
The Shalom Hartman Institute
  of North America
New York, NY, USA

ISBN 978-3-030-07271-1   ISBN 978-3-319-96917-6   (eBook)
https://doi.org/10.1007/978-3-319-96917-6

© The Editor(s) (if applicable) and The Author(s), under exclusive license to Springer Nature Switzerland AG 2018
Softcover re-print of the Hardcover 1st edition 2018
This work is subject to copyright. All rights are solely and exclusively licensed by the Publisher, whether the whole or part of the material is concerned, specifically the rights of translation, reprinting, reuse of illustrations, recitation, broadcasting, reproduction on microfilms or in any other physical way, and transmission or information storage and retrieval, electronic adaptation, computer software, or by similar or dissimilar methodology now known or hereafter developed.
The use of general descriptive names, registered names, trademarks, service marks, etc. in this publication does not imply, even in the absence of a specific statement, that such names are exempt from the relevant protective laws and regulations and therefore free for general use.
The publisher, the authors and the editors are safe to assume that the advice and information in this book are believed to be true and accurate at the date of publication. Neither the publisher nor the authors or the editors give a warranty, express or implied, with respect to the material contained herein or for any errors or omissions that may have been made. The publisher remains neutral with regard to jurisdictional claims in published maps and institutional affiliations.

Cover image: Amelia Rothwell/EyeEm - Getty Images
Cover design: Ran Shauli

This Palgrave Macmillan imprint is published by the registered company Springer Nature Switzerland AG
The registered company address is: Gewerbestrasse 11, 6330 Cham, Switzerland

EPIGRAPH

All the new thinking is about loss.
In this it resembles all the old thinking.

Robert Hass, "Meditation at Lagunitas"

Lo alekha hamlacha ligmor,
v'lo atah ben chorin l'hibatel mimenah.

(It is not on you to finish the work,
Nor are you free to desist from it.)

Pirkei Avot 2:21

A widely travelled sophist asks Socrates: "Are you still here and still saying the same thing? You are making light of the matter." Socrates answers: "No, you sophists are making light of it because you are always saying what's new and the very latest [news]. You always say something different. To say the same thing is what's difficult. To say the same thing about the same thing is the most difficult."

Martin Heidegger, *Zollikon Seminars*

ACKNOWLEDGEMENTS

This book, like all things mortal, is a record of events that are at once contingent and destinal, quotidian and sublime, disconsolate and gracious. And, like all things that endure for a little while, its calling is to say "yes"—yes to the possibilities suggested in the word "redemption," and yes to a redemption whose meaning is essentially riven. To say "yes" from the rift of Being for the rift of Being is to affirm that "love is strong as death" (Song of Songs 8:6)—and to dwell, as only a human being can, in the unique and paradoxical jointure named by that "*as.*" But more than this, it is to work at bearing a world where the psalmist's words are felt to be true. Acknowledgements are owed to each and all—blessedly too many to name—who have made and continue to make the strength of love so palpable. This work is but a translation of what I have learned from sharing in your song and dance.

George Pattison met me in "the clearing" where textual questions opened into existential questions of faith and poetry. Tom Sheehan, Judith Wolfe, Johannes Zachhuber, Graham Ward, Pamela Sue Anderson, Stephen Mulhall, Stephen Ross, and Evan Parks, offered incisive and supportive feedback along the way. Michael Gottsegen introduced me to Heidegger and the concept of Dasein and set me on an awe-inspiring course of study. This book was made possible by the generosity of the Rhodes Trust.

CONTENTS

CHAPTER 1

Introduction

This book is a work of constructive theology. Its aim is not to say something that the historical person, Martin Heidegger, would agree with, but instead to reframe some of his concerns within an explicitly ethical and theological context. In doing so, however, I also seek to defend Heidegger's thought against the common charge that it privileges ontology *over and above* ethics and theology, showing instead that it is most charitably and fruitfully read as an injunction to conduct ethics and theology non-metaphysically.[1] Heidegger's project, I argue, constitutes not the death of ethics and theology, but an invitation to conduct them in a way that is appropriate to the unique, historically situated, problems of modernity.

---

[1] The most influential proponent of the view that Heidegger privileges ontology over ethics is his student, Emmanuel Levinas, who famously and polemically titled one of his books *Otherwise than Being*. See Levinas, *Otherwise than Being, Or Beyond Essence*, trans. Alphonso Lingis (Duquesne University Press, 1998). The most influential proponent of the view that Heidegger privileges ontology over theology is the Catholic theologian, Jean-Luc Marion. Marion argues that theology should concern itself not with Being, but with the "God without Being." Fascinatingly, although Marion is largely critical of Heidegger, he builds his argument on Heidegger's own claim that, "If I were to write a theology—to which I sometimes feel inclined—then the word *Being* would not occur in it. Faith does not need the thought of Being. When faith has recourse to this thought, it is no longer faith." Quoted in *God Without Being*, trans. Thomas A. Carlson (Chicago: University of Chicago Press, 1990), 61. For the original quotation, see Heidegger, GA 15, 436.

© The Author(s) 2018
Z. Atkins, *An Ethical and Theological Appropriation
of Heidegger's Critique of Modernity*,
https://doi.org/10.1007/978-3-319-96917-6_1

One of the primary challenges posed to modern human beings, Heidegger argues, and I agree with him, is an inability to regard the phenomenon of "truth" non-instrumentally. Another, related problem, is an inability to recognize mortality—and finitude more generally—as the condition for meaningfulness, rather than as a categorically bad thing. And a third, related problem, is a culturally enforced understanding of the human being as "the most important raw material" (*der wichtigste Rohstoff*).[2] These problems have far-reaching geopolitical, ecological, and interpersonal consequences. Yet while Heidegger was good on the diagnosis, his own prescriptions remain mostly opaque and digressive. Heidegger's reluctance to offer direct prescriptions, I argue, is connected to his belief that our obsession with measurable solutions is a *symptom* of a problem that we can only address once we have undergone a paradigm shift, or embarked on what he calls in his *Contributions to Philosophy* (1936–1938) "the other beginning" (*der andere Anfang*).[3] Another reason for Heidegger's reluctance derives from his belief that only a thinking that is embodied and enacted "in-the-world," and thus, that is not simply restricted to the cognitive or the theoretical domain, can adequately address these problems.

These caveats, however, needn't be the last word. Instead, they offer a starting point for a response that takes their diagnostic kernel seriously, yet also develops their prescriptive implications. To that end, this book seeks to argue, where Heidegger himself did not, that listening and gratitude are core ways that we can authentically respond to the perils of modernity. Since these postures enact the very non-instrumental relationship to truth that Heidegger advocates, since they reveal finitude as a positive condition of meaningfulness, and since they bring to light the being of the human being in non-subjectivist and non-objectivist terms, they constitute nodes through which genuine ontological transformation can occur.[4]

---

[2] Heidegger, "Overcoming Metaphysics," in *The End of Philosophy*, trans. Joan Stambaugh (New York: Harper & Row, 1973), 104; GA 7, 91.

[3] Heidegger, GA 65, 171, 176–186, 205.

[4] The reader should note that my book follows the convention in Heidegger scholarship of using the same word "truth" (*Wahrheit*) to refer to something that, in fact, can be understood, according to Heidegger, in three distinct, yet interrelated ways. Roughly, these are (1) truth in the sense of correctness (or, in other words, propositional truth as defined by Aquinas as the "adequation of intellect and thing") (2) truth in the sense of intelligibility, meaningfulness, or fittingness when used to describe things, as in "it was a true hammer" and (3) truth in the sense of openness, unconcealdness, or

My argument is organized integumentally around one claim, namely, that ontology is not simply a cognitive or philosophical project, but an existential one. Of course, there is one sense in which "ontology" is a narrow, technical term denoting the thematic study of what "Being" means. And in this sense, ontology can be thought of as a philosophical sub-discipline that exists alongside other sub-disciplines such as "ethics," "logic," and "epistemology." Yet, there is another sense, and this is the sense emphasized by Heidegger in *Being and Time*, in which "ontology" denotes not a branch of philosophy, but a basic feature of the kind of being which we ourselves are, namely, "Dasein." On this definition, ontology simply means "to let Being be manifest," a claim that Heidegger sharpens when he writes, "*[o]ntology is only possible as phenomenology.*"[5] "Phenomenology," in turn, means, for Heidegger, "*apophainesthai to phenomena*—to let what shows itself be seen from itself, just as it shows itself from itself."[6] Understood as phenomenology, ontology therefore means: to let *beings* be manifest in their *being*. Heidegger further argues that phenomenology is not a disengaged study of phenomena, but an interpretative affair in which we ourselves are always implicated. As he writes, "phenomenology…is *hermeneutics* in the original signification of that word, which designates the work of interpretation."[7] Thus, ontology, phenomenology, and hermeneutics belong together, and they belong together because we ourselves are beings for whom our own Being is an issue. As Heidegger writes, "Da-sein is a being that does not simply occur among other beings. Rather it is ontically distinguished by the fact that in its being this being is concerned *about* its very being."[8] Whenever we interpret a situation, we do so by letting some aspect of it come into existential focus (while covering up other aspects of it). Thus, ontology (understood as existential, hermeneutical phenomenology) is something that, qua existing, we are "always already" doing in every moment. Engaging in ontology, therefore, does

---

disclosedness (*Erschlossenheit*) when used to refer to "Being" or the clearing. When I write of Heidegger's critique of the instrumental conception of truth, I am referring specifically to his critique of our tendency to forget or repress this third meaning of truth, that is, truth as the unconcealment of Being or the clearing as such.

[5] SZ, 35/ BT, 31.

[6] SZ, 34/ BT, 30.

[7] SZ, 37/ BT, 33.

[8] SZ, 12/ BT, 10.

not simply involve asking theoretical or descriptive questions about what the word "Being" signifies, but much more critically, coming to an embodied understanding of the phenomenon of Being as it is phenomenologically and hermeneutically filtered through and enacted concretely in our own "being-in-the-world" in each and every moment.

Thus, while it so happens that the man, Martin Heidegger, engaged in ontology by writing lots of books about "Being," one needn't be a professional philosopher or even someone who has heard of the word "ontology" to be engaged in ontology in a more holistic sense. Consequently, we can simply think of ontology as "care for Being"— Heidegger writes that "the being of Da-asein is care"—where care is meant to denote both something we can't but do (we are beings whose being is defined by care, according to Heidegger) and as a challenge that perpetually confronts us, and in the face of which our responses must always remain incomplete and questionable.[9] What this book seeks to examine are the repercussions of understanding ontology in this expansive way.[10] In the same way that my book makes an argument

---

[9] SZ, 284/ BT, 262.

[10] Read in an expansive way, "ontology," as I will be using it, refers not simply to the thematic study of "Being," or to the transcendental project of seeking to ground the ontic sciences in some kind of Aristotelian "first philosophy"—projects that Heidegger later abandons in favor of what he calls "metontology." (Heidegger describes "metontology" as an overturning [*Umschlag, metabolé*] of ontology that nevertheless "resides in the essence of ontology." See *The Metaphysical Foundations of Logic*, trans. Michael Heim (Bloomington: Indiana University Press, 1984), 157; GA 199–200). Instead, "ontology," as I seek to use the term, refers to the ever-imperfect practice of seeking to acknowledge and embrace our condition as, in Heidegger's words, "thrown projection" (*Geworfene Entwurf*). Read this way, ontology can be defined as the art of coming to understand—not just mentally, but holistically—that "Being" (meaningfulness) is not a thing or a property belonging to things, but is instead a field in which things can disclose themselves to us as meaningful. Ontology means learning to recognize this field as something to which we ourselves intimately belong, both because we are always already immersed in it and cannot unchoose it—it is the condition of our own capacity to care, that is, to take something *as* something—and because the texture of this field depends upon how we respond to it and bear ourselves within it. On the one hand, this broad conception of ontology seeks to resist the early Heidegger's Husserl-inflected definition of it as a "fundamental" discourse. On the other hand, however, it is in keeping with Heidegger's own later critique of metaphysics as "onto-theological," i.e., as an enterprise that is misguidedly directed by the desire to ground and secure a philosophical account of what things *are*. The question then becomes why I use the word "ontology" at all, a term that the later Heidegger comes to criticize. One reason is that I want to draw attention to the *continuity* between the early

for an expansive understanding of ontology, it also shows that the word "Being" is ultimately not a word that we should worry about defining propositionally. Instead, it is best encountered as a placeholder for that which language cannot but misspeak, a liturgical term that, if turned into a piece of philosophical jargon, risks becoming an instrument of metaphysics, rather than a poetic means toward resisting it. This book sticks to the word "Being" as a matter of convention, convenience, and communicative desire, even as it recognizes that for Heidegger, the term Being became woefully inadequate. At different stages in his development, Heidegger turns away from "Being," writing it as Beyng (*Seyn*) and ~~Being (*Sein*)~~. He also claims that Being has meant different things at different times to different cultures. For instance, for the ancient Greeks, their word for Being was *physis*.

It is a sign of the richness of Heidegger's thought that his terminology continued to evolve throughout his career, and that he strove for his language to be original so that it would open up a philosophical experience for himself and for the reader, rather than rest in the certainty of fixed definitions and propositional coherence. Yet the seeming chaos of Heidegger's vast language—a composite of neologisms (new words) and paleonymies (the repurposing of old words)—also presents many stumbling blocks and red herrings for readers, focusing their attention and labor on deciphering his terms and seeking a unified apparatus which might help them make sense of his "Heideggerese." Unfortunately, such

Heideggerian project of "fundamental ontology" and the later Heidegger's critique of metaphysics. Another is that I do not want to set up a false dichotomy between thematic, philosophical discourse (ontology as method of enquiry) and existence (ontology as living in a state of openness, reflexivity, and embodied care), but seek to show how these can reinforce and enrich each other. A refusal to separate life and philosophy, and instead a desire to insist that the stakes of philosophy are existential—just as the stakes of life are philosophical—is thus a position I draw from Heidegger, even as it also offers a basis for going beyond him. A third reason for preferring the word "ontology" to Heidegger's awkward, and highly technical "metontology" concerns audience. "Ontology" is already an austere, and potentially intimidating term. "Metontology" even more so. Thus, although there are certain risks in appropriating a term that Heidegger came to have reservations about, these risks are off-set by the possibility they grant to non-Heidegger-specialist readers of appreciating the importance of "thinking Being" (*Seinsdenken*). Even if "Being" is not ultimately what Heidegger's thought is about—as Thomas Shehan compellingly argues—coming to terms with the enigma so named is a necessary path for understanding, and coming to embody, that which is, in the words of Heidegger's critics, "beyond Being," and what Heidegger himself calls "the clearing" (*die Lichtung*) and "the Event" (*das Ereignis*).

attempts can have one of two negative consequences: either they entrap the reader in Heidegger's idiosyncratic terminology, making Heidegger's insights communicable only to those initiates willing to share in Heidegger's cult-like language, or else they lead the reader down the unnecessary task of translating Heidegger's terms into concepts that would be considered acceptable by the standards of analytic philosophy. Both approaches miss the poetic, existential heart of Heidegger's project; the former fall into the trap of making Heideggerian philosophy a form of "specialized" knowledge, while the latter fall into the trap of divesting the form of Heidegger's thought from its content.

This book offers a middle way, holding onto core Heideggerian terms, like ontology, phenomenology, Dasein, and Being (terms admittedly distinctive of the so-called early Heidegger) while also showing that the force and import of these poetic terms need not be constrained by Heidegger's own strictures about them. We can elucidate and follow Heidegger's arguments for the importance of ontology and the question of Being, even as we part company with his own specifications about how such a question should be asked.

Each chapter attempts to develop the implications of ontology, broadly understood, within and for a particular field. This introductory chapter looks at "metaphysics." Chapter 2 looks at "ethics." Chapter 3 looks at "history" and "poetry." Chapter 4 looks at "thinking." Chapter 5 looks at the everyday phenomenon of "being needed." And Chapter 6 looks at "gratitude." Each chapter seeks to expand our understanding of ontology's meaning and stakes, so that by the end, ontology simply proves to be a name for a way of being that is sensitive to the entrenched challenges of existence (as simultaneously personal, interpersonal, political, economic, ecological, etc.), yet which is nevertheless affirmative of our unique responsibility to work through these challenges.

Ontology matters, this book argues, because all of our questions— from the most exalted and abstract ("What is justice?" "What is good?") to the most everyday and personal ("How will I pay the bills this month?" "Where should I send my children to school?")—are questions that implicitly engage our understanding of what it means for us and others *to be*. And while ontology cannot give universal prescriptions or solutions to the many questions that confront us, it can magnify our ability to engage these questions *as questions of being*. In so doing, it offers us a helpful way to reframe and come to terms with the diverse range of questions that confront us as beings whose being is both singular and social, perplexing and familiar, historical and futural.

While I might have developed a similar argument from a more explicitly Christian perspective, by way of Bultmann, Tillich, or Rahner (who were deeply influenced by Heidegger), or from an explicitly Jewish perspective by way of Buber, Rosenzweig, or Heschel (who were also influenced by Heidegger, though to a lesser degree), and thus might have avoided direct engagement with a thinker whose religious record is ambiguous and whose political record is disturbing, I believe that Heidegger's thought holds the greatest potential to yield an ethics that can speak ecumenically to both theists and non-theists. Likewise, while the critique of instrumental rationality is a hallmark of Frankfurt school thinkers such as Adorno, Horkheimer, Marcuse, and, more recently, Habermas (who were all influenced more or less directly by Heidegger), these thinkers fail to develop this critique in the direction of a thinking that can be both poetic and religious. In fact, despite Habermas's welcome claim that ethics is a fundamentally discursive and communicative enterprise, his project remains avowedly rationalistic. His "theory of communicative action"—in contrast to the religious and poetic ethics that I develop out of Heidegger's thinking—is committed to grounding ethical norms in an appeal to their universality, albeit a universality that is linguistically mediated.[11] Moreover, his contention that the goal of communication is "mutual understanding" seems either to miss or to denigrate the density of the unsayable—something to which Heidegger's thinking, by contrast, gives more credence.[12]

In short, this project seeks to highlight the places where faith and ontology *converge*, that is, to show that the practice of ontology ("care for Being") can be understood as a (potentially) devotional enterprise, even as the terms on which such devotion are conducted remain open to further refinement, definition, and debate within and between particular faith traditions. For whatever the differences between them, ontology

---

[11] See Jürgen Habermas, *The Theory of Communicative Action: Reason and the Rationalization of Society*, trans. Thomas McCarthy (Cambridge: Polity Press, 1991), 75–101, 305–319.

[12] Jürgen Habermas, *Moral Consciousness and Communicative Action*, trans. Christian Lenhardt and Shierry Weber Nicholsen (Cambridge: MIT Press, 1995), 163.

and faith intersect in at least four key ways. First, both offer a rebuttal of the Cartesian conception of selfhood as a self-standing ego, while still averring individual responsibility. Second, both reveal that the primary meaning of truth is not scientific fact, logical correctness, practical utility, or metaphysical certainty, but—as Heidegger puts it—"unconcealment"—i.e., a temporally and historically constituted play *between* the hidden and the revealed.[13] Third, both expose finitude as the positive condition of meaningfulness, rather than as an obstacle to it. And fourth, both reveal that our proximity to and distance from God or Being are not mutually exclusive, but dynamically entwined. Articulated within the tradition of Judaeo-Christian faith, these insights can take the form of a covenantal theology, according to which humanity is elected by God to be a partner with God in the ongoing project of caring for the world.[14] Articulated within the more ecumenical language of ontology, they can take the form of what might be called a "covenantal phenomenology," according to which Dasein, understood as openness-to-Being, is charged with the task of letting "the truth of Being" be manifest in-the-world. As Heidegger writes,

> Man is [...] "thrown" from Being itself into the truth of Being, so that ek-sisting in this fashion he might guard the truth of Being, in order that beings might appear in the light of Being as the beings they are [...] Man is the shepherd of Being.[15]

My interpretation of ontology as a kind of non-dogmatic posture of faith is consistent with a number of passages in Heidegger's thought. First, Heidegger protests that reading his project either as metaphysically atheistic or as metaphysically theistic forces it into categories that his thought seeks to suspend:

> With the existential determination of the essence of man, therefore, nothing is decided about the "existence of god" or his "nonbeing," no more than about the possibility or impossibility of gods. Thus, it is not only rash

---

[13] SZ, 219/ BT, 202.

[14] See, for example, Abraham Joshua Heschel, *God in Search of Man: A Philosophy of Judaism* (New York: JPS, 1959).

[15] "Letter on Humanism," in *Basic Writings*, ed. and trans. David Farrell Krell (New York: HarperCollins, 1993), 234.

but also an error in procedure to maintain that the interpretation of the essence of man from the relation of his essence to the truth of Being is atheism.[16]

Second, Heidegger suggests that his refusal to privilege the ontic faith claims of a positive theological tradition as the starting point for his thinking might be more charitably read as a religious intervention against what he calls the "godlessness" of more traditional religious believers and theologians:

> It is preferable to accept the cheap accusation of atheism, which, when intended ontically, is completely justified. But might not the ostensibly ontic faith in God be fundamentally godless (*im Grunde Gottlosigkeit*)? And the genuine metaphysician more religious than the usual believers, "church" members, or even the "theologians" of each confession?[17]

Similarly, Heidegger proclaims that a "god-less thinking," which is not confined by the Western philosophical conception of God as *causa sui* [cause of itself] may be "closer to the divine god" than that thinking which posits God's existence in advance, yet treats God merely as a concept to be correctly represented.[18] The reason for this, Heidegger intimates, is that the God posited by philosophers is not a God to whom one could "pray," "bring sacrifices," "play music," "dance," or before whom one could "fall on [one's] knees in awe."[19] Heidegger makes a similar point in "The Question Concerning Technology," when he warns that

> [W]here everything that presences exhibits itself in the light of a cause-effect coherence, even God can, for representational thinking, lose all that is exalted and holy, the mysteriousness of his distance. In the light of causality, God can sink to the level of a cause, of a *causa efficiens*. He then

[16] Ibid., 223.

[17] GA 16, 211n3 (translation mine).

[18] *Identity and Difference*, trans. Joan Stambaugh (Chicago: University of Chicago Press, 2002), 72. On Heidegger's complex relationship to theology, see Lawrence Paul Hemming, *Heidegger's Atheism: The Refusal of a Theological Voice* (Notre Dame: Notre Dame University Press, 2002); and Ben Vedder, *Heidegger's Philosophy of Religion: From God to the Gods* (Pittsburgh: Duquesne University Press, 2006).

[19] *Identity and Difference*, 72.

becomes, even in theology, the god of the philosophers, namely of those who define the unconcealed and the concealed in terms of causality, of making, without ever considering the essential origin of this causality [unconcealment].[20]

Heidegger's worry in this passage seems to be that our capacity to encounter God is undermined by our desire to fit our understanding of "him" to a particular, metaphysical worldview. In particular, what is lost, Heidegger claims, is "the mysteriousness of his distance." These lines of criticism, directed primarily at Thomistic metaphysics—the philosophical tradition in which Heidegger was schooled from a young age—can also be found in Heidegger's introduction to *Being and Time*:

> Theology is slowly beginning to understand again Luther's insight that its system of dogma rests on a "foundation" that does not stem from a questioning in which faith is primary and whose conceptual apparatus is not only insufficient for the range of problems in theology but rather covers them up and distorts them.[21]

Here, what Heidegger critiques is not theology as such, but rather its foundationalist assumptions and aspirations, and its "conceptual apparatus," which he suggests obstruct the kind of questioning one would pursue if one were guided by "faith." Thus, we can conclude that while Heidegger is a critic of rationalist theology, he needn't be read as an anti-religious thinker.[22] At the same time, it would be a mistake to read Heidegger's critique of rationalism as a simple reversion to fideism. In

---

[20] "The Question Concerning Technology," in *The Question Concerning Technology and Other Essays*, trans. William Lovitt (New York: 1977, Harper & Row), 3–35, 26.

[21] SZ, 10/ BT, 8.

[22] Elliot Wolfson makes a similar argument through a close, analytic reading of the later Heidegger's term "the last God." See Elliot R. Wolfson, "*Gottwesen* and the De-Divinization of the Last God: Heidegger's Meditation on the Strange and Incalculable," in *Heidegger's Black Notebooks and the Future of Theology*, ed. Marten Björk and Jane Svenungsson (New York: Palgrave, 2017), 211–255. I agree with Wolfson that "the last God" does not refer to a transcendent entity, but instead, counter-intuitively, to the impossibility of theological or philosophical closure, a permanent deferral of our ability to fix the referent of the divine. My work departs from his, however, in that it seeks to offer a poetic response to and positive appropriation of Heidegger's thought, rather than a systematic exposition of its opaque terminology.

Being and Time, Heidegger states his intention to steer a middle path between both of these extremes:

> Existentially and ontologically there is not the slightest justification for minimizing the "evidence" of attunement by measuring it against the apodictic certainty of the theoretical cognition of something merely objectively present. But *the* falsification of the phenomena, which banishes them to the sanctuary of the irrational, is no better. Irrationalism, as the counterpart [counterplay, *Gegenspiel*] of rationalism, talks about the things to which rationalism is blind, but only with a squint.[23]

Here, Heidegger argues that rationalism and irrationalism are two sides of the same metaphysical coin. Rationalism fails to acknowledge the importance of affect or attunement [*Befindlichkeit*] in how we come to know things, but irrationalism fails to acknowledge that what our attunements disclose is always something phenomenal, that is, apparent and meaningful within a meaning-giving context. In short, both rationalism and irrationalism overlook the extent to which discourse is interpretive, and as such, animated by a tension between manifestation and hiddenness.

Another reason Heidegger criticizes both fideism and rationalism is his contention that regardless of their relative and practical coherence, none of the narratives they offer, can make Dasein's being any less mysterious:

> Even when Da-sein is "sure" of its "whither" in faith or thinks it knows about its whence in rational enlightenment, all of this makes no difference in the face of the phenomenal fact that mood brings Da-sein before the that of its there, which stares at it with the inexorability [lit. relentlessness, *unerbittlicher*] of an enigma.[24]

As is evident from this passage, Heidegger's critique of "[creedal] faith" and "rational enlightenment" is not that they are wrong, but that, to the extent that they offer surety, they lead Dasein down a path of self-denial, away from the abyssal source of its wonder, what Heidegger sometimes calls "the nothing" (*das Nichts*), because it is quite literally, *no thing*. In "What Is Metaphysics?" Heidegger explains:

[23]SZ, 136/ BT, 128.
[24]SZ, 128/ BT, 135.

Only on the ground of wonder—the revelation of the nothing—does the "why?" loom before us. Only because the "why" is possible as such can we inquire into grounds, and ground them. Only because we can inquire and ground is the destiny of our existence placed in the hands of the researcher.[25]

As such, our research can only be a response to, never, a substitute for, our encounter with no-thing-ess, which is why Heidegger can say, "The question of the nothing puts us, the questioners, in question."[26]

Confronting the originary no-thingness that motivates our most basic questions, however, should not lead us to discard our inherited theological and philosophical narratives and become "nihilists." Instead, I will show, it should help us engage our inheritance and the inheritance of others hermeneutically, understanding that while no discourse can get around or behind the essential mystery of our being here, our attempts to reckon with the mystery of being are always illuminating and worthwhile.

Thus, this book seeks to affirm a positive role for theology, while at the same time restricting the ambit of its concern to our being-in-the-world, and in particular to our being-in-the-world as it is inflected by the legacy of modern metaphysics. While my attempt to speak across the "believer"/"non-believer" divide risks alienating both camps, my hope is that the religious ethics I articulate can contribute to redrawing the terms of this divide *away from* debates about *what* beliefs are factually correct or morally valid *towards* a debate about *how* we might aspire to embody and enact our beliefs as historically situated mortals.[27] My

---

[25] "What Is Metaphysics?," in *Basic Writings*, 109, 89–111.

[26] Ibid.

[27] While I affirm the gravity of the differences in stance between the believer and non-believer, I also contend that Heidegger's thought is relevant and supplemental to both positions. Heidegger himself is not so easily pinned down to one side of this divide. On the one hand, he is a great critic of religious fundamentalism, in the school of Nietzsche, and for that matter, many a philosopher; but, like Nietzsche, his arguments against thoughtlessness are also easily accommodated by, if not outright welcomed by, many religious thinkers. Moreover, Heidegger's criticisms of religious thought are not restricted to "believers." He is often and equally critical of secular pieties, claiming overtly, that even atheism is premised on a certain metaphysics. The antagonism between Heidegger's philosophical orientation and that of the fundamentalist believer is real, but is also no more pronounced than the

contention is that, despite the crucial differences between those who profess belief in a personal, theistic God and those who profess disbelief in such a God, there is an important conversation to be had about what it means to treat the world—understood not objectively as "things out there" or subjectively as "things in here," but non-dualistically and phenomenologically as the "clearing" wherein things "come to presence"—as a phenomenon worthy of awe and love. Such a conversation is warranted, moreover, by the fact that, as this book will show, the challenges of modernity cannot simply be remedied by substituting one set of beliefs for another, but instead require a more holistic transformation of our being. Such a transformation may be facilitated by—or obstructed by—the adoption of certain beliefs, but unless our dispositions and practices—and the conditions that engender our dispositions and practices—also change, the challenges of modernity will continue to run their course. As Heidegger argues in his essay "The Age of the World Picture," the decisive question for modern human beings is not *which* picture of the world they should hold, but whether it is possible for them to regard the world as something other than a thing that can be pictorially represented. As Heidegger writes,

> [The phrase] world picture, when understood essentially, does not mean a picture of the world but the world conceived and grasped as a picture. What is, in its entirety, is now taken in such a way that it first is in being and only is in being to the extent that it is set up by man, who represents and sets forth.[28]

In other words, even if our picture of the world happened to be correct or effective—however, we might define these terms—it would still be problematic, since it would be premised on reducing the world to

---

perennial antagonism between philosophy and theology. If Maimonides, a leading Jewish thinker, could read the Torah as an Aristotelian in the thirteenth century, who is to say he couldn't have read it as a Heideggerian in the twentieth century, assuming he believed Heidegger's philosophy to be the most compelling? My point in asking such a hypothetical question is to highlight that the challenges of speaking across the believer/non-believer divide are not unique to Heidegger, but emerge out of more fundamental questions concerning the definition and tasks of philosophy and faith.

[28] Heidegger, "The Age of the World Picture," in *The Question Concerning Technology*, 129, 115–154.

an object-sphere for human manipulation. The deeper question, then, according to Heidegger, is whether and how we in the modern age might encounter the world according to a different understanding.

In his essay "The Turning," Heidegger brings a similar set of concerns to bear on the problematic of theology, claiming that the central religious question for modern times is not whether one can believe in or experience God, but on what *terms* and *assumptions* one can do so. As Heidegger writes, albeit more opaquely,

> Whether the god lives or remains dead is not decided by the religiosity of men and even less by the theological aspirations of philosophy and natural science. Whether or not God is God comes disclosingly to pass from out of and within the constellation of Being.[29]

As I interpret this passage, Heidegger is saying something along the lines of, "The possibility or impossibility of living our lives with a sense that transcendence makes a binding claim on us is not significantly dependent upon how sincerely we, either as individuals or local communities, believe or disbelieve in God's existence, and is even less dependent upon whether philosophical or scientific discourse can offer good arguments in favor of God's existence or non-existence. Rather, the deciding factor in determining whether transcendence, qua transcendence, can be experienced as making binding claims on us is if it comes to pass independently of our own ego-centric efforts. (Otherwise, transcendence would cease to be transcendence, and would simply be a way of dressing up our own subjective will)". Another more Kuhnian (rather than Barthian) way to state this point would be to say that the possibility of living a genuinely religious life is not determined by whether one takes "a leap of faith" or reasons one's way to God's existence, but is instead determined by whether one lives in an age in which the historically reigning paradigm grants the claims of transcendence ontological legitimacy.

This last point is one that Heidegger sharpens, when he writes, "The loss of the gods [*Entgötterung*] is so far from excluding religiosity that rather only through that loss does the relation to the gods change into mere 'religious experience' (*Erlebnis*)."[30] With this formulation, Heidegger is making two counter-intuitive points. The first is that

---

[29] "The Turning," in *The Question Concerning Technology*, 49, 36–49.

[30] "The Age of the World Picture," 117.

what he calls "the loss of the gods," and what I am more directly calling the loss of a cultural paradigm that lets us take claims about transcendence seriously, is an issue that concerns not *whether* people can identify as religious, but *how* the terms of their religious identity are constructed. The second is that modern appeals to "religious experience"—with their subjectivist connotations of privacy and interiority—do not occur *in spite of* "the loss of the gods," but *because* of it. As Heidegger's use of the pejorative "mere" suggests, "religious experience" is a term that belongs to an age in which transcendence can only be taken seriously as an instrumental good, that is, as something to be consumed by subjects, and legitimated as a means to the advancement of their own ends. The upshot of this claim is that the meaning and stakes of what it means to be religious in the modern world are not primarily epistemic but ontological. One of Heidegger's sharpest claims to this effect can be found in his essay "The Word of Nietzsche: 'God Is Dead'":

> Unbelief in the sense of a falling away from the Christian doctrine of faith is [...] never the essence and the ground, but always only a consequence of nihilism; for it could be that Christendom itself represents one consequence and bodying-forth of nihilism.[31]

In suggesting that lack of belief is a symptom of "nihilism," rather than its cause, Heidegger suggests that the most pressing question for contemporary human beings is not whether we can or should believe in God, but whether we can relate to anything (be it God, ourselves, another person, or our local environment) in a way that doesn't degrade it by turning it into an object whose value depends simply on our own subjective esteem for it. As Heidegger explains in a commentary on Nietzsche, "The ultimate blow in the killing of god is perpetrated by metaphysics, which, as the metaphysics of the will to power, accomplishes thinking in the sense of value-thinking."[32]

Heidegger's claim—that the stakes of modernity are primarily ontological, and not simply epistemic—yields two interrelated demands, I am arguing, for the disciplines of ethics and theology. The first is that they must address themselves primarily to human *being*, and not simply

---

[31] "The Word of Nietzsche: 'God Is Dead,'" in *The Question Concerning Technology*, 65, 53–112.

[32] Ibid., 107–108.

to human *faith* or *reason*, which are aspects of human being, but not exhaustive of it. And the second is that they must seek to be existentially transformative, and not simply correct. In this conclusion, I am in strong agreement with the theologian Merold Westphal, who—also coming out of Heidegger—writes, "The theological project betrays itself when it abstracts the project of getting it right from the task of becoming righteous."[33]

It is with sensitivity to these challenges that I have taken up Heidegger's thought, and in response to which I believe a post-denominational, post-a/theistic theology is a legitimate, and even much needed, response. Drawing on Heidegger's claim that "logos," more than simply meaning "account," "statement," "study," or "science" means "showing," "dis-closing," "letting-appear," and "gathering," my book will seek to advance a model of doing "theo-logy" that redistributes our attention from debating what "God" *is*, toward thinking about what it might mean to let God "come to presence."[34] Yet since, as Heidegger shows, presence and absence, revelation and concealment, manifestation and hiddenness, and nearness and farness, belong together, part of what it will mean to do theo-logy, I will also be arguing, is to hold open a space where both of these dimensions can be affirmed.

To the extent that this book is deemed persuasive, it will show that Heidegger's ambivalence about theology and ethics allows for the

[33] Merold Westphal, *Overcoming Onto-Theology: Towards a Postmodern Christian Faith* (New York: Fordham University Press, 2001), 299.

[34] As Heidegger writes, "*Logos* means, much more originally than 'to speak': *to let* presence [*Anwesen* lassen.]" *Four Seminars*, trans. Andrew Mitchell and François Raffoul (Bloomington: Indiana University Press, 2003), 39; GA 15, 70–71. In *Being and Time*, Heidegger writes, "*logos* as speech really means *deloun*, to make manifest 'what is being talked about' in speech...*Logos* lets something be seen (*phainesthai*), namely what is being talked about, and indeed *for* the speaker (who serves as the medium) or for those who speak with each other." SZ, 32/ BT, 28. Finally, in his 1944 seminar on Heraclitus, Heidegger writes, "The common meaning of *legein* and *logos*—in the sense of statement [*Aussage*], saying [*Sagen*], speech [*Rede*], word [*Wort*], and word-meaning [*Wortsinn*]—does not bring the primordial essence of *logos* to manifestation [*nicht das ursprüngliche Wesen des logos zum Erscheinen bringt*]...[T]he common meaning of *logos* as speech [*Rede*] and statement [*Aussage*] is not appropriate [*nicht geeignet*] for making the...essence of *logos* as harvesting and gathering [*Lesen und Versammlung*] accessible [*zugänglich*] and intelligible [*verstehbar*]." GA 55, 270 (translation mine). Note that Heidegger is here playing up a double-meaning of *Lesen* as both "reading" (in the ordinary sense) and "harvesting" (in the archaic sense).

development of a deeply religious and ethical posture, one that strives to acknowledge both the phenomenological reality of destitution and the phenomenological possibility of grace. This may not be the only way to interpolate Heidegger's project, but it is strongly supported by his remarks in "A Letter to a Young Student" (1950), where Heidegger writes,

> The default of God and the divinities is absence. [*Der Fehl Gott und des Göttlichen ist Abwesenheit*]. But absence is not nothing [*Allein Abwesenheit ist nicht nichts*]; rather it is precisely the presence [*Anwesenheit*], which must first be appropriated, of the hidden fullness [*verborgenen Fülle*] and wealth of what has been and what, thus gathered, is presencing, of the divine in the world of the Greeks, in prophetic Judaism, in the preaching of Jesus. This no-longer is in itself a not-yet of the veiled arrival of its inexhaustible nature. Since Being is never the merely precisely actual, to guard Being can never be equated with the task of a guard who protects from burglars a treasure stored in a building. Guardianship of Being is not fixated upon something existent.[35]

There are three points I want to draw out from this passage. The first is that Heidegger does not seem to be too concerned with drawing strong distinctions between the insights of ancient Greece, prophetic Judaism, and Christianity. Instead, he suggests that all three traditions hold a wealth of possibilities that it would behoove anyone in the modern West to appropriate.[36] We can only add, where Heidegger here did not, that other ancient traditions might likewise be regarded in this way. The second is Heidegger's emphasis that the truth of a tradition is indexed to the future and not simply to the present. Potentiality, not actuality, is what makes a tradition great. Extending Heidegger's claim, we can thus say that the primary question for believers and non-believers should not be "Does God, or do gods, exist?"—since this presumes a conception of God that ties "him" to actuality—but "How can we be

---

[35] Heidegger, "The Thing," *Poetry, Language, and Thought*, trans. Albert Hofstadter (New York: Harper & Row, 1971), 182; GA 7, 185.

[36] This was also the view of Heidegger's contemporary, the Jewish theologian, Franz Rosenzweig, who argues that paganism, Christianity, and Judaism, each bear profound phenomenological insight into the meaning of "God," "Man," and "World." See Rosenzweig, *The Star of Redemption*, trans. William W. Hallo (New York: Holt Rhineheart & Winston, 1970).

guardians of a world in which the divinity that was once palpable for our ancestors might again be palpable (albeit in a different way) for our descendents?"[37] The third point to be emphasized in this passage is that Heidegger's examples—"the world of the Greeks," "prophetic Judaism," and "the preaching of Jesus"—underscore that divine presence is crucially dependent upon us, even if it remains non-identical to us. What Heidegger stresses as the import of Christianity in this passage is Jesus's teaching—his worldly wisdom—and not his metaphysical status as the son of God. Likewise, what Heidegger stresses as the import of Judaism is not the Exodus from Egypt or the entering of the Israelites into the promised Land—events in which God acts "with a mighty hand and an outstretched arm"—but rather the human side of the covenant, the attempts of human beings to serve as God's translators in the everyday world. Likewise, for Heidegger, it is "*the world* of the Greeks" that matters, and not what gods they believed in, or whether these gods can be said, by scientific standards, to exist. When we emphasize these points, we come to see that for all the crucial doctrinal differences between Christian theology, Jewish theology, and Greek theology—as well as Buddhist, Hindu, Taoist, and Islamic theology—common to all of these traditions is the difficult task of living out these theologies. As a diagnosis of the particular challenges that modernity poses to such a task, Heidegger's thought, I contend, holds ecumenical relevance.

Non-confessional Theology

As should now be clear, the theological intention of this book is not confessional. Instead of aspiring to be a work of specifically Jewish or Christian theology, it seeks to offer more general reflections on what it means to speak appropriately about God. This move will no doubt elicit objection from many, including, most recently, the proponents of "radical orthodoxy," who argue that such reflections would be impossible without the explicit support and motivation of a positive theological tradition.[38] Yet there are just as many thinkers—as diverse as Hegel (dialectical rationalism), Buber (dialogical mysticism), Mark Taylor

---

[37] For an excellent theological work on the meaning of God as possibility, see Richard Kearney, *The God Who May Be: A Hermeneutics of Religion* (Bloomington: Indiana University Press, 2001).

[38] See, for instance, John Milbank, "The End of Dialogue," in *The Future of Love: Essays in Political Theology* (London: SCM Press, 2009).

(deconstruction), and Elizabeth Schüssler Fiorenza (feminist "the*logy")—who reject this argument.[39]

Among the more compelling articulations of this approach is Franz Rosenzweig's suggestion—inspired by his Kabbalistic predecessors—that the content of divine revelation is simply revelation itself, and that the Torah in its written and transmitted form simply constitutes a human attempt to give practical and logistical shape to a moment of unspeakable density. As Rosenzweig writes,

> [R]evelation is certainly not Law-giving. It is only this: Revelation. The primary content of revelation is revelation itself. "He came down" [on Sinai]—this already concludes the revelation; "He spoke" is the beginning of interpretation, and certainly "I am."[40]

Here, Rosenzweig suggests that Scripture can only be a *commentary* on the event of revelation, and this to such a radical extent that even imputing the sentence—"I am"—to God constitutes a fundamentally interpretive gesture. This is not to discount Scripture or tradition as "merely" commentary, but to affirm that, even within the terms of a positive theological tradition such as Judaism, one can come to the conclusion that the truth of revelation is essentially language-resistant, and that even the word "God" can constitute a decisively human attempt to grapple with the unsayable. While Rosenzweig's account is contentious, it at least offers an alternative to radical orthodoxy's claim that we must choose *between* "faith" and "nihilism."[41] For on Rosenzweig's view, the essence

---

[39] For these respective strategies see Hegel, *Lectures on the Philosophy of Religion: Volume 1*, trans. R.F. Brown, P.C. Hodgson, and J.M. Stewart (Berkeley: University of California Press, 1984); Martin Buber, *I and Thou*, trans. Ronald Gregor Smith (New York: Schocken, 1958); Mark C. Taylor, *Erring: A Post-modern A/Theology* (Chicago: University of Chicago Press, 1987); and Elisabeth Schüssler Fiorenza, "G*d—The Many-Named—Without Place or Proper Name," in *Beyond Transcendence*, ed. John D. Caputo and Michael Scanlon (Bloomington: Indiana University Press, 2007), 109–128. For a compelling approach similar to Taylor's, yet one that calls itself "a hermeneutics of the desire for God," see John D. Caputo, *The Weakness of God: A Theology of the Event* (Bloomington: Indiana University Press, 2006), 291, 283–299.

[40] Rosenzweig, "Revelation and Law," in *On Jewish Learning*, ed. Nachum Glatzer (Madison: University of Wisconsin Press, 2002), 118.

[41] The opposition between "faith" or "theology" and "nihilism" seems to be a hallmark of radical orthodox theology. This is strikingly evident in the Catholic theologian Lawrence Paul Hemming's claim that "Nihilism is that situation from out of which I am called to redemption, it is the experience of the world apart from God." See Hemming, "Nihilism:

of faith is presented precisely as a capacity to embrace and appreciate the fundamental emptiness of revelation.[42]

None of this, of course, *settles* the initial question of whether it is possible to conduct theology non-confessionally. But this is no shortcoming of my book. Rather, it speaks to a more general methodological impasse between those who think theology should aspire to *confirm* what is given first through a particular faith tradition and those who think theology should aspire to *prepare* its readers only for the *possibility* of living faithfully. For at issue in this debate is whether philosophy itself can say anything meaningful independent of the epistemological privileges granted by a particular divine revelation. For those who believe that only faith in a Judaeo-Christian God can liberate philosophy from its sinful prejudices no argument to the contrary will be convincing. Just as, likewise, there is little one can persuasively say to those who are convinced that ideas are little more than the vestiges of oppression and power-struggles. In both cases, a posture of suspicion ensures its own invincibility in advance, while rejecting out of hand any argument that does not submit to its terms. Yet even if this approach were justified on the basis of its correctness, it risks forfeiting the alethic possibilities that can only emerge through dialogue with "the other."

Heidegger and the Grounds of Redemption," in *Radical Orthodoxy: A New Theology*, ed. John Milbank, Catherine Pickstock, and Graham Ward (London: Routledge, 1999). Or as John Milbank puts it even more directly, "[O]nly Christian theology now offers a discourse able to position and overcome nihilism itself. This is why it is so important to reassert [Christian] theology as a master discourse; [Christian] theology, alone, remains the discourse of non-mastery." See John Milbank, *Theology and Social Theory: Beyond Secular Reason*, 2nd ed. (Oxford: Blackwell, 2006), 6.

[42] Rosenzweig articulates this point in *The Star of Redemption* even more forcefully when he writes, "Revelation climaxes in unfulfilled wish, in the cry of an open question." And, "Revelation is of the present, indeed it is being-present itself." See Rosenzweig, *The Star*, 184, 186. For a similar claim made from an Eastern perspective, one might look to Keiji Nishitani's Heidegger-influenced *Religion and Nothingness*, trans. Jan van Bragt (Berkeley: University of California Press, 1982). For a similar argument made by a Heidegger-influenced Christian theologian, see John Macquarrie, *Principles of Christian Theology* (London: SCM Press, 1966), who writes, "faith is not primarily assent to propositions, but an existential attitude of acceptance and commitment; and...revelation is not primarily given in the form of statements, but it is rather the self-giving or self-communication of being," and "'God exists' is a way of asserting what would perhaps be more exactly expressed as the holiness of being." 94, 109.

To clarify: Heidegger's thought is not incompatible with a confessional theological approach. Consider, for example, Lawrence Paul Hemming's explicitly Catholic engagement with Heidegger, which is replete with insights that are simultaneously existential and Christian:

> Tradition, *the traditio* or "handing over," is not simply something which is handed over to me, but rather something over to which I am first delivered, am "proper to." In this sense "I" am constitutive for the tradition as being in an intimate dialogue with it: I am the potential horizon of its being made actual, its realization. Thought in terms of salvation, my being is the place where, through this conversation, this "being proper to..." God comes to be, which means the 'how' of my being Christian will indicate something about me (from the perspective of my growth and maturity in Christ) and something about God (how God comes to be found in me by others)...Faith in God, specifically in the God of Christianity, makes God real within the horizon of my "I," which is to say faith in God makes me the horizon where God is made real and so expressed. In this sense my time with God is not just something I spend (in church, in prayer and so on) but time I create, as a way of being in the world.[43]

Hemming shows—and enacts—how Heidegger's insights into the existential meaning of tradition can speak directly not only to what it might mean *to be* Christian, in the sense of belonging to a Christian tradition, but even more sharply, to what it might mean *to be* saved, in the sense of allowing God's presence to infuse all aspects of one's being-in-the-world. Hemming shows that a religious life is one that involves an existential partnership and dialogue with God. Yet Hemming is also careful to point out—and this is where Heidegger's influence is apparent—that this existential dialogue with God always occurs *in*-the-world. As he writes,

> [A]ny claims to a purely "private" or "personal" experience of God apart from "world" are shown to be nonsensical. This does not mean I cannot pray privately; it means that even when I pray on my own, in the privacy of my room, I pray in a "world" as a being whose coming about is as lingual or even "logos-ed." I pray *as* a worlded being, never in some interior, subjective or "noumenal" space.[44]

[43] Hemming, "Nihilism: Heidegger and the Grounds of Redemption," 92.
[44] Ibid., 104.

Yet it is precisely this conclusion—articulated from *within* a stance of confessional theology—that motivates my own desire to conduct theology in a non-confessional (or perhaps, more accurately, post-confessional) vein. For once we admit that there is no such thing as a pure religious experience that can occur outside of language or culture—or, in short, "world," in the ontological and phenomenological sense—we must still ask if the distinctions that we draw between one culture and another or one "world" and another (e.g., the world of orthodox Christian faith and the world of secular, liberal nonbelief, or the world of the young and the world of the elderly) are as meaningful as the commonalities between them. Deciding this, however, will always be a matter of interpretation and contestation, and therefore cannot simply be settled by pointing out some particular set of differences between "us" and "them." For at issue is not whether there is difference—there is always difference—but what scale is most appropriate for assessing the importance of this difference. And this is also contestable, because the circumstances that call for such distinctions are both multiple and dynamic. The point, then, is that even if we were to grant that there is an ontological (and not just ontic) difference between Christian Dasein and non-Christian Dasein (or, for Heidegger, German Dasein and non-German Dasein), we still would not have answered the larger question of whether this difference is the *only* or even *most significant* difference that might be emphasized. And, in fact, there are many who argue that categories such as race, class, gender, sexuality, or disability, are just as important as the categories of religious identity, thereby challenging the confessional theologian's claim that faith marks the originary access point to the meaning of being.

From the fact that people disagree about what terms of their identity should be considered most salient, we can conclude that the terms of our being-in-the-world are plural—sometimes overlapping, and sometimes conflicting. We can also conclude that the categories of "difference" and "sameness" are effects of our understanding, and are not simply "real" in the sense that they exist "out there." It is meaningful to articulate and define differences, but to take these articulations as *evidence* of the metaphysical reality of those differences is to ignore the extent to which difference is always contextual.

Given the above argument, the following are the grounds on which one might defend a non-confessional theological approach to Heidegger. First, even if one were orthodox, one would still have to come to terms with the "world" in which one seeks to live an orthodox life. And this requires an appreciation for the unique challenges that modernity poses to our ontological welfare writ large, and not just to our hermeneutic commitments. Second, since each of us is characterized by a multiplicity of traditions and understandings, and since these traditions and understandings are themselves historically fluid, it is not helpful to insist that one tradition—represented as monolithic and mutually exclusive of others—offers the *sole* way to diagnose and respond to the modern human condition. And third, the fact that one does not belong to a positive faith tradition does not mean that one cannot encounter "God" (leaving open what this word signifies).

Of course the terms of one's engagement with God, as well as one's understanding of what "God" signifies, matter a great deal. But do they matter "all the way down"? When approached as a metaphysical or political question, the answer remains debatable. But when approached phenomenologically, the answer tilts toward "no," for the simple fact that communication with those who do not share all of our basic beliefs and commitments, however constrained, is still possible. The fact that our views and commitments can and do change—and that they often do when we are confronted by another person or by an unfamiliar situation—testifies to the fact that, phenomenologically speaking, our "world" remains open to revision. And to the extent that our world is open, no single discursive tradition can offer an exhaustive response to our condition.

In short, the limits of both confessional and non-confessional approaches to theology are precisely what allow them to be meaningful. The limitation of confessional theology is that its accessibility to insiders is in tension with its inaccessibility to outsiders. The more salient it is for those who are already "in," the more exclusive it is of those who are "out." Meanwhile, the limitation of non-confessional theology is that its inclusivity can make it seem either relativistic or else falsely inclusive. Given that both approaches have limits, the question is not which is more correct, but which is most appropriate to the situation at hand. Within the scope of this book, the situation at hand is taken to be the affliction wrought by modernity's philosophically entrenched and culturally enforced legacy, particularly with regards to three issues: (1) an instrumentalist conception of "truth", (2) an inability to recognize finitude as the condition of meaningfulness, and (3) an anthropology that overstates the meaning of human agency (subjectivism), while simultaneously reducing the being of the human being into an object (objectivism). To the extent that this situation affects both theists and non-theists, Christians and non-Christians, a non-confessional theological approach that can speak across these distinctions is in order. This being said, I will now address some of the methodological and philosophical challenges that my project faces. In the first section, I describe my position in the field of Heidegger studies, with particular attention to the work of Thomas Sheehan and the question of how to read Heidegger's critique of metaphysics. In the second section, I discuss my justification for a constructive approach to Heidegger's thought. In the third section, I discuss my position on Heidegger and Nazism. In the fourth section, I discuss my reasons for relying primarily on the texts of the later Heidegger. In the fifth section, I describe the relevance that *Being and Time* plays in my interpretation of Heidegger's later texts. And in the sixth section, I offer an elucidation of the significance of the book's subtitle, "Unframing Existence."

BEING, MEANINGFULNESS, AND FINITUDE

This book assumes a deep continuity between the projects of the early and later Heidegger. It also follows Thomas Sheehan's claim that when Heidegger says "Being," he means the "meaning" into which Da-sein is continuously "thrown" and "projecting," and not some metaphysical entity, cause, or substance standing behind, above, or between things. As Sheehan writes, "When [Heidegger] uses the language of 'being,' he means 'being' as phenomenologically reduced, i.e., as meaningfulness."[45] "The basic question motivating all of Heidegger's work is quite simply 'How does meaning occur at all?'"[46] I also agree with Sheehan that Heidegger's answer to this question is not "Being," but rather "the clearing" (*die Lichtung*), or what Heidegger elsewhere calls "Welt," [world] "Da" [openedness], "Ereignis" [the event of appropriation], and "es gibt" [it gives/there is].[47]

[45] Thomas Sheehan "Dasein," *A Companion to Heidegger*, 197. See also, Sheehan, "A New Paradigm in Heidegger Research," *Continental Philosophy Review* 34 (2002): 183–202.

[46] Sheehan, "The Turn," in *Martin Heidegger: Key Concepts*, ed. Bret Davis, 85, 82–97.

[47] Sheehan, "The Turn: All Three of Them," in *The Bloomsbury Companion to Heidegger*, ed. François Raffoul and Eric S. Nelson (London: Bloomsbury, 2013), 31, 31–37; Sheehan, "A New Paradigm in Heidegger Research," 138.

Where Sheehan overstates his case, however, is in matters of inflection. According to Sheehan, "meaningfulness," "Being," and "intelligibility" are synonyms.[48] Sheehan's view is well supported by Heidegger's claim in *Being and Time* that "when we ask about the meaning of being, our inquiry does not become profound and does not brood on anything which stands behind being, but questions being itself in so far as it stands within the intelligibility of Da-sein" (*Verständlichkeit des Daseins*).[49] Nevertheless, Sheehan's conflation of meaning and intelligibility, I argue, can be misleading if we do not also consider Heidegger's suggestion in "The Origin of the Work of Art" (1936) that "Truth [*Wahrheit*], in its essence, is un-truth [*Unwahrheit*]."[50] Thus, my book also endorses Julian Young's claim that, "[t]hough there is indeed *a* sense of *Sein* in which it is just presence (truth as disclosure…intelligibility), there is another sense in which what is crucial about it is precisely the opposite—*un*intelligibility ("untruth")."[51] While such gnomic formulations have the disadvantage of sounding gratuitously provocative, they testify to something important, namely, that the occurrence of meaning bears an ineliminable residue of disorientation and bewilderment. This is a point, moreover, which is clearly very dear to Heidegger, who describes truth not as the triumph of comprehension over incomprehension, but as that which emerges only in and as the "strife" between them. As Heidegger writes, "truth is the opposition of clearing and concealing […] and does not exist in itself beforehand, somewhere among the stars, only subsequently to descend elsewhere among beings."[52]

If this still sounds like a philosophically indefensible—or "merely" poetic position—consider Heidegger's formulation in *Being and Time* that "understanding" is always already "attuned," which makes the same point more concretely.[53] For in arguing that understanding and mood are interlinked, Heidegger also implicitly shows that intelligibility is

---

[48] Sheehan, "The Turn: All Three of Them," 31.

[49] SZ, 152/ BT, 142.

[50] Heidegger, "The Origin of the Work of Art," in *Basic Writings*, ed. David Farrell Krell (New York: HarperCollins, 1993), 179.

[51] Julian Young, *Heidegger's Later Philosophy* (Cambridge: Cambridge University Press, 2002), 12.

[52] "The Origin of the Work of Art," 186.

[53] SZ, 143/ BT, 134.

always colored by something that is itself not fully intelligible. Which is another way of saying that human reason is not autonomous—our reasons for thinking and feeling something always develop *in response* to a situation whose meaning is in excess of what we can say and know of it in any given moment.

Appreciating the irreducible non-ipseity of meaningfulness, I contend, is crucial if we are to grasp how Heidegger's ontology, far from being "totalizing," as Levinas charges, can show us the extent to which a total understanding is impossible.[54] Even more significantly, it can help us confront an issue that is typically marginalized in the secondary literature on Heidegger, namely, that the aim of Heidegger's ontology is not merely greater *conceptual cognition* of the meaning of Being, but also, if not more importantly, a transformed *existential orientation* to Being.[55] That this is Heidegger's position is strikingly evident in the high esteem he grants to poets, poetry, and works of art: "The essence of poetry," Heidegger writes, "is the founding of truth."[56] Why? Drawing an explicit connection between the importance of poetry and the essential hiddenness of the source of meaning, Heidegger writes, "In the familiar appearances, the poets call the alien as that to which the invisible imparts itself in order to remain what it is—unknown."[57] What is key here, as in so much of Heidegger, is that the task of ontology is argued to be not the demystification of the world, but, on the contrary, a renewed capacity to regard the familiar itself as an unquenchable source of awe. Heidegger makes this injunction acutely evident in his "Letter on Humanism," where he creatively translates Heraclitus's fragment 119— *ethos anthropoi daimon*—as "The (familiar) abode for man is the open region for the presencing of god (the unfamiliar one)" [*der (geheure) Aufenthalt ist dem Menschen das Offene für die Anwesung des Gottes (des*

---

[54] As Levinas writes, "In Heidegger coexistence is, to be sure, taken as a relationship with the Other irreducible to objective cognition; but in the final analysis it also rests on the relationship with *being in general*, on comprehension, on ontology." *Totality and Infinity: An Essay on Exteriority*, trans. Alphonso Lingis (Pittsburgh: Duquesne University Press, 1969), 67. My argument, contra Levinas—and this explains why my disagreement with Sheehan is important—is that ontology is not simply the same as comprehension.

[55] For an exceptional work that does take this point seriously, see David Wood, *Time After Time* (Bloomington: Indiana University Press, 2007).

[56] Heidegger, "The Origin of the Work of Art," 199.

[57] "...Poetically Man Dwells...," in *Poetry, Language, and Thought*, 223.

Un-geheuren)].[58] With this translation, Heidegger intimates that the familiar and the unfamiliar are not opposites, but companions. Or to say it more poetically, we can be hosts of meaningfulness only because we are also at the same time guests of meaningfulness.

Of course, Sheehan would not disagree with what has been said so far, but he would urge us to exercise great caution in talking about the essential foreignness of the source of Being, lest we fall back into metaphysics. As Sheehan writes, "*Ereignis* is not Big Being...operating from some Beyond and heteronomously 'appropriating' us into a place other than ourselves. Rather, it is our finitude that opens the open..."[59] "Our finitude, and it alone, is the intrinsically hidden mystery, overlooked in fallenness and embraced in resolve."[60] For Sheehan, our awe should be directed at the sheer fact that things make sense, and not at trying to explain this fact by appealing to a theological account of Creation.[61] For Sheehan, there is a clear line to be drawn between the Heideggerian project, which is human-centric, and religious projects, which, in their theistic guises, define the human being as the beloved offspring of an omni-benevolent God, and in their nontheistic guises define the human being as mere organ in a cosmic, conscious whole. On Sheehan's view, attempting to use Heidegger's vocabulary to substantiate a cosmological view of any kind constitutes a hermeneutic abuse, and should be rejected not only because it misrepresents Heidegger's project, but because, more importantly, it overlooks "the matter itself" (*die Sache selbst*)—"our finitude as opening up the world/clearing/open that we essentially are."[62]

Sheehan's injunctions are compelling. And there is no doubting the strong textual evidence he brings to defend his vision of Heidegger as a kind of updated version of Kant (and Nietzsche). Nevertheless, I take issue with the opposition Sheehan sets up between attributing mystery to "some Beyond" and attributing mystery to "our finitude" on a number of grounds. First, it is not clear that attributing mystery to "our finitude" is any less metaphysical than attributing it to a "Beyond." Each formulation is at risk of sounding like a causal explanation. At the same time,

[58] "Letter on Humanism," 234.

[59] Sheehan, "A New Paradigm in Heidegger Research," 199.

[60] Ibid.

[61] See Sheehan, "Astonishing! Things Make Sense!," *Gatherings: The Heidegger Circle Annual* 1(2011): 1–25.

[62] Sheehan, "A New Paradigm in Heidegger Research," 200.

there is nothing in the terms themselves that requires us to read them this way. It is just as possible to attribute mystery to a "Beyond" without reifying it, as it is to hypostasize finitude. The fact that one word is capitalized—and the other not—is not enough to guarantee that we know how to read them with the appropriate inflection. Second, it is questionable whether the dichotomy Sheehan sets up between "finitude" and the "Beyond" holds up phenomenologically. Why must we assume that these are two distinct categories, rather than simply two different words for the same nondual enigma? Why not say that the language of "finitude" helps us grasp the essential irresolvability of our most basic questions, while the language of "a Beyond" helps us remember that these questions are not arbitrary, one-sided projections, but emerge in *response to* a situation that calls for questioning? Such would also be in keeping with Heidegger's own maxim, cited by Sheehan, *verschiedene Namen für dasselbe* ("many names for the same").[63] Third, and this relates to the first two issues, it is doubtful whether Sheehan can modify "finitude" with the possessive article "our" without falling into subjectivism himself, and thus going expressly against Heidegger's claim that "[t]he resoluteness intended in *Being and Time* is not the deliberate action of a subject but the opening up of human being, out of its captivity in beings, to the openness of Being."[64] Sheehan is not wrong to claim that there could be "no opening up" without finitude, but, to the extent that he conflates this finitude with the finitude *of a subject*, he is putting the cart before the horse, since, for Heidegger, subjectivity and ownership are modalities of finitude, and not the other way around. If, however, Sheehan really makes no such conflation, and would be happy to accept that subjectivity is a modality of finitude rather than synonymous with it, then it seems he is overstating his differences with those scholars he criticizes as too metaphysical. At the very least, it would be unfair of him to criticize them for hypostasizing "the clearing" since such would simply be the inevitable outcome of any attempt to put the a priori into words.

From these observations, two conclusions can be drawn. The first is that the task of Heidegger scholarship cannot simply be to interpret Heidegger's thought in such a way that one avoids metaphysical language altogether. This is a point which Heidegger himself explicitly confirms

---

[63] Ibid., 199; GA 65, 331.
[64] Heidegger, "The Origin of the Work of Art," 192.

when he writes, "[m]etaphysics cannot be abolished like an opinion. One can by no means leave it behind as a doctrine no longer believed and represented."[65] And the second is that, given the impossibility of avoiding metaphysics, one should read the metaphysical language of others charitably, rather than simply writing it off as naïve (To vocalize this point in the Biblical language of commandment, we could say, "Let she who is without metaphysics cast the first stone"). Of course, one can wield the Heideggerian project like a weapon with which to attack anything that sounds like a denial of finitude, but in doing so, one may simply be avoiding finitude oneself. Thus, Heidegger's discovery that finitude is the condition for the possibility of meaningfulness is one that cuts both ways. It can be used to expose our "master narratives" as evasions from "the thing itself," but it can also become its own master narrative.

In short, the language of finitude speaks to an *aporia*, and cannot simply be used as a tactic for stamping out anything we condemn as metaphysics. This would only be to perpetuate the very metaphysics one seeks to abolish. Heidegger formulates this point at a general level when he writes, "Everything 'anti' thinks in the spirit of that against which it is 'anti,'"[66] as well as a point that he sharpens in his particular quarrel with Nietzsche:

> [T]he reversal of Platonism, according to which for Nietzsche the sensuous becomes the true world and the suprasensuous becomes the untrue world, is thoroughly caught in metaphysics. This kind of overcoming of metaphysics...is only the final entanglement in metaphysics.[67]

The upshot of these claims, to repeat, is that Heidegger's critique of metaphysics must be understood not as a call for the dissolution of metaphysics, but instead as an attempt to bring about a healthier relation to metaphysics. The implications of this point are significant. To see what they are, let's look at Sheehan's definition of metaphysics. Sheehan writes, "Metaphysics gives an ontic answer to the question about being."[68] Or in other words, it answers the question, "What is

---

[65] Heidegger, "Overcoming Metaphysics," *The End of Philosophy*, 85.

[66] Heidegger, *Parmenides*, 52–53; GA 54, 77.

[67] "Overcoming Metaphysics," 92.

[68] Sheehan, "Dasein," 195.

meaningfulness?" by pointing to a meaningful entity, thereby deflecting the initial question. Sheehan's definition is perfectly consistent with the one that Heidegger gives in his "Letter on Humanism" when he writes, "Metaphysics...thinks the Being of beings...[but] it does not think the difference [between Being and beings]."[69] Yet in light of my claim that metaphysics is a basically unavoidable condition, both Sheehan's and Heidegger's critical definitions of metaphysics, I argue, can also be inflected positively. Read positively, they might be interpolated as saying something like this: "Our access to the phenomenon of meaningfulness cannot and should not be divorced from our access to meaningful things in all of their singularity and contingency. Thus, recognizing the ubiquity of meaningfulness—or the clearing that we ourselves are—is not something that we do in spite of ontic things, but thanks to them." This conclusion is, in fact, one of the crucial points that Heidegger makes in his essay "The Thing," in which he describes how a jug can be a vessel not just for holding or serving liquid, but for bringing us into greater intimacy with Being.[70] Of course, Heidegger does not state this point so directly in that essay, yet in his concise phrase, "the thing things world," he intimates that ontic entities can play an essential role in attuning us to the ontological dimension of our being.

Thus, if metaphysics goes too far by over-privileging meaningful things, while forgetting meaningful*ness*, we should not go too far in the other direction by abandoning our attachment to meaningful things so as to focus exclusively on the phenomenon of meaningfulness. Instead, a healthy relationship to metaphysics will involve the affirmation of meaningful things, while also recognizing that no individual meaningful thing or collective arrangement of them can exhaust or explain what the phenomenon of meaningfulness itself involves.

From these observations, two counter-intuitive conclusions follow. First, one can embrace a Heideggerian worldview and still be thoroughly engaged in the kind of "calculative" and "representational" thinking that Heidegger criticizes.[71] Second, one can profess belief in God, salvation, or the immortality of the soul and still affirm that the *meaningfulness* of these terms would be impossible without the presence of human

[69]Heidegger, "Letter on Humanism," in *Basic Writings*, 226.

[70]Heidegger, "The Thing," *Poetry, Language, and Thought*, 161–185.

[71]For a succinct articulation of Heidegger's critique of "calculative" and "representational" thinking see "The Age of the World Picture," 148–150.

finitude. In both cases, the health of one's relationship to metaphysics would be determined less by the content of one's beliefs than by the quality of how one embodies them.[72]

This last point is not one that Heidegger always makes directly, but is a point that can be appreciated once we recognize that Heidegger himself uses the word "metaphysics" ambiguously. On the one hand, Heidegger uses metaphysics broadly to refer to any particular way of understanding things at all. As Heidegger writes, "Metaphysics grounds an age, in that through a specific interpretation of what is and through a specific comprehension of truth it gives to that age the basis upon which it is essentially formed."[73] On this definition, "metaphysics" refers most basically not to a doctrine about the suprasensuous, but to any understanding whatsoever. It is in this sense that Heidegger says in his essay, "What is Metaphysics?" (1929) "[M]etaphysics belongs to the 'nature of man.' It Is neither a division of academic philosophy nor a field of arbitrary notions. Metaphysics is the basic occurrence of Dasein. It is Dasein itself."[74] On the other hand, however, Heidegger uses metaphysics in the narrow and more pejorative sense to refer to a particularly Western and acutely modern way of understanding that is premised on the desire for security and order. As Heidegger writes, "the metaphysics of the modern age begins with and has its essence in the fact that it seeks the unconditionally indubitable, the certain and assured [*das Gewisse*], certainty."[75] Heidegger tells different stories about how this understanding came to prominence, sometimes emphasizing Plato as the turning point where things went wrong; sometimes emphasizing the Roman empire as the moment when the radical spirit of Greek thinking was lost; sometimes emphasizing Thomism and the medieval Christian worldview as the moment of decline; and sometimes emphasizing Descartes' desire for an indubitable first principle as the primary expression of the problem. Common to each of these moments, though, according to Heidegger, in his essay, "The Onto-Theo-Logical Constitution of Metaphysics," is that their underlying desire for security and order obstructs their capacity to

---

[72]For an excellent argument that makes parallel claims, see Merold Westphal, *Overcoming Onto-Theology*, 285–303.

[73]"The Age of the World Picture," 116.

[74]Heidegger, "What Is Metaphysics?," in *Basic Writings*, 110.

[75]"The Word of Nietzsche," in *The Question Concerning Technology*, 83.

---

appreciate—and make room for—an understanding of Being *as* fundamentally groundless. As Heidegger explains,

> The Being of beings is thus thought of in advance [by metaphysics] as the grounding ground. Therefore all metaphysics is at bottom, and from the ground up, what grounds, what gives account of the ground, what is called to account by the ground, and finally what calls the ground to account.[76]

And it is this aspect of metaphysics—metaphysics understood as grounding, or in his more technical parlance, "onto-theology"—that Heidegger claims requires critique.[77] The force of this critique, however, is not, I contend, to condemn this tendency as such, but only to show that, so long as it is unchecked and taken for granted, it may lead to a vicious cycle of repression and insecurity.

This conclusion is further supported by Heidegger's suggestion that metaphysics is so deeply encoded in the structure of Western language that even if we wanted to soften its grip we would have to do so by learning to listen to our language differently, and not simply by changing our vocabulary. As he writes,

> Our Western languages are languages of metaphysical thinking, each in its own way. It must remain an open question whether the nature of Western languages is in itself marked with the exclusive brand of metaphysics, and thus marked permanently by onto-theo-logic, or whether these languages offer other possibilities of utterance—and that means at the same time of a telling silence.[78]

In other words, Heidegger suggests that, to the extent that Western language is redeemable, it will involve making room for "a telling silence,"

---

[76] Heidegger, *Identity and Difference*, 58.

[77] What Heidegger means by "ontotheology," Iain Thomson convincingly shows, is a mode of thinking that combines two different ways of grounding or explaining what an entity is, namely, ontology (defining something "from the inside out") and theology (defining something "from the outside in"). Thomson, *Heidegger on Ontotheology: Technology and the Politics of Education* (Cambridge: Cambridge University Press, 2005), 2. To clarify, this does not mean that "ontology" or "theology" must be defined reductively in this way, but only that this is what these terms, in their classical sense, can be taken to mean.

[78] Heidegger, *Identity and Difference*, 73.

and that means, one in which metaphysics can manifest *as* metaphysics. The point, then, of a critique of metaphysics would be to clear a space for metaphysics to be revealed *as* metaphysics, rather than simply perpetuated without reflection, a conclusion that is explicitly endorsed by a number of passages in Heidegger. "The step back from the representational thinking of metaphysics does not reject such thinking, but opens the distant to the appeal of the trueness of Being in which the responding always takes place."[79] And, "[f]or transitional thinking, what matters is not an 'opposition' to 'metaphysics,' since that would simply bring metaphysics back into play; rather, the task is an overcoming of metaphysics out of its ground."[80] In both of these passages, Heidegger suggests that the decisive question is not whether our words, thoughts, and deeds are structured by metaphysics, but whether, by acknowledging our entrenchment in metaphysics, we can make room for a non-metaphysical encounter with the enigma of Being.

Having seen that metaphysics is not reductively a bad thing, but is instead an entrenched human tendency, structurally encoded in all events of meaningfulness, we can now see that the critical element in Heidegger's critique of metaphysics also has a positive dimension. In the remainder of this section, I will attempt to spell out what this dimension involves, although it will be for the remaining chapters to argue it more thoroughly. I suggest that the critique of metaphysics testifies to the importance of a non-dualistic approach to discourse, whereby we come to recognize that the words of others can be both true and untrue at the same time—true to the extent that they open up the world, and untrue to the extent that they repress other ways of opening up the world, including, typically, the fact of world-opening itself. By recognizing that *all discourse* is a site of strife between truth and untruth, however, we can also come to receive the concerns of others with a hermeneutics of generosity. This is crucial, I argue, not only to Heidegger scholarship but also to ethical life more generally. And so by enacting such a hermeneutics of generosity in my reading of Heidegger, I hope that my book can model the kind of hermeneutic generosity that it enjoins more broadly. A hermeneutics of generosity—or what I call, in my own words, "an ethics of grateful listening"—does not require that we agree with or accept

---

[79] "The Thing," in *Poetry, Language, and Thought*, 183.

[80] *Contributions to Philosophy (Of the Event)*, trans. Richard Rojcewicz and Daniela Vallega-Neu (Bloomington: Indiana University Press, 2012), 136; GA 65, 172.

every discourse as correct or right, but it does require us to regard the words of others—regardless of our positive or negative judgments about them—as sites of world-disclosure.

Thus, while I strongly agree with Sheehan's *presentation* of Heidegger's project, accepting it does not require following him in judging other Heidegger scholars' work as simply wrong or incorrect.[81] Instead, I believe that the most fruitful way to read Heidegger is in a more constructive way, a topic I address in the next section.

DEFENDING A CONSTRUCTIVE APPROACH TO HEIDEGGER'S THOUGHT

The philosophical and theological response to Heidegger's thought has been greatly divided. On the one hand, Heidegger has been widely recognized as one of the most insightful thinkers of the twentieth century, and on the other hand, he has been widely condemned as a pagan, a relativist, an irrationalist, a nihilist, and a fascist. Thanks to Heidegger's large body of work, the idiosyncrasy and variety of its language, the contentiousness of its reception and translation, and the great amount of notoriety and mystique that surrounds his name, it is unlikely that this disparity will ever be resolved.

This is not, prima facie, a bad thing, but it does mean that the question of *how to read Heidegger*, so important for the kind of Heidegger one ends up with, will be circular. Generous readings of Heidegger will produce a Heidegger that demands generosity, while suspicious readings of Heidegger will produce a Heidegger that demands suspicion. In both cases, the interpreter's "fore-conception" (*Vor-griff*)—to use Heidegger's phrase—will determine, in advance, which aspects of Heidegger's thought are to be disclosed (and which are to remain concealed).[82]

This is not surprising. As Heidegger argues in *Being and Time*, all investigations are defined in advance by the assumptions and aspirations that are brought to bear on it.[83] It is why all discoveries, however new

---

[81] Cf. Sheehan, "A Paradigm Shift in Heidegger Research," 188.

[82] SZ, 150/ BT, 141.

[83] SZ, 148–153/ BT, 139–144.

and surprising they may seem, already make *some* sense to us, as well as why it is impossible to find what one is not, on some level, already looking for. Or to say this point differently, it is why we can never discover things *outside* of our meaning-giving context.

This is not to say that our meaning-giving context isn't incredibly robust or flexible, but only to show why critics and defenders of Heidegger alike frequently find themselves unable to convince each other: their discussions about the meaning and import of Heidegger's thought are typically about much more than Heidegger. It is this "much more," however, that needs to be made explicit if the practice of reading and thinking with Heidegger is to break through this impasse. But this will mean that both exegetical readings and historicizing readings of Heidegger will have to be put in the service of asking constructive questions—questions, that is, which are not limited to "getting Heidegger right."

One example of an impasse in the secondary literature on Heidegger that is in fact about much more than Heidegger is the debate about whether Heidegger should be read as a pragmatist or a transcendentalist. Allan Bloom argues that Heidegger's pragmatism leads him down the path of relativism, blaming him and Nietzsche for "The Closing of the American Mind."[84] Meanwhile, Richard Rorty and Stanley Cavell argue just the opposite, namely that where Heidegger went wrong was in not being enough of a pragmatist. To the extent that Heidegger's thought is helpful, these thinkers claim, his thought must be appreciated as continuous with the projects of William James, Ralph Waldo Emerson, and John Dewey, and its metaphysical slippages seen as just as that, slippages.[85] What is evident from this example is that one's answer to the descriptive question "What is Heidegger's thought all about?" cannot be separated from one's answer to the evaluative question "In what ways is Heidegger's project right (good) or wrong (evil)?" Yet because the answer to these evaluative questions remains intensely polarized,

---

[84] See Allan Bloom, *The Closing of the American Mind* (New York: Simon & Schuster, 1987), 149–154, 309–314.

[85] Stanley Cavell, "Aversive Thinking: Emersonian Representations in Heidegger and Nietzsche," in *Emerson's Transcendental Etudes* (Stanford: Stanford University Press, 2003), 110–141; Richard Rorty, "Heidegger, Contingency, and Pragmatism," in *Essays on Heidegger and Others: Philosophical Papers Volume 2* (Cambridge: Cambridge University, 1996).

answering the first question becomes equally contentious.[86] A constructive approach, by contrast, can admit that it is a response to, rather than a representation of Heidegger's thought, and thus may be able to avoid some of this controversy, while refocusing the scholarly discourse on a question far broader than Heidegger's own thinking, namely, "What are the *stakes* of ontology?" Does—or should—ontology matter? And if yes, how? My own answer, in agreement with Heidegger, is that ontology matters a great deal, and that the stakes of ontology concern how we understand and relate to ourselves, others, and our environment. For ontological enquiry, I argue, leads us not just to ask about Being in the abstract, but about the various circumstances that challenge us as historical and contemporary beings.

Among the questions that ontology raises are: How can we can let our words, gestures, and silences bestow a world rich with meaning and concern within a system that privileges the generic over the inimitable, the correct over the revelatory, the valid over the profound, the productive over the playful, and the novel over the sustaining? Can we maintain the world as a place of generosity, receptivity, and deep conversation? Can we inhabit it with a sense of openness and wonder rather than with an *unflinching* will to dominate, secure, and control? Can we regard our own lives and the lives of others as more than just businesses to be managed, the goal of which is to achieve some maximal aggregate value? Can we encounter things without *utterly* instrumentalizing, objectifying, and commodifying them? How, in the simplest, most perennial, and yet elusive terms, can we wake up? These are not questions that Heidegger asks directly or comprehensively, yet they are the kinds of existential questions that his thought prompts us to consider.

This brings us to our second reason for defending a constructive approach to Heidegger's thought, namely, that this is how Heidegger himself indicated he should be read. As Heidegger writes in *Kant and the Problem of Metaphysics* (1929), "[W]ith any philosophical knowledge in general, what is said in uttered propositions must not be decisive. Instead, what must be decisive is what sets before our eyes as still unsaid,

---

[86]For a good study on how the opacity of Heidegger's thought, combined with the notoriety of Heidegger's life-politics, facilitated a wide range of (mis)readings of it, see Martin Woessner, *Heidegger in America* (Cambridge: Cambridge University Press, 2010).

in and through what has been said."[87] Or as Heidegger told his audience more straightforwardly in his 1935 lecture course, "Introduction to Metaphysics," "'Being and Time' means...not a book, but a task" (*nicht ein Buch...sondern das Aufgegebene*).[88] This task, Heidegger clarifies, is "not something that we genuinely know," but is something that we can "know, always only *questioningly, as* a task."[89] In short, Heidegger regarded the essence of his thought—and thought more generally—to consist not just in the specificity of its arguments, but more importantly in the routes it gives others to think.

That Heidegger saw his thought—and all serious thought—as demanding not just exposition, but more significantly, existential appropriation and translation is also evident in the testimony of his students, many of whom themselves became important twentieth century thinkers (e.g., Hannah Arendt, Herbert Marcuse, and Hans Georg-Gadamer). As Richard Wolin sums up this testimony, "The leitmotif of Heidegger's [lecture] courses [was] Augustine's *mea res agitur*: "my life is at stake," in which "doing philosophy ceased to be an exercise in disembodied, scholarly exegesis" and became a "momentous, hermeneutical encounter between the historical past and...contemporary being-in-the-world."[90]

What Wolin implies, but not does not say directly here, is that in exposing his students to the existential stakes of thinking, Heidegger in effect rejects the idea that the *primary* task of philosophy should be to find solutions and instead proposes that the task of philosophy should be to prepare students for a lifelong existential engagement with their intellectual tradition. The pedagogic consequences of such a view are striking, and, I am arguing, deeply relevant for Heidegger scholarship. First, it demands that the task of the philosophy teacher is to help students become lifelong learners. And second, it shows that the purpose of a philosophical education is integrity—the ability to draw out philosophical insights from—as well as bring them to bear on—all aspects of one's life. In terms of the relevance for scholarship, the implication

---

[87] Heidegger, *Kant and the Problem of Metaphysics*, 5th ed., trans. Richard Taft (Bloomington: Indiana University Press, 1997), 140.

[88] GA 40, 215.

[89] Ibid.

[90] Richard Wolin, "Introduction: What Is Heideggerian Marxism?," in *Heideggerian Marxism: Herbert Marcuse*, ed. Richard Wolin and John Abromeit (Lincoln: University of Nebraska Press, 2005), xiii.

is that likewise, the task of a work on Heidegger—at least according to
Heidegger—is not simply to present Heidegger's ideas accurately but
to bring them into conversation with the author's own existentially and
contemporarily situated concerns. As Heidegger puts it, "a thinker is not
beholden to [another] thinker—rather, when he is thinking, he holds on
to what is *to be thought*..." (my emphasis).[91]

While the referent of "what is to be thought" is admittedly elusive,
and is, in a circular sense, precisely that which remains *to be thought*,
Heidegger's larger point is clear: thinking is a dialogical enterprise. That
is why Heidegger warns that a "flight into tradition...can bring about
nothing in itself other than self-deception and blindness in relation to
the historical moment,"[92] and why he says that "any mere 'back to'
[movement] is a self-deception..."[93] For these attitudes miss the importance of the present in mediating the significance of the past. The key,
by contrast, Heidegger says, is to be "transport[ed]...into that 'between'
in which [we both] belong to Being and remain...strangers amid that
which is."[94] This enigmatic injunction seems to suggest something along
these lines: the conceptual dichotomies we set up between constancy and
change, universality and singularity, and ordinariness and extraordinariness, are false. The fact of the matter is that the phenomenon of meaningfulness presupposes both, and it is precisely the co-presence of both
that makes our existence an unending source of mystery. Consequently,
the task of thinking must be to *maintain* this tension—to hold open a
"between"—and not simply collapse one side into the other.

Another argument in favor of reading Heidegger's thought not as
a fixed body of propositions, but instead as a path of questioning, can
be supported by Heidegger's remarks on Hölderlin. Hölderlin's poetry,
Heidegger writes, "is a destiny for us" only as "that which awaits our
mortal correspondence with it."[95] And, as Heidegger put it, in 1968,

---

[91] Heidegger, *What Is Called Thinking?*, trans. J. Glenn Gray (New York: Harper & Row, 1968), 95.

[92] "The Age of the World Picture," 136.

[93] Heidegger, *Hölderlin's Hymn "Der Ister,"* trans. William McNeill and Julia Davis (Bloomington: Indiana University Press, 1996), 66; GA 53, 81.

[94] Ibid.

[95] Heidegger writes, "Hölderlin's Dichtung ist für uns ein Schicksal. Es wartet darauf, daß die Sterblichen ihm entsprechen." GA 4, 195. See also GA 39, 1, 6, where Heidegger refers to Hölderlin as "our most futural *thinker*" ("unser zukunfstigster *Denker*").

it is "still not yet so near to us that his word has reached us" (*immer noch nicht so nahe, daß sein Wort uns erreicht*).[96] In raising the possibility that a text, like wine, requires time to age, Heidegger may also be suggesting that his own thought, too, remains only *en route* to maturation. Accordingly, the label "Heidegger's thought" would have to be understood not as the thought that belongs to the man, Martin Heidegger, but rather as the thought to which the man, Martin Heidegger, sought to belong. This, anyways, is how Heidegger conceives of the relationship between the poet and poetry, when, commenting on Hölderlin's poem, "Germanien," he suggests that we must interpret the poet's self not as a detached subject existing above or before language, but instead as a site of concern that is brought into play by language itself. After quoting three different lines in which Hölderlin's text speaks in the first-person, Heidegger asks, "Who is this 'I'? Hölderlin? As the author [*Verfasser*] of the poem—yes, in so far as the author brings the whole poem to language as formed language [*Sprachgebilde*] ...but really [*eigentlich*] nobody speaks [*spricht da niemand*] here."[97] In describing the poem as the speech of language itself, and not as the creation of an ego-like object, Heidegger offers a model of reading that can apply to his own texts as well.

Commenting on Heidegger's remark that "there is no philosophy of Heidegger," Phillippe Lacoue-Labarthe articulates the implications of Heidegger's attempt to wrest the enterprise of reading from the twin ideologies of subjectivism and objectivism:

> To be or call oneself "Heideggerian" does not mean anything...any more than being or calling oneself "anti-Heideggerian." Or rather, both mean the same thing, that one has missed the essential thought and is destined to remain deaf to the question that, through Heidegger, is posed by this era.[98]

In his lecture course "Introduction to Metaphysics," Heidegger articulates an even more polemical version of this point:

[96] GA 4, 182; *Elucidations of Hölderlin's Poetry*, 209.

[97] GA 39, 42 (translation mine).

[98] Phillippe Lacoue-Labarthe, *Heidegger, Art, and Politics: The Fiction of the Political*, trans. Chris Turner (Hoboken: Wiley-Blackwell, 1990), 481–482.

Philosophy is essentially untimely because it is one of those few things
whose fate it remains never to be able to find a direct resonance in their
own time, and never to be permitted to find such a resonance. Whenever
this seemingly does take place, whenever a philosophy becomes fashion,
either there is no actual philosophy or else philosophy is misinterpreted
and, according to some intentions alien to it, misused for the needs
of the day.[99]

Interpreters of Heidegger do well, then, to consider Heidegger's
injunction that "all true thought remains open to more than one interpretation—and this by reason of its nature...multiplicity of meanings
is the element in which all thought must move in order to be strict
thought."[100] Attempts to reduce Heidegger's thought to a coherent
philosophy—whether to save it or condemn it—in other words, subordinate what Heidegger called "the *task* of thinking" to a desire for security
and order. Like Dostoevsky's "Grand Inquisitor," they turn the name of
a revolutionary into an ideological banner. While it is a truism that all
post-Heideggerian thought can be so only by being post-*Heideggerian*,
and that all post-*Heideggerian* thought can be so only by being *post*-
Heideggerian, what is particularly striking is that this double-movement
of faithfulness in infidelity and infidelity in faithfulness that would characterize any work of reading seems to belong, in the case of Heidegger,
not merely to the nature of interpretation writ large, but to what one
name's "Heidegger's thought" "itself."

The only way to put this strange conclusion is that Heidegger's
thought "itself" is post-Heideggerian, which is also to say that
Heidegger's thought is post-itself more primordially than it is itself. Yet
this suggestion is strangely consistent with Heidegger's claim in *Being
and Time* that "Da-sein is always already *ahead* of itself in its being," and
"always already 'beyond itself,' not as a way of behaving toward beings

---

[99] Heidegger, *Introduction To Metaphysics*, trans. Gregory Fried and Richard Polt (New
Haven: Yale University Press, 2000), 9; GA 40, 6. The melancholy of this passage is of
a piece with Walter Benjamin's reading of Paul Klee's painting, *Angelus Novus*, in which
he describes an angel, trapped in a storm that is blowing from paradise, and that propels
it towards a future to which its back is turned. See Benjamin, *Illuminations*, trans. Harry
Zohn (New York: Schocken, 1969) 257–258.

[100] *What Is Called Thinking?*, 71.

which it is *not*, but as being toward the potentiality-for-being which it itself is."[101]

This being so, we should entertain Heidegger's claim that "every great thinker thinks only one thought" as saying both more and less than what it says.[102] That is to say, rather than taking the phrase "one thought" to refer to a single identifiable book or idea, perhaps we should understand it as a stand-in phrase for a non-numerical, non-categorical negativity—neither one nor many, neither particular nor universal— that paradoxically refuses thought at the same time that it demands and nourishes it, in other words, as what Heidegger elsewhere calls, "an unthought." Such an "unthought," Heidegger suggests,

is not a lack inherent in [a thinker's] thought. [Rather], what is *un*-thought is there in each case only as the un-*thought*. The more original the thinking, the richer will be what is unthought in it. The unthought is [thus] the greatest gift that thinking can bestow.[103]

Heidegger maintains that this paradox also holds for "great" poetry. On the one hand, he writes, "Every great poet creates his poetry out of one single poetic statement only," and on the other hand, he writes, "The poet's statement remains unspoken. None of his individual poems, nor their totality, says it all."[104]

With claims such as these, Heidegger is suggesting that the generosity of thinkers and poets consists not in their positive findings themselves, but in what their commitment to a particular path of thinking and poetizing gives us to think through and incant responsively for ourselves. As Heidegger puts it, "What a thinker has thought can be mastered only if we refer everything in his thought that is still unthought back to its originary truth" (*ursprüngliches Wahrheit*).[105] Thus, a body of thought or poetry is "great" not simply because its project is coherent, but because its incongruities can draw us into "thoughtful dialogue" with it and with ourselves.[106]

[101] SZ, 192/ BT, 179.
[102] *What is Called Thinking?*, 50.
[103] Ibid., 76.
[104] *On the Way to Language*, 160.
[105] Ibid., 54.
[106] Ibid.

During a 1969 interview on public television, Heidegger cautioned,

> A coming thinker, who will perhaps be faced with the task of taking over this thinking that I am only attempting to prepare, will have to accommodate the words which were written by Heinrich von Kleist…'I step back before one who is not yet here, and bow, a millennium before him, to his spirit.'[107]

These words simultaneously enjoin and enact a most audacious humility—on the one hand, to recognize the task of thinking as preparatory, not accomplishable, and, on the other hand, to consider that this preparatory task is of an almost cosmic, world-historical importance. They suggest a kinship between thinkers across the vicissitudes of epochal difference, or else, simply bestow a hope, an oblique promise—a possibility whose vastness we can intimate only in prayer, in a saying so reticent it can be said only as a gesture.

Regardless of whether we accept Heidegger's rhetoric or dismiss it as hyperbole, we should acknowledge that he regarded his thought not simply as a set of propositions to be evaluated, but instead as a varied path of questioning whose work remains for others to continue.[108] It is for this reason that I see a constructive or appropriative reading of Heidegger's thought as not just warranted by it but even demanded by it.

Nevertheless, it is worth acknowledging the risks of culling ethical and theological insight from a thinker who put his thought in the service of Nazism. In what follows I shall offer my own preliminary account of how we may read Heidegger's thought charitably while also taking seriously its complicity in one of the most reactionary and repugnant ideologies of the twentieth century (For a more sustained examination of these issues, see Chapters 2 and 5).

---

[107] Martin Heidegger, "The End of Philosophy and the Task of Thinking." http://www.youtube.com/watch?v=qouZC17_Vsg (accessed March 18, 2013). For the Kleist quotation see "Brief an Ulrike Kleist vom 5. Oktober 1803," in *Sämtliche Werke und Briefe*, ed. Helmut Sembdner (Munich: Hanser, 1985), 2: 735–737, as cited in Gerhard Richter, *Afterness: Figures of Following in Modern Thought and Aesthetics* (New York: Columbia University Press, 2011), 244n8.

[108] George Pattison, following George Steiner, helpfully suggests that we read Heidegger's thought not as a single book but rather as a fugue. George Pattison, *The Routledge Philosophy Guidebook to The Later Heidegger* (London: Routledge, 2000), 22–23.

HEIDEGGER AND NAZISM

If we trust the conclusion of commentators such as Victor Farías, Emmanuel Faye, Richard Wolin, and Tom Rockmore, as well as Heidegger's Jewish students, Emmanuel Levinas and Hans Jonas, then Heidegger's thought is not just circumstantially implicated in Nazism, but is essentially and irredeemably so.[109] Even Philippe Lacoue-Labarthe, a more sympathetic reader of Heidegger, seems to lend their position support when he writes, "[Heidegger's] political involvement of 1933 is neither an accident nor a mistake...but completely consistent with his thought."[110] Heidegger's own comments on the matter only make such a view more plausible, as for instance, when he told the German newspaper, *Der Spiegel*, in a 1966 interview (which he insisted be published posthumously), that he was still "not convinced [that] democracy [is the best political system]."[111]

The posthumous publication of Heidegger's famed "Black Notebooks" in 2014 has raised the specter of Heidegger's Nazism anew, with many of Heidegger's long-standing critics arguing that these writings prove definitively that anti-Semitism is intrinsic to Heidegger's philosophical worldview. Indeed, these writings make clear that Heidegger's anti-Semitic prejudices form a deep part of both his personal and philosophical identity. As Peter Gordon writes, "[Heidegger's] anti-Semitism turns out to have been far more pronounced than one might have imagined."[112] The historical record now shows that Heidegger unequivocally thought of World Jewry in essentialist, conspiratorial terms, often

[109] Victor Farías, *Heidegger and Nazism*, ed. Joseph Margolis and Tom Rockmore, trans. Paul Burrell (Philadelphia: Temple University Press, 1989); Emmanuel Faye, *Heidegger: The Introduction of Nazism into Philosophy in Light of the Unpublished Seminars of 1933–1935*, trans. Tom Rockmore (New Haven: Yale University Press, 2011); Richard Wolin, *The Politics of Being: The Political Thought of Martin Heidegger* (New York: Columbia University Press, 1992); Tom Rockmore, *On Heidegger's Nazism and Philosophy* (Berkeley: University of California Press, 1992); Emmanuel Levinas, "Reflections on the Philosophy of Hitlerism," trans. Sean Hand, in *Critical Inquiry* 17, no. 1 (1990): 63–71, 63; and Hans Jonas, *The Phenomenon of Life: Towards a Philosophical Biology* (Evanston: Northwestern University Press, 2001), 247.

[110] See Philippe Lacoue-Labarthe, "Neither an Accident Nor a Mistake," trans. Paula Wissing, *Critical Inquiry* 15, no. 2 (1989): 481–484, 482.

[111] *The Heidegger Controversy: A Critical Reader*, ed. Richard Wolin (Cambridge: MIT, 1993), 104.

[112] Peter Eli Gordon, "Heidegger in Black," October 9, 2014.

blaming this group for all that he found wrong and untenable with his contemporary world. Here is one of his more famously scandalous statements, quoted by Richard Wolin, a stalwart anti-Heideggerian, in *The Jewish Review of Books*:

> Contemporary Jewry's ... increase in power finds its basis in the fact that Western metaphysics—above all, in its modern incarnation—offers fertile ground for the dissemination of an empty rationality and calculability, which in this way gains a foothold in "spirit," without ever being able to grasp from within the hidden realms of decision.[113]

We can remark, easily enough, about sentences like this, that Heidegger's broad-stroked use of terms like "Contemporary Jewry" is wrong—factually, intellectually morally, and politically. We can also affirm that Heidegger's writing contains elements that are toxic and paranoid (a quality not unique to Heidegger, but shared by many thinkers who attempt to offer a totalizing wordlview). But the question remains: must we throw out the baby of Heidegger's insights with the bathwater of his personal, rhetorical, and philosophical failings? As Peter Gordon writes, "None of [Heidegger's anti-Semitic writings] would necessarily modify our political judgments of the author, since we knew the basic contours of the story even before the black notebooks appeared."[114] Even regarding the above-quoted passage, we can ask, does Heidegger's association of "Contemporary Jewry" with the "empty rationality" and "calculability" of Western metaphysics require us to condemn Heidegger's critique of these aspects of metaphysics as anti-Semitic? Perhaps the problem with Heidegger's philosophically inflected, anti-Semitic writings is only the fact that he unnecessarily, unrigorously, and pathetically scapegoats a group of people for phenomena that he himself, in many other areas of his thought, acknowledges cannot be blamed on any individual or group, since they are merely part of the epochal destiny of Being's self-disclosure.

My contention is that Heidegger's path of thinking can be saved, even if some of the particular aspects of it must be discarded or challenged. To be clear, I am not making the argument that the daughter of a fallen

---

[113]Richard Wolin, "National Socialism, World Jewry, and the History of Being: Heidegger's Black Notebooks," in *The Jewish Review of Books*, Summer 2014.

[114]Gordon, ibid.

rabbi in the Talmud makes about her father: "Remember his Torah, but not his deeds," since the issue is Heidegger's thought itself.[115] Instead, I am making the proposal that what we call "Heidegger's thought" is not reducible to the way Heidegger himself thought.[116]

Heidegger's thought no more belongs to Heidegger the person who wrote *Being and Time* and the *Black Notebooks* than it does to us who seek to read Heidegger in our own context. Heidegger the particular man of flesh and blood offered a particular interpretation of his thought, but his interpretation is only one among many possible interpretations. It is our opportunity and responsibility as readers of Heidegger to show that interpreting Heidegger's thought as fascistic, racist, and prejudiced is not only bad philosophy but is, as it odd as it might seem, "bad Heidegger."

Such a hermeneutic approach might be called "oral Torah," the Jewish-rabbinic idea that the written Heidegger (the words on the page in his collected works) do not constitute the living essence of Heidegger's philosophy, but merely an archive of clues, traces, and moments of thought, that must be brought to life through our existential intervention in it, the way in which we allow its questions of us and our own questions of it to form something new.[117] For Heidegger's thought to become philosophical, and thus to be read on the terms which it asks and deserves to be read, we cannot treat it reductively as an object of historical curiosity or political opprobrium.

The totalizing, rejectionist conclusion of the anti-Heideggerians, is an understandable psychological and political impulse, but is ultimately an anti-philosophical move. I don't contest the anti-Heideggerian charge on the grounds that it is false, or even that it is poorly argued, but on the ground that it undersells the richness and polyvocality of thought, which always offers more than any single interpretation can fix. As Elliot

[115] Babylonian Talmud, *Chagigah*, 15b.

[116] My approach, here, is aligned with that of Elliot Wolfson, who argues that Heidegger's thought should be interpreted in light of what is "unthought" in it. See Elliot Wolfson, *The Duplicity of Philosophy's Shadow: Heidegger, Nazism and the Jewish Other* (New York: Columbia University Press, 2018), 6.

[117] The meaning of "oral Torah" is too complex and contentious to define, but suffice it to say that it is the hermeneutic mechanism through which readers of the "written Torah" (Scripture) can synthesize their moral universe with the moral universe apparently described in the Bible, without having to either throw out the Bible as antiquated or else tamp down on their own contemporary truths in favor of a regressive antiquarianism.

Wolfson notes, "a dogmatic rejection of dogmatism is no more acceptable than the dogmatism it rejects."[118] Moreover, as Hans Sluga argues in *Heidegger's Crisis*, the intellectual diversity of philosophers who supported Nazism shows that the connection between philosophy and politics is complex.[119] To say that Heidegger was a Nazi *because* of what he thought is to give his thought too much credit. But to say that Heidegger thought what he thought *because* he was a German nationalist and anti-modernist is to give his thought too little credit. No doubt, these aspects of Heidegger's identity figure in his thought, but they are not what make Heidegger's thought all that it is. If they did, it would be difficult to explain the ongoing and diverse appeal that Heidegger's thought has enjoyed. The question, then, is not *whether* Heidegger's thought is implicated in Nazism, but *how*.

There are undeniable anti-democratic and anti-liberal aspects of Heidegger's thought—often in some of his most compelling texts— that should not be dismissed. In particular, Heidegger's language of leadership and guardianship take on an ominous tenor when we think about the historical context in which he uttered these words. It seems to me, however, that these odious elements of Heidegger's thought can be attributed to a prejudice that is *posited*, rather than *argued for*, by Heidegger, and which, though linked to his philosophical concerns, are not necessitated by them. This prejudice, not unique to Heidegger or Nazism, is simply that "greatness" or "authenticity"—be it philosophical, poetic, political, or existential—is the provenance of exceptional individuals, whereas most people are, by constitution, simply too weak to ever achieve it on their own. As Heidegger told his students in 1935, "The true is not for everyone, but only for the strong" (*das Wahre ist nicht für jedermann, sondern nur für die Starken*).[120] What follows from this doctrine, Richard Wolin argues, is that the daring few have an imperative to impose their will on those too cowardly to enact their own, a claim that Heidegger reads directly out of Plato's allegory of the cave.[121] Even

---

[118] Wolfson, *The Duplicity of Philosophy's Shadow*, 168.

[119] Hans Sluga, *Heidegger's Crisis: Philosophy and Politics in Nazi Germany* (Cambridge, MA: Harvard University Press, 1993).

[120] GA 40, 142.

[121] Wolin, *The Politics of Being*, 46, 96. For an excellent examination of how Heidegger's reading of the cave allegory morphs from being authoritarian in 1931 to being more democratic in 1947, see Mary-Jane Rubenstein, *Strange Wonder: The Closure of Metaphysics and The Opening of Awe* (New York: Columbia University Press, 2009), 25–56.

in the case where the projected goal is egalitarian—authenticity for all—the means endorsed are authoritarian and violent. Such a view becomes particularly dangerous when the leader is charged not just with looking after the people's material welfare, but also with their spiritual liberation since this does away with all standards to which the leader might be held accountable besides his own enforced charisma. And it is even more dangerous when this charisma is wedded to an essentialist conception of peoplehood whereby resident aliens are regarded as a cultural and spiritual threat to the "native" people's purity. Paradoxically, then, Heidegger's very attempt to save the modern West from positivism by embracing his own idiosyncratic conception of National Socialism ends up looking like its own inverted form of positivism. As Peter Sloterdjik polemically articulates this point, "It is precisely by doing away with the myth of objectivity that Heidegger's existential-hermeneutical analysis produces the hardest 'depth positivism.'"[122] And yet there is much in Heidegger's thought that would call into question the philosophical rigor of the aforementioned moves. Heidegger's basic assumption that authenticity or greatness is the exclusive property of enlightened subjects, for instance, is strongly undercut on a number of *Heideggerian* grounds. In what follows, I will focus on five of them.

First, Heidegger's critique of Cartesian subjectivism makes it clear that the self is a complex phenomenon and cannot simply be identified with the ego. Thus, it is a mistake to attribute greatness, one-sidedly, to individual constitution, while minimizing the fact that Dasein is fundamentally a being that shares its being *with* others. In fact, Heidegger's language of "being-in-the-world" makes it clear that the categories of self and other, content and context, identity and difference, cannot be disentangled. But if this is so, then can Hölderlin's greatness really mean the greatness owned or possessed by the person named Hölderlin, or is it not rather, a greatness *attested to* by Hölderlin's poetry, yet preserved by his readers, interpreters, and translators? As Heidegger writes in his essay on the "Origin of the Work of Art," "Not only the creation of the work is poetic, but equally poetic, though in its own way, is the preserving of the work..."[123] This preservation occurs, moreover, according to Heidegger, only as a give-and-take between the work and

[122] Peter Sloterdjik, *Critique of Cynical Reason*, trans. Michael Eldred (London: Verso, 1998), 195–210.

[123] Heidegger, "The Origin of the Work of Art," 199.

the interpreter—that is, when we "move into what is disclosed by the work so as to bring our own essence itself to take a stand in the truth of beings."[124] But once we accept that the greatness of poetry consists in this back-and-forth, then, Heidegger concludes, we will have to give up our metaphysical attachment to the reified artistic conception of greatness otherwise known as "genius."[125] Extending this argument, we should say that the same holds for political leaders as well. Political leadership must be characterized by a capacity to engage in and honor dialogue, something that is simply incompatible with regimes that violently enforce censorship and genocide.

A second reason to chafe against the "great man" view of leadership is supplied by Heidegger's oft-repeated claim that Nietzsche's "will to power" is the culmination of metaphysics, and is thus a symptom of, rather than a cure for, our modern malaise. Thus, even if we want to read *Being and Time* as a work that equates authenticity with decisionism, we must come to terms with Heidegger's later critiques of Nietzsche, in which authentic decision-making involves something much more complex than simply asserting one's will with resoluteness.

Third, and related, is Heidegger's claim, intimated in *Being and Time*, but also advanced in his *Contributions to Philosophy* and *Country Path Conversations*, that authenticity involves reticence (*Verschweigung*), restraint (*Verhaltenheit*), repose (*Ruhe*), and releasement (*Gelassenheit*), terms that denote openness, receptivity, humility, and non-aggression. As Heidegger writes, "restraint is the ground of care" ("*Die Verhaltenheit ist der Grund der Sorge*").[126] Heidegger's turn to such a receptive model of leadership is also of a piece with his famous use of the Biblical motif of the shepherd in his 1946 "Letter on Humanism," who, in contrast to the figure of the warrior, is a figure of peace and gentleness.

Fourth is Heidegger's ontological definition of the human being as a *potentiality of being* (*Seinskönnen*). As Heidegger writes, "Da-sein is not something objectively present which then has as an addition the ability to do something, but is rather primarily being-possible. Da-sein is always what it can be and how it is its possibility."[127] Such a non-essentialist

---

[124] Ibid.

[125] Ibid., 200.

[126] *Contributions to Philosophy*, 29; GA 65, 35.

[127] SZ, 143/ BT, 134.

understanding of who we are can be read as a rebuke against both genetic and cultural determinism, as well as of any ideology that would want to fix a person's identity to any ontic properties such as blood or soil. And it could be used, moreover, as a way of checking the common tendency to overlook the complexity and dynamism of individuals and groups by attempting to paint them in monolithic moral terms as *either* good *or* bad, helpful *or* harmful.

Fifth is Heidegger's claim "that there is translating within one and the same language," a claim that can be read as not only undercutting linguistic essentialism, but as actively insisting on the primacy of linguistic alterity and difference.[128] It is a claim, moreover, that maintains the irreducible singularity of any given linguistic event without letting this become an excuse for linguistic chauvinism. Finally, Heidegger's claim shows that the politics of translation go beyond just questions of linguistic fidelity to the heart of what it means to share meaning with others. In defining translation as a hermeneutic and existential matter, Heidegger underscores that the true challenge of translation is not finding the most semantically or syntactically appropriate words, but rather of opening up a dialogue between understandings that, though incommensurable, can nevertheless speak to each other. Recognizing the primacy and ineluctability of translation, in other words, is part and parcel of an ethics of humility. It is to understand that translation is not an obstacle to disclosure, but the only way that disclosure can occur.

While these observations may not redeem Heidegger's thought *tout court*, they offer positive directions in which Heidegger's thought can be taken beyond itself. That Heidegger himself did not put these aspects of his thought in the service of self-examination, but instead held fast to an ideological post-war German narrative that saw American liberalism as no better than Nazism, is lamentable, but not a reason, in my estimation, to dismiss the thought itself. The essentialist streaks of Heidegger—embodied in the grand narratives Heidegger loves to tell about the destiny of the Greeks and the Germans—are part of the pathos of his philosophical conceit, but they should not lead us to forget what Fred Dallmayr calls "the other Heidegger," the Heidegger whose thought can help expose these very postures as evasions of finitude.[129] As Veronique Foti

[128] Heidegger, *Der Ister*, 62; GA 53, 75.
[129] Fred C. Dallmayr, *The Other Heidegger* (Ithaca: Cornell University Press, 1993).

argues, "Heidegger's strong nationalistic tendencies become tempered by the realization that the retrieval of *aletheia* [unconcealment] undercuts ideologies of national identity."[130] Or as Heidegger himself put it, "Every nationalism is metaphysically an anthropologism, and as such subjectivism."[131]

More complex, however, is the issue of whether Heidegger's agonistic conception of truth condemns his thought as fascist or opens it up for progressive appropriation. What, for instance, are we to make of Heidegger's claim—inspired by a reading of Heraclitus's fragment 53 ("war is the king of all things")—that "Beings are in their constancy and presence only if they are preserved and governed by struggle [*polemos*] as their ruler"?[132] Does such a claim amount to a celebration of violence or does it hold out the promise of an agonistic model of democracy?[133] We can see, even in the writing of the Levinasian philosopher and liberation theologian, Enrique Dussel, that the answer is far from simple:

> From Heraclitus to Karl von Clausewitz and Henry Kissinger, "war is the origin of everything," if by "everything" one understands the order or system that world dominators control by their power and armies. We are at war—a cold war for those who wage it, a hot war for those who suffer it, a peaceful coexistence for those who manufacture arms, a bloody existence for those obliged to buy and use them [...] Space as a battlefield, as a geography studied to destroy an enemy, as a territory with fixed frontiers, is very different from the abstract idealization of empty space of Newton's physics or the existential space of phenomenology. Abstract spaces are naïve, nonconflictual unrealities. The space of a world within the

---

[130] Veronique Foti, "*Aletheia* and Oblivion's Field: On Heidegger's *Parmenides* Lectures," in *Ethics and Danger: Essays on Heidegger and Continental Thought*, ed. Arlene Dallery and Charles E. Scott (Albany: SUNY Press, 1992), 78, 71–82.

[131] "Letter on Humanism," 244.

[132] *Being and Truth*, trans. Gregory Fried and Richard Polt (Bloomington: Indiana University Press, 2010), 73; GA 37, 90–92. For an extended analysis of this question, see Gregory Fried in *Heidegger's* Polemos: *From Being to Politics* (New Haven: Yale University Press, 2000).

[133] A similar set of questions haunts the reception of the Nazi jurist and political theorist, Carl Schmitt. See, for example, Chantal Mouffe, *The Democratic Paradox* (London: Verso, 2005); Gopal Balakrishnan, *The Enemy: An Intellectual Portrait of Carl Schmitt* (London: Verso, 2002).

ontological horizon is the space of a world center, of the organic, self-conscious state that brooks no contradictions—because it is an imperialist state.[134]

On the one hand, Dussel seems to accuse Heraclitean-Heideggerian ontology of supporting imperialism and realpolitik. On the other hand, Dussel acknowledges that to regard our world in neutral terms would be "naïve." Rather than come down on one side or another, I simply want to note that this question is not restrictively an exegetical question. As Samuel Moyn shows, the widespread emphasis on crisis and struggle as loci of self-discovery was part of a larger historical trend that began in post-WWI Germany, thanks, in large part, to the influence of Karl Barth by way of Kierkegaard.[135] That Barth, who embraced a language of crisis and struggle parallel to Heidegger, and yet wrote a personal letter of protest to Hitler, shows, at minimum, that there is no essential link between crisis philosophy and fascism. It is also worth noting that some thinkers, such as Schelling, have gone so far as to argue that agonism is the only way to achieve some kind of intersubjective liberation: "If there were no conflict, love could not become real."[136] Thus, however scandalizing certain aspects of Heidegger's thought maybe, we should consider that they speak to a more general *aporia* about violence and responsibility. One way to articulate the problem in which Heidegger's thought, like all thought, is caught, is how or whether we can engage in non-violent resistance in a world whose structures automatically implicate us in networks of unthinkable exploitation and domination?[137]

[134] Enrique Dussel, *Philosophy of Liberation*, trans. Aquilina Martinez (New York: Orbis Books, 1985).

[135] See Samuel Moyn, *The Origins of the Other: Emmanuel Levinas Between Revelation and Ethics* (Ithaca: Cornell University Press, 2005), 168–70. For a look at how similar trends effected German-Jewish thinkers, see Benjamin Lazier, *God Interrupted: Heresy and the European Imagination Between the World Wars* (Princeton: Princeton University Press, 2008).

[136] F.W.J. Schelling, *Philosophical Enquiries into the Nature of Human Freedom*, trans. James Gutmann (La Salle: Open Court, 1992), 374/50.

[137] For an excellent examination of the twentieth and twenty-first century philosophical debates on this question, and in particular of Walter Benjamin's enigmatic, yet influential essay, "The Critique of Violence," see Richard Bernstein, *Violence: Thinking Without Banisters* (Cambridge: Polity, 2013).

Without purporting to solve this problem, this book shows that in understanding the task of thinking as a poetic one, we make room for a way of discoursing that allows the marginal and marginalized to reveal themselves as part of "the truth of Being." And in so doing, we are on the way to an ethics of humility.

This being case, there is still one more set of issues that must be discussed, namely Heidegger's post-war silence. According to George Steiner, the most troubling question is not how to make sense of Heidegger's early involvement in Nazism, but how to make sense of his inability or unwillingness to apologize for it after the war.[138] For Steiner, it is this omission that testifies to the failure of Heidegger's thought more generally: "Lacking an ethic, self-maimed in the face of the inhuman," Steiner writes, "Heidegger's ontology remains an overwhelming fragment."[139] Richard Bernstein goes even further than Steiner, arguing that Heidegger's silence is attributable to his philosophical essentialism, which, by necessity, must flatten all particular evils by reading them as merely symptomatic of more fundamental, ontological problems.[140] If these critics are right, then Heidegger's ontology—even as it is articulated in his later texts—is ethically compromised. For the implication would be that ontological concerns and ontic concerns stand in diametric opposition to each other, and that, facing a tradeoff between ontological profundity, on the one hand, and ontic sobriety on the other, we must choose the latter. This is a serious charge and one that I discuss at greater length in the next chapter. For now, I simply want to state my disagreement with this claim. Hopefully, my book will convince the reader that the ontological and the ontic are interlinked, and that the question is not which of them we must choose, but how we can integrate them without effacing their distinction.

[138] See, for example, George Steiner, *Martin Heidegger* (Chicago: Chicago University Press, 1989), xxxiv.

[139] Ibid.

[140] Richard J. Bernstein, "Heidegger's Silence?: Ethos and Technology," in *The New Constellation: The Ethical-Political Horizons of Modernity/Postmodernity* (Cambridge: MIT Press, 1991), 79–141.

A NOTE ON THE TEXTS

My book is guided by two questions, one negative, and one positive. The negative question is: "What are the *challenges* that the philosophical assumptions of modernity (as analyzed by Heidegger) pose to human and planetary welfare?" and the positive question is: "What contribution can such a diagnosis make toward the construction of an ethics capable of responding to these challenges?" These two questions correlate with two prominent motifs in the writings of the later Heidegger, the first being "the danger" posed by what he calls "The Essence of Technology" (*das Wesen der Technik*), and the second being "the saving power" of what he calls poetry (*Dichtung*). How, in short, can Poetry (ontologically defined) be a radical and transformative response to Technology (ontologically defined)?

The answer, I argue, can be found in Heidegger's contention that (1) our understanding of—and relationship to language is decisive in determining the kind of world that we inhabit and (2) that there is a critical difference between a technological understanding of language, which treats language as an instrument for transmitting meaning, and the poetic understanding of language, which calls attention to the fact that in every utterance it is "language itself [that] speaks."[141] Stated more simply, there is a difference between language that conceals the fact of its being language and language that reveals the fact of its being language. The former reduces meaning to information, turning speaker and listener (or text and reader) into mere inputs and outputs, while the latter allows meaning to remain open, turning speaker and listener (or text and reader) into participants in an event of meaningfulness.

That our relationship to language is at the center of Heidegger's larger concerns is something Heidegger states directly in his "Letter on Humanism"—the essay that he wrote in response to Jean Beaufret's question, "When will you write an ethics"? Heidegger writes, "The widely and rapidly spreading devastation of language not only undermines aesthetic and moral responsibility in every use of language; it arises from a threat to the essence of humanity."[142] In other words, Heidegger claims, our ethical considerations must include not just questions of right

---

[141] Heidegger, "Language," in *Poetry, Language, Thought*, 191.

[142] Heidegger, "Letter on Humanism," 222.

and wrong *action*, but of *the terms* by which we evaluate our actions as right or wrong. How we speak, think, and communicate—Heidegger here suggests—is of paramount significance to human and planetary welfare, and therefore it is insufficient and even dangerous to sequester ethical questions from our consideration of the discursive conditions that make their discussion possible.[143] The same, I will be arguing by extension, holds for theology.

Consequently, the focus of my textual attention will be on those places where Heidegger discusses these interrelated themes of technology, poetry, and language. These include "The Origin of the Work of Art" (1935–1936), *Elucidations of Hölderlin's Poetry* (1936–1968), *Hölderlin's Hymn "Der Ister"* (1936), "The Age of the World Picture" (1938), "Overcoming Metaphysics" (1936–1946), "What Are Poets For?" (1946), "The Letter on Humanism" (1946), "The Turning" (1949), "The Thing" (1950), "Language" (1950), "Building Dwelling Thinking" (1951), "...Poetically Man Dwells..." (1951), *What Is Called Thinking?* (1951), and "The Question Concerning Technology" (1953).

THE CRITICAL CONTRIBUTION OF *BEING AND TIME*: "DASEIN"

In spite of my emphasis on these texts, however, it will be obvious to the reader that certain aspects of *Being and Time* also play a critical role in my presentation of Heidegger's thought. This is in keeping with Heidegger's own remarks that his early thought and his later thought should be read in light of each other. As he famously told William Richardson,

> The distinction...between Heidegger I and Heidegger II is justified only on the condition that it be constantly kept in mind: only by way of what [Heidegger] I has thought does one gain access to what-is to-be-thought

---

[143] The concept of ethics I employ throughout this book is not an overtly directive or normative ethics; it is certainly not Kantian. And yet a major feature of my argument is that Heidegger's critique of traditional ethical philosophy does not eviscerate normativity altogether, but offers a poetic meditation on human flourishing, one that he hoped, and we can hope, may lead to a better condition for the human being. Heidegger's "utility," to use a word he rails against, is not at the level of prescribing answers to the trolley problem, but at the level of reflection.

by [Heidegger] II. But the thought of [Heidegger] I becomes possible only if it is contained in the thought of [Heidegger] II.[144]

Consequently, it is worth mentioning here just a few insights of *Being and Time* that I believe are helpful for grasping the significance of Heidegger's later work, and which I unpack in more depth in subsequent chapters. The first concerns Heidegger's ontological definition of Dasein, and the second concerns what I will call "the paradox of authenticity."

By defining the human being as Dasein, Heidegger effectively short-circuits the debate between realism and idealism (see section §43) as well as related debates about whether truth is subjective or objective (see section §45). For by using this term, Heidegger wants to claim that all of the traditional interpretations of the human being are only possible on the basis of a more primordial phenomenon, namely what he calls "Being" (*Sein*). Yet as noted above, Thomas Sheehan shows that "Being" is simply Heidegger's phenomenological way of saying "meaningfulness." Therefore, Heidegger's definition of the human being as Dasein amounts to saying that to be a human being is to be confronted by the primordial and ineluctable fact of meaningfulness. In other words, meaningfulness is the condition for both perception and action and without it there could be neither. Conversely, it would be impossible to perceive or do something that is completely without meaning. More than this, though, Heidegger's term "Dasein" suggests that meaningfulness always unfolds within a particular existential space or "Da"—literally a "here" or "there." That is to say, that meaningfulness is not just inexorable, but that it is always inexorably *here*. Or better yet, every "here" can be "here" only because it is shot through with meaningfulness. Thus, the term "Dasein" also succinctly suggests—though it is the merit of *Being and Time* to argue this point at length—that time and space are indexed to meaningfulness long before they can be indexed to any particular system we have for measuring them, such as the clock or the ruler. It is because of a particular understanding of meaningfulness, in other words, that we can measure time and space as we do, Heidegger argues, and not the other way around.

---

[144]Quoted in William J. Richardson, *Heidegger: From Phenomenology to Thought* (New York: Fordham University Press, 2003), xxxii–xxxiii.

A number of further things can be said about the primordiality of meaningfulness. One is that meaningfulness is always meaningfulness *for me*. That is to say, it is *jemeinig*, mine. At the same time, however, the fact that meaningfulness is always mine—always mediated by my projective sense of who I *can be* as well as by my thrown sense of *having been*—does not mean that meaningfulness is simply arbitrary or interior. Heidegger's insight that Dasein is always already "being-*in-the-world*," as well as his claim that Dasein is always already *Mitsein*—being-with (-others)—makes it clear that mineness is not the sole or exclusive mediator of meaningfulness. Instead, who I am—my capacity to perceive, understand, and act—is always also socially and ecologically determined. This is true in the obvious sense that we *develop* into Dasein only through a long and complex process of education and socialization, and that, from a young age, the terms of our sense of self are explicitly *given to* us by others—parents, elders, teachers, and peers. But it is also true in the sense that, even as adult Dasein, part of what it means to aspire and to understand ourselves in terms of our own projects is to see ourselves as part of a community and a story that is larger than our own egos. In Heidegger's evocative language, having such an understanding means having a "Destiny" (see §74). Heidegger contends that having a destiny is not just an incidental thing that could happen to Dasein, but a possibility that is structural to its being what it is. As he writes, "the fateful destiny of Da-sein in and with its 'generation' constitutes the complete, authentic occurrence of Da-sein."[145] Heidegger clarifies, "Destiny is not composed of individual fates, nor can being-with-one-another be conceived of as the mutual occurrence of several subjects. These fates are already guided beforehand in being-with-one-another in the same world..."[146]

Thus, my projects are never just for *me*, even if the non-substitutability of my own death means that I am the sole person that can formulate them and carry them out. This is an important point, though it is one that is typically lost on those interpreters who regard Heidegger's emphasis on the authenticity of being-toward-death as somehow solipsistic. As Lawrence Hatab convincingly argues, *Being and Time* is best read as an attempt to bring the ideals of liberalism and communitarianism

[145] SZ, 385/ BT, 352.
[146] SZ, 384/ BT, 352.

together, rather than as an argument in favor of one tradition over the other.[147] Hatab's argument is succinctly captured by Heidegger's own remark that individuation (or what he calls "existential solipsism") should not be mistaken for ethical or epistemological solipsism. As Heidegger writes,

> *Angst* individualizes and thus discloses Da-sein as '*solus ipse*.' This existential 'solipsism,' however, is so far from transposing an isolated subject-thing into the harmless vacuum of a worldless occurrence that it brings Da-sein in an extreme sense precisely before its world as world, and thus itself before itself as being-in-the-world.[148]

In other words, while meaningfulness is always *mediated* by my own acute, inimitable, and idiosyncratic perspective, the terms of my perspective are at the same time *given* to me, or in Heidegger's more charged language, "thrown" upon me.[149] Even this language is imprecise, insofar as it makes it seem as though there were a stable, identifiable "me" onto whom certain demands and possibilities are thrown when instead it would be more accurate to say that my egoic sense of self arises only as and in the constant interplay between individuation and sociality. Moreover, as the passage quoted above indicates, true individuation does *not* mean detachment from the world, but instead, the discovery and clarification of one's place in it. Thus, while there is a sense in which Dasein is singled out by the ineluctability of its own death (and therefore, life), there is another sense in which this singling out can occur only in response and in relationship to others. In short, it is only when we equate Dasein with the ego that we imagine that an ethics of authenticity necessarily constitutes an ethics of selfishness. In fact, however, such a misunderstanding is precisely what characterizes Dasein in its inauthentic mode. As Heidegger writes, "The they-self [*Das Man*] keeps on saying 'I' most loudly and frequently because at bottom it is

---

[147]Lawrence J. Hatab, *Ethics and Finitude: Heideggerian Contributions to Moral Philosophy* (Oxford: Rowman & Littlefield, 2000), 176–178. See also Lawrence Vogel, *The Fragile We: Ethical Implications of "Being and Time"* (Evanston: Northwestern University Press, 1994), 103–124.

[148]SZ, 188/ BT, 176.

[149]SZ, 135/ BT, 127.

not *authentically* itself and evades its authentic potentiality-of-being."[150] And, in a direct challenge to the Cartesian tradition, Heidegger writes that "[s]elf-understanding should not be equated formally with a reflected ego-experience."[151]

The consequence of understanding Dasein as a locus of meaningfulness that includes a sense of mineness, but is also not reducible to it, I will be arguing in subsequent chapters, is that our responsibility is dialogical, not monological. In being responsible for our own being, we must necessarily take responsibility for our being-in-*the-world*, and for our *being-with*-others. And even if we understand that "world" for Heidegger is an existential category, meaning something like "*my* meaning-giving context," this does not mean that it is only subjective. Instead, my meaning-giving context is, by necessity, always also *our* meaning-giving context. Understanding this does not guarantee that we will behave morally or compassionately toward all beings—it may be possible to have an authentic self-understanding, and *for that very reason*, come to eugenic conclusions—but it does enjoin us to exercise moral consideration and compassion toward *some others*. And in doing so, we may come to discover that, although there are practical and epistemological limits to our capacity to care for everyone, this does not mean that we shouldn't aspire toward creating a world where all Dasein are cared for *as* Dasein, that is, as singular loci of meaningfulness who share a common destiny. The consequences of treating others *as Dasein*, I will show, tilt toward love and compassion, even as the particular dilemmas that confront us in our attempts to enact such love and compassion remain insoluble.

We have just seen that how we understand who we are and how we understand Being more generally are crucially interrelated, a point that Heidegger makes explicitly in his lecture course "What Is Called Thinking?" when he says, "as soon as I thoughtfully say, 'man's nature,' I have already said relatedness to Being. Likewise, as soon as I say thoughtfully: Being of beings, the relatedness to man's nature has been named."[152] Consequently, this means that forgetting one necessarily entails forgetting the other. When we forget Being, we forget who

---

[150] SZ, 322/ BT, 296.

[151] Heidegger, *Basic Problems of Phenomenology*, 175.

[152] Heidegger, *What Is Called Thinking?*, 179.

we truly are (Dasein), and when we forget who we truly are, we forget Being. This is why *Being and Time* pursues "the question of the meaning of Being" as an analysis of Dasein ("What is primarily interrogated in the question of the meaning of being that being which has the character of Da-sein") as well as why it claims that it is only by understanding Dasein in its authentic mode, that this analysis can be completed.[153] Yet this raises a series of questions: how can Dasein *become authentic* if Dasein is not simply a synonym for the ego, but is instead a unique site of world-disclosure? What would it take for Dasein to understand itself not just conceptually, but *existentially*, as Dasein? Or in other words, what connection can be drawn, if any, between reading *Being and Time* and taking its wisdom to heart? It is here that *Being and Time* seems to be elliptical. For what *Being and Time* sketches is simply what some of the features of an authentic self might involve—"Angst," "anticipatory resoluteness"—not how to *become* authentic. In fact, while *Being and Time* discusses the inauthentic structures of Dasein that constantly inhibit its capacity to be itself, Heidegger is also very clear that inauthenticity is *not* to be regarded as though it were a synonym for "illusory" or "fake." As Heidegger writes,

> [I]nauthentic and non-authentic by no means signify "not really," as if Da-sein utterly lost its being in this kind of being-in-the-world. Inauthenticity does not mean anything like no-longer-being-in-the-world, but rather it constitutes precisely a distinctive kind of being-in-the-world, which is completely taken in by the world and the *Mitda-sein* of the others in the they. Not-being-itself functions as a *positive* possibility of beings which are absorbed in a world, essentially taking care of that world. This *nonbeing* must be conceived as the kind of being of Da-sein nearest to it and in which it mostly maintains itself.[154]

In other words, "Not-being-itself" is still a mode of being Dasein, and therefore cannot simply be opposed to being-itself. Heidegger maintains a similar logic in his late essay, "...Poetically Man Dwells..." There he writes that "dwelling can be unpoetic only because it is in essence poetic.

[153] SZ, 41, 231/ BT, 36, 213.
[154] SZ, 176/ BT, 164.

For man to be blind, he must remain a being by nature endowed with sight. A piece of wood can never go blind."[155]

Heidegger's argument that inauthenticity is a structural feature of Dasein helps us appreciate why, for him, authenticity and inauthenticity are not to be interpreted as moral designators. As he writes,

> [Fallenness, *Verfallenheit*] does not signify the Fall of man understood in a 'moral-philosophical' and at the same time secularized way; rather it designates an essential relationship of man to Being within Being's relation to the essence of man. Accordingly, the terms 'authenticity' and 'inauthenticity,' which are used in provisional fashion, do not imply a moral-existential or an 'anthropological' distinction but rather a relation which...has yet to be thought...[namely,] an 'ecstatic' relation of the essence of man to the truth of Being.[156]

Heidegger repeats a variation of this claim again in his "Letter on Humanism," when he writes, "What is said in *Being and Time*...about the "they" [*das Man*] in no way means to furnish an incidental contribution to sociology. Just as little does the "they" mean merely the opposite, understood in an ethical-existentiell way, of the selfhood of persons."[157]

What follows from these remarks is strange and paradoxical. If inauthenticity and authenticity are integral to Dasein's being—i.e., something that Dasein cannot help but be modified by—then to interpret them as something that Dasein *ought to be modified by* is to make a category mistake. Or said another way, it is to take the being of Dasein as something objectively present, and thus to miss the essence of Dasein itself. The paradox, then, is that Heidegger construes inauthenticity as both an inhibition to our true selves and as a structure of our true selves. Meanwhile, authenticity is paradoxically defined as both an exceptional modality of Dasein, and something that is fundamental to Dasein.[158]

---

[155] "...Poetically Man Dwells...," 225.

[156] SZ, 175–176/ BT, 164.

[157] "Letter on Humanism," 221–222.

[158] For a similar argument that shows the parallels between Heidegger's account of authenticity and the Zen idea of "the gateless gate" see Joan Stambaugh, "An Inquiry into Authenticity and Inauthenticity in *Being and Time*," *Research in Phenomenology* 7, no. 1 (1977): 153–161. For a work that picks up on this paradox, but treats it as an inconsistency to be resolved, see Hubert Dreyfus, *Being-In-The-World: A Commentary on Heidegger's Being and Time, Division I* (Cambridge: MIT Press, 1991), 333. The reason Dreyfus thinks Heidegger's account of authenticity is "incoherent," is the result of his believing

Michael Lewis captures this paradox well when he writes,

> Too often Dasein is misunderstood as a state, indeed as an entity, an individual man, while in fact [Dasein] is the very process of individuation itself—the formation of an individual self-relating entity—and one which is always incomplete because Dasein is never exclusively being-towards-death. If there were such a thing as an authentic Dasein then it would no longer be Dasein, for Dasein exists as the process which stretches *between* the authentic and the inauthentic, pulled towards its own death but also pulled in the other direction, towards a birth which is common to everyone and which amounts to our factual arrival in a particular world. Without these two vectors tugging at one another the tearing that is Dasein would not occur.[159]

Lewis's characterization of Dasein as a "process of individuation" and as a "tearing," and *not* as an entity, shows that the meanings of authenticity (*Eigentlichkeit*) and inauthenticity (*Uneigentlichkeit*)—both etymologically connected to ownership and possession—must be understood dialectically.[160] For even if we translate authenticity as being-oneself and inauthenticity as not-being-oneself (or, according to the etymology, as self-possession and self-dispossession), the point is that the "self" of this oneself is not something that we can point to, but is instead a field of ever-changing tensions, and it is only on this basis that pointing itself can occur.

Thus, to summarize what we have said so far, there are two strange features of Dasein. First, Dasein is an openness to Being

---

that authenticity depends on Dasein's "motivation," a position that, as we will see, the later Heidegger rejects as subjectivist.

[159] Michael Lewis, *Heidegger and the Place of Ethics* (London: Continuum, 2005), 14–15.

[160] Let me be clear here that my use of the term "dialectic" in this book follow Adorno's definition of dialectics as a permanent struggle, and not the more conciliatory definition typically attributed to Hegel. As Adorno writes, "[t]o proceed dialectically means to think in contradictions, for the sake of the contradiction once experienced in the thing, and against that contradiction. A contradiction in reality, it is a contradiction against reality." Adorno, *Negative Dialectics*, trans. E.B. Ashton (Routledge: London, 1973), 145. In other words, the essence of dialectical thinking is to think—paradoxically—*both* "for the sake of" and "against" contradictions. While Heidegger himself does not characterize his thinking in this way, and while Adorno even argues that Heidegger's thought is expressly at odds with dialectical thinking—see ibid., 155—my contention is that Adorno's definition of dialectics offers a helpful way to show what is positive in Heidegger's own inconsistencies.

(meaningfulness) that is colored by a sense of mineness and a sense of belonging to others (and to a realm of meaning that is larger than itself). Second, while Dasein can be itself—can recognize itself *as* Dasein—only when it is authentic, an integral part of what it means for Dasein to be itself is to be inauthentic. This means that even when Dasein misunderstands itself and is not itself, it is still itself. And even more peculiarly, it is only when Dasein misunderstands itself that it regards authenticity as a goal or an ideal that it must somehow achieve.

As I will show in the coming chapters, this complex understanding of the human condition offered in *Being and Time* anticipates a number of deep and deeply dialectical conclusions argued by the later Heidegger. As we saw above, one such conclusion was that it is precisely a hallmark of metaphysical thinking to aspire to overcome metaphysics, whereas a genuinely post-metaphysical thinking must be capable of recognizing the structural necessity of metaphysics. The paradox here is that the "way out" of metaphysical thinking is not actually a way out, but a way in. This paradox is also formulated in Heidegger's later writings on *Gelassenheit*, often translated as "releasement" or "letting-be." On the one hand, Heidegger declares that *Gelassenheit* is a posture of non-willing, one in which the ego does not interfere with the disclosure that is occurring. At the same time, however, to will non-willing—to desire to be non-willing—is to interpret *Gelassenheit* from an egoic perspective as a goal, and thus to miss the essence of *Gelassenheit*, namely that it is always already happening, and therefore not simply something that the ego needs to do. As "The Scholar" in one of Heidegger's philosophical dialogues puts it, "Non-willing...means: to willfully renounce willing. *And*...that which does not at all pertain to the will"[161] (emphasis added). The paradox, here, is that the ego operates as both an obstruction to authentic perception, and, as simply another texture of authentic expression. In other words, it is only from an egoic perspective that the ego is seen to be in need of overcoming, whereas from a posture of releasement, the ego is simply there as one texture of meaningfulness among others.

Heidegger's most famous articulation of this paradoxical structure appears in his commentary on Hölderlin's poetic statement, "But where danger is, there grows/The saving power also" (*Wo die Gefahr ist, da wächst/das Rettende auch*). Glossing these lines, Heidegger writes,

---

[161] Heidegger, *Country Path Conversations*, 69; GA 77, 106.

"Where the danger is as the danger, there the saving power is already thriving also. The latter does not appear incidentally. The saving power is not secondary to the danger. The self-same danger is, when it is *as* the danger, the saving power."[162] In other words, according to Heidegger, the danger of forgetting who we are/forgetting Being is also something that, when acknowledged, becomes the very path toward self-remembrance/remembrance of Being. Moreover, without the very danger of forgetting Being, there could be no possibility of remembering Being. Paradoxically, then, it is when we recognize obstacles to authenticity as endemic to the structure of our being that they cease to be obstacles. It is for this reason, I argue, that Heidegger's critique of metaphysics must also be understood in a positive light. For it is by recognizing the ways in which metaphysics obstructs our capacity to be ourselves that we can begin to discover its saving power. Whereas, if we simply ignore metaphysics—or else, if we understand it *only* as a worldview, rather than as a structural tendency of Dasein—we remain caught up in its dualistic logic. The point, then, of a critique of metaphysics, I am arguing, is to recognize that the *opposition* metaphysical thinking sets up between the "danger" and the "saving power" need not be authoritative. Instead, it is just as possible to regard the danger and the saving power as two different ways to make sense of the same enigmatic phenomenon.[163] As my book will show in subsequent chapters, this ontological understanding also carries ethical and theological import. In learning to regard Being/ourselves non-dualistically (which does not mean anti-dualistically), we can become more capable of listening and responding to the calls of others, as well as more capable of encountering the divine in and as a play of nearness *and* farness, revelation *and* hiddenness.

In the next chapter, I will show how and why such an understanding can be characterized as "ethical." Before doing so, however, a few concluding words are in order about the meaning of this book's subtitle, "Unframing Existence."

---

[162] Heidegger, "The Turning," 42.

[163] For a sustained argument of this point, see Iain Thomson, "Understanding Technology Ontotheologically, or The Danger and The Promise of Heidegger, an American perspective," in *New Waves in Philosophy of Technology*, ed. Jan Kyrre Berg Olsen Friis, Evan Selinger, and Søren (London: Palgrave Macmillan, 2009), 147–166. For a more general argument on "aspect-seeing" in Heidegger, see Stephen Mulhall, *Wittgenstein and Heidegger: On Seeing Aspects* (London: Routledge, 1990).

UNFRAMING EXISTENCE

"Unframing Existence" offers a play on Heidegger's concepts of "Enframing" (*Gestell*) and "Unconcealment" (*a-letheia*).[164] It emphasizes first that the key to a non-instrumental relation to truth requires us to check our desire for frames—i.e., for narratives whose primary imperatives are security and order—and instead learn to recognize an unframable dimension of existence, namely the sheer enigma that there is meaningfulness at all; and second, that unframing is *both* something we must do to our conceptions of what it means for us to exist *as well as* something for which existence itself always already beckons (qua *un*canny). Finally, the "-ing" suffix in "unframing" signifies that the practice of unframing is always in progress, and never concluded or conclusive. Moreover, it signifies that "unframing" always transpires in relation to an entrenched set of counter-tendencies toward framing and reframing, so that the question is *not* how do we immunize ourselves to all frameworks—an impossible feat—but rather, how do we allow ourselves to recognize frameworks *as* frameworks? Or, in other words, how do we operate *within* frameworks without losing our appreciation for the fact that these frameworks are always mediated and motivated by finitude? For the model of unframing existence for which I am arguing is not that we abandon the frames through which our understanding is colored, but that we appreciate the extent to which our sense of who we are is both inherited, something into which we are "thrown," and revisable, something we must always reinterpret in light of a uniquely anticipated future. In short, "unframing existence" means maintaining an awareness of the richness and irrepressibility of potentiality. Such a posture is not strictly synonymous with ethical behavior or with faith, but, as this book will show, it is nevertheless a crucial feature of an ethical and religious life.

[164] The English word, "Enframing" is a particularly awkward and jargony way to render *Gestell*, which in German, simply means, "frame," "rack," or "stand," i.e., that which holds something up, and gives it structure. Therefore, it is best to think of *Gestell*, per Joan Stambaugh's translation, as "The Framework." See *Identity and Difference*, 35. Nevertheless, for the sake of scholarly consistency, and for the sake of highlighting that it is, for Heidegger, a philosophical designation, I will stick to William Lovitt's "Enframing."

CHAPTER 2

Ontological Ethics as a Restoration of Questionability

Being able to question means being able to wait, even for a lifetime. But an age for which the actual is only whatever goes fast and can be grasped with both hands takes questioning as "a stranger to reality," as something that does not count as profitable. But what is essential is not counting but the right time—that is, the right moment and the right endurance.[1]

In the previous chapter, we saw that Heidegger's project is best read as an invitation to think in new ways, rather than simply as a theory about the meaning of "Being." We also saw that part of what makes Heidegger's project radical—and therefore impossible to definitively interpret—is that it asks us not simply to cognize the meaning of Being, but to enact and embody that understanding in the world. We saw how this claim was borne out in Heidegger's critique of metaphysics, to the extent that its primary charge was not that we abandon metaphysical language and argument altogether, but instead that we learn to recognize it as an entrenched human tendency, and thereby allow it to come to presence *as metaphysics*. And finally, we saw that Heidegger's definition of authenticity similarly involves not the dispelling of inauthenticity, but an ability to come to terms with it as a structure that is paradoxically integral to who we are. The question of this chapter, however, is whether, or in what way, such an ontological posture can be construed as

---

[1] *Introduction to Metaphysics*, 157; GA 40, 221.

ethical (and, conversely, whether or in what way, ethical life can be said to include and even require an ontological dimension).

As a question of Heidegger scholarship, the relationship between ontology and ethics is a divisive one, with compelling arguments on both sides. As a constructive question, however, it is one that, I will show, can be answered affirmatively: ontology and ethics are categorically distinct, yet existentially and phenomenologically imbricated.[2] Ethics presupposes ontology, because how we understand our being-in-the-world is critical to our capacity to live responsibly in it. Meanwhile, ontology presupposes ethics, because our understanding of being, rather than being fixed, is something we must continuously *renew, return to*, and *answer for* in each moment. In short, the stakes of ontology are ethical and the stakes of ethics are ontological. A sketch of the reasons for this

---

[2] It will help the reader to note that my use of the term "ethics" in this and subsequent chapters differs from the conception of ethics typically assumed in the field of normative ethics. The main difference is that normative ethics concerns *action*, whereas ethics in the broad sense that I seek to use it, concerns how we *bear ourselves* more generally, a category that includes, but cannot be limited to our actions. To be sure, how we act and how we bear ourselves can never be completely disentangled from each other. Nevertheless, it would be too hasty to try to derive or develop a positive, normative framework about right and wrong actions on the basis of the kind of ethical discussion that this book pursues. One reason for this is that ethics in the sense that I am using it refers not to rule-based decisions, but to the more general practice of living well. In this sense, my use of the word "ethics" is closer to that definition presupposed by virtue ethics, where the emphasis is not simply on obedience or outcomes, but on developing a kind of individuated, yet collectively situated practical wisdom. Moreover, where normative ethics is oriented around an axis of right/wrong, ethics in the sense that I am using it seeks to emphasize the extent to which we make choices not between right and wrong, but between right and right, i.e., choices where there is no simple right answer, but where different possibly right answers can nevertheless conflict with each other, forcing us to make difficult choices. Where normative ethics allows us to keep a good conscience by enabling us to justify our decisions as "the best," ethics in the sense that I am pursuing it, seeks to maintain a space for us to recognize an essentially tragic structure in many of our decisions. Existential questions regarding the extent and limits of our capacity to compromise cannot be settled by appealing to normative ethics, yet they are the kinds of questions that an ontological ethics such I pursue in this chapter and beyond can help clarify. Here the temptation may arise to call what I am doing "metaethics" rather than "ethics." Since, however, these questions do not occur beyond or outside of our everyday questions about how to live, but are instead the questions that most basically concern us, calling them "metaethical" seems disingenuous. If anything, it is the mathematical-logical approach to ethics, evinced in the classic variations of the trolley dilemma that should be construed as metaethical, since such an approach can only come after an immersion in ethical life itself.

conclusion (four from the side of ontology, and four from the side of ethics) can be found below:

1. Ontology can help us appreciate that the field of ethics is much broader than just the science of values or morally correct behavior, but is always constituted by the much more difficult question of what it means *to be* ethical, i.e., what it means to conduct oneself with care and compassion in a world that is complex and mediated.
2. Ontology can help us become sensitive to the problematic assumptions on which traditional ethical theories are based, not as a way of discounting these other theories, but as a way of endowing *us* with responsibility for the inherent tensions that constitute our being-in-the-world (e.g., the tensions between self and other, giving and taking, acceptance and judgment, norms and exceptions).
3. Ontology can help us encounter ourselves and others in a non-calculative and noninstrumentalizing way, thereby enjoining us to recognize and respond to our needs and the needs of others at a holistic, ontological level, rather than simply at an isolated, and objectifying level.
4. Ontology can make us aware of the complexity of our condition in such a way that it helps us embrace ambiguity, indeterminacy, and pluralism in the way we approach understanding a given situation.
5. Ethics reminds us that understanding our condition is not enough. Rather, we are always obliged to enact this understanding in the world, and to make difficult, time-bound and context-specific choices about how to respond most appropriately to the situation at hand.
6. Ethics reminds us that, although on one level, we cannot but be who we are, on another level, we remain alienated from who we are, and therefore called upon to "become who we are."
7. Ethics reminds us that authenticity is not an individual or egocentric affair, but a matter of being able to be present for and with those others with whom we share a world.
8. Ethics reminds us that, however paradoxical and problematic the following terms may be, the aspiration of ontology is the emancipation, freedom, redemption, and/or healing of *beings*.

Before we can come to a full understanding of the above proposal, however, we need to examine Heidegger's own position on this question as well as the common criticisms leveled against his ontology. In particular, we need to engage with the following accusations: (1) Ontology is too utopian, privileging a "pure and empty horizon of possibility" over and above anything actual, concrete, and positive.[3] (2) Ontology prioritizes authenticity to self over obligation to the other.[4] (3) Ontology is morally relativistic, formally empty and insufficiently directive.[5] (4) Ontology is actively hostile to everyday life.[6] (5) Ontology is an ideology of false consciousness—Adorno calls it "corny exoticism."[7] (6) Ontology is an idiosyncratic discourse that "lacks public utility."[8] While many of these criticisms hold some traction, the argument of this chapter is that they need not be read as refutations of ontology as such. Instead, they can be more positively considered as a set of questions that can clarify the stakes, limits, and risks of ontological ethics. Thus, rather than taking them as a *verdict* on Heidegger's thought, we should take them, I argue, as *testimony* to the challenges of appropriating it. Taking the criticisms of ontology seriously, I hope to show, can itself be considered an onto-ethical posture, as it makes room for us to encounter the essential questionability of our condition. In the next section, we open this discussion by examining Heidegger's ambivalence about calling his thought an ethics.

HEIDEGGER'S AMBIVALENCE

Heidegger's most famous remarks on the relationship between ontology and ethics can be found in his "Letter on Humanism":

[3] Hans Blumenberg, *Work on Myth*, trans. Robert M. Wallace (Cambridge: MIT Press, 1990), 224.

[4] Levinas, *Entre Nous: Thinking-Of-The-Other*, trans. Michael B. Smith and Barbara Harshav (New York: Columbia University Press, 1998), 116.

[5] See Jonas, *The Phenomenon of Life*, 235–261; Werner Marx, *Is There A Measure on Earth?: Foundations for a Nonmetaphysical Ethics*, trans. Thomas J. Nenon and Reginald Lilly (Chicago: University of Chicago Press, 1987), 248–249; and Richard Rubenstein, "The Philosopher and the Jews: The Case of Martin Heidegger," *Modern Judaism* 9, no. 2 (1989): 179–196, 181.

[6] Stephen K. White, "Heidegger and the Difficulties of a Postmodern Ethics and Politics," *Political Theory* 18, no. 1 (1990): 83, 80–103.

[7] Adorno, *Negative Dialectics*, 68.

[8] Richard Rorty, *Contingency, Irony, and Solidarity* (Cambridge: Cambridge University Press, 1989), 118–120.

If the name "ethics," in keeping with the basic meaning of the word *ethos*, should now say that "ethics" ponders the abode [*Aufenthalt*] of man, then that thinking which thinks the truth of Being as the primordial element of man, as one who ek-sists, is in itself the originary ethics [*Ursprüngliche Ethik*]. However, this thinking is not ethics in the first instance, because it is ontology.[9]

This passage captures Heidegger's ambivalence about calling his thought an ethics. On the one hand, Heidegger claims that his thought is "an originary ethics." On the other hand, Heidegger claims that it is *not* ethics, *because* it is ontology, implying that, at least in his own conception, ontology and ethics are mutually exclusive (in terms of the boundaries of academic disciplines). What are we to make of this apparent contradiction? One possible solution is to emphasize that Heidegger is struggling in this passage with an ambiguity in the word "ethics." On the one hand, Heidegger seeks to redefine and reclaim this word, as suggested by the fact that he opens this passage with the conditional: "If the name 'ethics' [...] should now say [...]." On the other hand, however, he seems to appreciate that his idiosyncratic and archaic definition of ethics will not be able to substitute for the ordinary understanding of ethics as a science of values or moral rectitude, and thus recoils from his initial suggestion that his thinking constitutes an ethics. Thus, strangely, Heidegger simultaneously says that his thinking is an "originary ethics" and that it is not an ethics.

A similar ambiguity, also bracketed by the conditional, can be found in Heidegger's 1933 lecture course "Being and Truth": "[I]f we ask about the good as we would ask about a good thing, then we will not find it, we will always run up against *the nothing*. The good can never be found at all among beings or Being. It requires that we ask in a different way."[10] The first two sentences suggest that ontology is not interested in "the good." The reason Heidegger gives is that ontological enquiry must confront "the nothing," and in so doing, must drop its metaphysical pretensions of being a science of values. Ontology cannot speak of "the good" because to do so would be to presuppose a Platonic realm that stands above the vicissitudes of temporality, language, and embodiment—in short, finitude. Moreover, in seeking out "the good"

---

[9] "Letter on Humanism," 258; GA 9, 356–357.

[10] *Being and Truth*, 154; GA 37, 199.

as an entity that can be identified and studied, it would be degrading "the good" into one object amongst many. On the other hand, however, Heidegger's negative statements needn't be interpreted as a wholesale dismissal of ethical enquiry, for his conclusion remains positive: asking about the good "requires that we ask in a different way."

We will come back to what it means to "ask in a different way" at the end of this section. For now we need to look further at why Heidegger was so reluctant to characterize his thought as an ethics. In his "Letter on Humanism" Heidegger states one of his primary motivations for avoiding the word "ethics": "Even such names as 'logic,' 'ethics,' and 'physics' begin to flourish only when originary thinking comes to an end."[11] This passage suggests that for Heidegger the rise of philosophical subdisciplines such as "logic," "ethics," and "physics" is the result of an unhealthy breakdown of thinking. Accordingly, when questions that should be thought *together* are corralled into separate domains and treated in abstraction from their fundamental unity in the human condition, the most urgent question is *not* "How should I behave?" but "How can we come to regard ethical, physical, and logical questions as *existential* questions?" Or, "How can we inhabit a world where thoughtfulness, rather than just goal-oriented or calculative thinking counts as legitimate?"

Heidegger makes a version of this last point explicitly in his lecture course *What Is Called Thinking?*:

> The organizations of social life, rearmament in moral matters, the grease paint of the culture enterprise—none of them any longer reach what is. With all the good intentions and all the ceaseless effort, these attempts are no more than makeshift patchwork, expedients for the moment. And why? Because the ideas of aims, purposes and means, of effects and causes, from which all those attempts arise—because these ideas are from the start incapable of holding themselves open to what is.[12]

Heidegger's rhetoric is heavy and provocative, but by including "rearmament in moral matters" along with "the grease paint of the culture enterprise," he seems to suggest that ethical thought—at least understood as a science of values and morals—is complicit in fomenting the

---

[11] Heidegger, "Letter on Humanism," 219–220.
[12] Heidegger, *What Is Called Thinking?*, 66.

perils of modernity. In particular, Heidegger highlights that the "ideas of aims, purposes and means, of effects and causes" which are the bread and butter of metaphysical ethical theories are unable to come to terms with or make room in their discourse for "what is." Heidegger, of course, does not say himself in this passage "what is," but ostensibly this is what ontology asks about.

Heidegger's concern that our attachment to goal-oriented thinking is in conflict with our ability to understand Being in non-calculative and noninstrumentalist terms is a common theme in his later work. As he writes, "The will to action, which here means the will to make and be effective, has overrun and crushed thought."[13] And, "No mere action will change the world, because Being as effectiveness and effecting closes all beings off in the face of The Event."[14] Unpacking the assumptions underwriting passages such as these, we can see that part of Heidegger's reluctance to call his thought an ethics can be traced to his belief that the rhetoric of self-assertiveness, willing, and achievement, leaves little to no room for recognizing the legitimacy of thoughtfulness, i.e., of an encounter with "what is" that is not pervaded by the imperatives of instrumental reason.

The conclusion to which this leads him is that "if man is to find his way once again into the nearness of Being he must first learn to exist in the nameless."[15] In other words, rather than worry about whether ontology is ethically oriented, we should be concerned with learning to loosen our attachment to metaphysical categories and instead try to reencounter the world without imposing our labels on it. Thus, Heidegger cautions,

[E]thics as a mere doctrine and imperative is helpless unless man first comes to have a different fundamental relation to Being—unless man of his own accord, so far as in him lies, begins at last *to hold his nature open for once to the essential relation toward being* (emphasis added).[16]

---

[13] Heidegger, *What Is Called Thinking?*, 25.

[14] Heidegger, "Overcoming Metaphysics," 110: "Keine bloße Aktion wird den Weltzustand ändern, weil das Sein als Wirksamkeit und Wirken alles Seiende gegenüber dem Ereignis verschließt." GA 7, 97.

[15] *What Is Called Thinking?*, 223.

[16] Ibid., 89.

Thus, we can see that what Heidegger criticizes under the name ethics is "ethics as a mere doctrine and imperative." What Heidegger advocates, however, as an "originary ethics" is a commitment to open ourselves to an "an essential relation towards being." What the above passage suggests is that too much reliance upon a narrow conception of ethics may come into conflict with this more holistic conception of ethics. For in reducing ethical questions to a matter of fixed doctrine, we forget that part of what it may mean to *live* ethically is to *be open* to the questions and challenges that confront us in each moment, and for which ethical discourse can itself only be a guide, not a surrogate.

Thus, one reason that Heidegger might have been reluctant to call his thought by the name of "ethics" is his contention that thinking should not aspire to be authoritative, but instead to hold open a space for questions to remain questionable: "There are no authoritative assertions in the realm of thinking. The only measure for thought derives from the matter which is to be thought. This matter, however, is what is questionable before all else..."[17] And, "We must guard against the blind urge to snatch at a quick answer in the form of a formula. We must stay with the question."[18] And, "One can answer...questions very straightforwardly and thereby demonstrate they are not serious questions worth asking."[19] Or finally, "the ontological penetration to the 'origin' does not arrive at things which are ontically self-evident for the 'common understanding, but rather it is precisely this that opens up the questionability of everything self-evident."[20] In each of these passages, Heidegger indicates that ontology must be concerned less with the enterprise of justification than with the practice of questioningly meditating on what eludes justification. Heidegger's most famous claim to this effect is that "questioning is the piety of thought," a claim which suggests that ontological thinking requires a posture of *not knowing*.[21] Thus, to the extent that ethical enquiry is intent on proposing answers, be they theoretical or practical, it misses the originary task of encountering their mysterious, and ever questionable source, namely, "what is to be thought."

[17] "*Der Spiegel* Interview with Martin Heidegger," in *The Heidegger Reader*, 332.
[18] *What Is Called Thinking?*, 48.
[19] *Der Ister*, 93.
[20] SZ, 334/ BT, 307.
[21] "The Question Concerning Technology," 35.

Another reason Heidegger might have been reluctant to call his thought an ethics can be traced to his claim in *Being and Time* that once we analyze the being of the human being in terms of Dasein—and not, say, according to the terms of the ontic disciplines such as anthropology, theology, physics, biology, law, or ethics—we must recognize that questions pertaining to the specifics of morality, justice, and obligation can only be derivative of ontological questions.[22] Since Heidegger defines Dasein most basically as "the being for whom its being is an issue" this means that ethical questions can only be understood as extensions of a more basic issue, namely, Dasein itself.[23] The consequence of this, Charles Scott explains, is that "in the context of the question of ethics… the 'essence' of human being is not susceptible to conceptual grasp and hence not to definitive judgments concerning it."[24]

And yet for all of his numerous criticisms of ethics, at least in the traditional sense of the term, Heidegger remained compelled to hold onto a positive meaning of the term. In his 1944 lecture course on Heraclitus, Heidegger offers a holistic definition of "ethics" as that which "concerns [itself with] man not as a lone object amongst other objects, but [rather] considers man in regards to his relationship to beings as a whole, and beings as a whole in regards to their relationship to man."[25] And, in 1968, Heidegger told a crowd of medical students that "[t]o stand under the claim of Being [*Anspruch des Sein*] is the greatest claim made upon the human being. It is ethics."[26] What is "the claim of Being" we should ask, and why is standing under it, in spite of all of the aforementioned caveats, an *ethical* posture? These are questions that we will come to in the final section of this chapter once we have reviewed the secondary literature on Heidegger and ethics. For now, we need simply note that answering these questions is not at all a matter of deciphering what Heidegger meant by these terms, since, as we have seen, Heidegger was himself quite vague and inconsistent in defining them.

---

[22] See SZ, 16/ BT, 14.

[23] SZ, 12/ BT, 10.

[24] Charles E. Scott, *The Question of Ethics: Nietzsche, Foucault, Heidegger* (Bloomington: Indiana University Press, 1990), 134.

[25] GA 55, 214 (translation mine).

[26] Heidegger, *Zollikon Seminars: Protocols—Conversations—Letters*, ed. Medard Boss, trans. Franz K. Mayr and Richard K. Askay (Evanston: Northwestern University Press, 2000), 217; GA 89, 273.

Instead, answering them will require a constructive approach, or as we saw Heidegger enjoin above, "ask[ing] in a different way."

Having seen that Heidegger was conflicted about calling his thought an ethics, we can now draw some helpful distinctions between the kind of ethics that Heidegger's thought might support and the kind of thought it might contest, rather than simply arguing whether Heidegger's thought is or isn't ethical. What Heidegger's thought seems to chafe against is the dominant traditions of metaphysical thinking which treat ethical action as a *means* to achieving some result, but are unable to give voice to the tensions that constitute our capacity to care in the first place. Meanwhile, the kind of ethical thinking that Heidegger's thought might support is one which seeks to ask how, precisely *as* beings structured by finitude, we might comport ourselves responsibly and sensitively to "what is," in all of its complexity and singularity.

In his essay "Building Dwelling Thinking," Heidegger gives two interrelated suggestions as to what this may involve, one negative and one positive. First, he says, that "by the means-end schema we block our view of [...] essential relations," meaning that the task for those who seek to be ontologically responsible is to learn how to regard things non-instrumentally or non-teleologically.[27] Second, he says, sharpening this point, that "building is not merely a means towards dwelling, to build is in itself already to dwell."[28] What does it mean to regard building not as a *means* toward dwelling, but as an embodiment of it? In part it means recognizing that our building projects are already structured in advance by our capacity to care. The reasons we have for building, and for building in the particular ways that we do are already rooted in a certain understanding of the world, which can be called, our "abode" or "dwelling place" (*ethos*) in the most basic, ontological sense. In other words, we shouldn't just think of houses, apartments, skyscrapers, homeless shelters, and refugee camps as instrumental goods, but as particular enactments of our very understanding of who we are. As Heidegger puts this point, "Building...is a distinctive letting-dwell" and "All planning remains grounded on this responding."[29] While Heidegger's example here is architecture (Heidegger delivered the lecture as a response to the

---

[27] "Building Dwelling Thinking," 144.
[28] Ibid.
[29] Ibid., 126.

postwar housing shortage), his point can be taken most broadly to refer to any kind of activity. Rather than regard our creative activities simply as a means toward achieving certain outcomes we should regard them as rooted in a more basic and ineliminable care for Being.

A second illustration of the meaning of ontological ethics can be educed from a story about Heraclitus that Heidegger introduces in his "Letter on Humanism in his attempting to expound the meaning of Heraclitus's gnomic fragment *"ethos anthropoi daimon"* ("man's *ethos* [is] a/the *daimon*")."

> The story is told of something Heraclitus told some strangers who wanted to come visit him. Having arrived, they saw him warming himself at a stove. Surprised, they stood there in consternation—above all, because he encouraged them, the astounded ones, and called for them to come in with the words, "here too the gods are present."[30]

On Heidegger's interpretation, what is striking about this story is that the strangers visiting Heraclitus expect him to be doing something extraordinary (because they imagine that philosophy is supposed to be something outwardly spectacular), yet instead find him doing something utterly mundane: warming himself by the fire. And yet, this very gesture is precisely what makes Heraclitus a profound thinker, namely that even in doing something as quotidian as warming himself by the fire, he is able to discern that "here too the gods are present." What this story demonstrates for Heidegger is that the greatness of thinking consists in its capacity to show that the ordinary is—or can, in its own way be—extraordinary. From this conclusion, Heidegger proposes that Heraclitus's fragment, *"ethos anthropoi daimon,"* can be more properly understood as saying "The familiar (abode) is for man the open region for the presencing of god (the unfamiliar one)."[31]

How does Heidegger's strange translation of Heraclitus—and his interpretation of the story of Heraclitus warming himself by the fire— relate to ethics? The answer, according to Heidegger, is that it is from Heraclitus's conception of "ethos" that we must understand the meaning of ethics in its most "originary" sense. Indeed, it is Heidegger's discussion of Heraclitus that serves as the prologue to his claim—which we

---

[30] "Letter on Humanism," 233; GA 9, 355–356.
[31] "Letter on Humanism," 234.

examined above—that "If the name 'ethics,' in keeping with the basic meaning of the word *ethos*, should now say that "ethics" ponders the abode of man, then…[it] is in itself the originary ethics." Putting these pieces together, we can see that for Heidegger, "ethics" in the original sense means coming to a particular understanding of human being as the locus in which the familiar and the unfamiliar interpenetrate. Ethics, in this basic sense, will mean making space for the recognition that unfamiliarity and uncanniness are an integral part of living and meaning-making and are therefore not simply something to be pushed aside. Meanwhile, it will also involve, as Heraclitus's act of warming himself by the fire demonstrates, an ability to recognize and affirm the depth and magnificence of our being precisely in its quality of ordinariness.

Thus, to summarize, ontological ethics or originary ethics has so far been shown to be a way of being-in-the-world that is conducted by an understanding of and appreciation for a noninstrumental relation to "what is" and by an understanding of and appreciation for the meaning of human existence as both a locus of ordinariness and extraordinariness. The question that remains to be examined, however, and which we turn to in the next section, is whether or how such a broad conception of ethics can be said to relate to ethics in a more narrow and traditional sense.

Is Ontology Ethical?

The claim that Heidegger's thought is saturated by ethical concerns may not come as a surprise to sympathetic readers of Heidegger. Numerous interpreters, even critics, have recognized an ethical dimension in Heidegger's thought. Fred Dallmayr writes that "[c]ontrary to his speculative reputation (and his own occasional disclaimers), Heidegger's entire opus is suffused with ethical preoccupations."[32] Jeffrey Malpas, Nicholas Dungey, Julian Young, and Alberto Perez-Gomez, have all elucidated Heidegger's work as an "ethics of dwelling."[33] Malpas elaborates Heidegger's project as an ethics that is concerned specifically with issues

[32] Dallmayr, *The Other Heidegger*, 109.

[33] Jeffrey Malpas, *Heidegger's Topology: Being, Place, World* (Cambridge: MIT Press, 2007); Nicholas Dungey, "The Ethics and Politics of Dwelling," *Polity* 39, no. 2 (2007): 234–258, 254; Julian Young, *Heidegger's Later Philosophy*; and Alberto Perez-Gomez, *Built Upon Love: Architectural Longing After Ethics and Aesthetics* (Cambridge: MIT Press, 2006).

of place and placedness. Charles Guignon and Michael Zimmerman have each interpreted Heidegger's work as an "ethics of authenticity."[34] Iain Thomson has more recently argued that Heidegger's philosophy can be understood as a "perfectionist ethics."[35] Frederick Olafson has located a "ground of ethics" in Heidegger's account of *Mitsein* [Being-with] in *Being and Time*, and Michael Lewis has interpreted "the place of ethics" in Heidegger's meditations on "the ontological difference."[36] Jean-Luc Nancy similarly claims that Heidegger's ontology can be read to support an ethics that acknowledges our being as both singular and plural.[37] Dennis Schmidt has argued that Heidegger's thought can be appreciated as an attempt to grapple with the meaning of ethics after Hegel.[38] Meanwhile, Joanna Hodge and Reiner Schürmann have argued that Heidegger's work can be read as an attempt to restore the ethical vision of Greek tragedy in a post-Christian age.[39] François Raffoul and Lawrence Hatab have educed Heidegger's work as an ethics of finitude.[40] William McNeill argues that Heidegger's thought can be read as a modernized version of Aristotelian virtue ethics.[41] Ruth Irwin has recently argued that Heidegger's ontology can "reinvigorate ways of being and knowing that do not rely narrowly on [...] consumerism," and that could help us come to more creative solutions to the problem

[34] Charles Guignon, "Philosophy and Authenticity: Heidegger's Search for a Ground for Philosophizing," in *Heidegger, Authenticity, and Modernity: Essays in Honor of Hubert Dreyfus, Volume 1*, ed. Mark Wrathall and Jeff Malpas (Cambridge: MIT Press, 2000), 79–103; Michael Zimmerman, *Eclipse of the Self: Developments of Heidegger's Concept of Authenticity* (Athens: Ohio University Press, 1981).

[35] Thomson, "Heidegger on Ontological Education: Or How We Become What We Are," *Inquiry* 44, no. 3 (2001): 261, 243–268.

[36] Frederick A. Olafson, *Heidegger and the Ground of Ethics: A Study of Mitsein* (Cambridge: Cambridge University Press, 1998).

[37] Jean-Luc Nancy, *Being Singular Plural*, trans. Robert Richardson and Anne O'Byrne (Palo Alto: Stanford University Press, 2000).

[38] Dennis Schmidt, "On the Sources of Ethical Life," *Research in Phenomenology* 42, no. 1 (2012): 35–48. For a mixed evaluation of Heidegger on the topic of post-Hegelian ethics, see John McCumber, *Poetic Interaction: Language, Reason, and Freedom* (Chicago: University of Chicago Press, 1989).

[39] Joanna Hodge, *Heidegger and Ethics* (London: Routledge, 1995); Reiner Schürmann, *Broken Hegemonies*, trans. Reginald Lilly (Bloomington: Indiana University Press, 2003).

[40] François Raffoul, *The Origins of Responsibility* (Bloomington: Indiana University Press, 2010).

[41] William McNeill, *The Time of Life: Heidegger and Ethos* (Albany: SUNY Press, 2006).

of climate change.[42] Mary-Jane Rubenstein argues that Heidegger's thought can be seen as a postmodern ethics whose "wondrous openness to alterity" necessarily entails "a tireless refusal to ground once and for all the identity of the self, the other, our god, this nation, or that people."[43] And Mechthild Nagel argues that Heidegger's thought can be read in the service of articulating a postmodern feminist ethics.[44]

Nevertheless, these accounts do not seem to have done much to shake the opinions of more skeptical readers. Graham Harman writes of "Heidegger's avoidance of ethics," while Theodore DeBoer writes of Heidegger's "ethical indifference."[45] Levinas's indictments—the inspiration for many of the suspicious readings of Heidegger—are among the most famous and influential: "In subordinating every relation with existents to the relation with Being, Heideggerian ontology affirms the primacy of freedom over ethics."[46] "A philosophy of power, ontology is, as first philosophy which does not call into question the same, a philosophy of injustice."[47]

> To affirm the priority of *Being* over *existents* is to already decide the essence of philosophy; it is to subordinate the relation with *someone*, who is an existent, (the ethical relation) to a relation with the *Being of existents*, which, impersonal, permits the apprehension, the domination of existents (a relationship of knowing), subordinates justice to freedom.[48]

And, again, "In Heidegger coexistence is, to be sure, taken as a relationship with the Other irreducible to objective cognition; but in the final analysis it also rests on the relationship with being in general, on

---

[42] Ruth Irwin, *Heidegger, Politics, and Climate Change: Risking It All* (London: Continuum, 2008).

[43] Mary-Jane Rubenstein, *Strange Wonder: The Closure of Metaphysics and the Opening of Awe* (New York: Columbia University Press, 2009), 134.

[44] Mecthild Nagel, "Thrownness, Playing-in-the-World, and the Question of Authenticity," in *Feminist Interpretations of Martin Heidegger*, 289–308.

[45] Graham Harman, *Tool-Being: Heidegger and The Metaphysics of Objects* (Peru, IL: Open Court, 2002), 236–237; Theodore DeBoer, "An Ethical Transcendental Philosophy," in *Face to Face with Levinas*, ed. Richard A. Cohen (Albany: SUNY Press, 1986), 108, 83–116.

[46] Levinas, *Totality and Infinity*, 45.

[47] Ibid., 46.

[48] Ibid., 45.

comprehension, on ontology."[49] Finally, against Heidegger's claim in *Being and Time* that death is unsubstitutably my own, Levinas markedly calls the ethical opening of responsibility to the Other [person] anterior to any ontology, "substitution."[50] In each of these formulations, Levinas seems to suggest that ontology is a "totalizing" enterprise, more interested in coming to a detached understanding of *Being* than in an engaged life of commitment to *beings,* and in particular to the marginalized and vulnerable human "other."

Edith Wyschogrod follows Levinas's criticisms of Heidegger when she accuses Heidegger's philosophy of being monological. In particular, she criticizes Heidegger's account of "the call of conscience" in *Being and Time* on the grounds that it reminds Dasein of its primordial guilt, rather than of something it has actually done. One effect of this view of guilt, suggests Wyschogrod, is that "from the perspective of the death event... the guilt of victim and agent are equalized."[51] Wyschogrod maintains that Heidegger's indifference to the plight of the victim, already evident in the *Daseinanalytik* of *Being and Time,* can be found even more intensely in his later thought:

> Since [Heidegger] starts from the point of view of man's relation to the being of things, [he] sees the primary distortions resulting from technique as blighted landscapes, urban sprawl, and dreary industrial complexes. The destruction of persons for him becomes a secondary phenomenon.[52]

Like Wyschogrod and Levinas, Herman Philipse charges that Heidegger's ontology is not just incidentally devoid of ethical content, but is necessarily and consistently so. Philipse claims, even further, that the monological element in Heidegger's thought explains his authoritarianism before, during, and after WWII:

---

[49] Ibid., 67.

[50] See Levinas, *Otherwise Than Being,* 99–129.

[51] Edith Wyschogrod, *The Spirit in Ashes: Hegel, Heidegger, and Man-Made Mass Death* (New Haven: Yale University Press, 1985), 174. Hannah Arendt makes a similar point when she writes, "It apparently never occurred to Heidegger that by making all men who listen to the 'call of conscience' equally guilty, he was actually proclaiming universal innocence: where everybody is guilty, nobody is." Arendt, *The Life of the Mind* (New York: Harcourt Brace, 1978), 184.

[52] Ibid., 203.

In each phase of his philosophical career, Heidegger endorsed an authoritarian view of ethics: only decisions carry authority and ethical discussion
is held in disrepute. With regard to moral theory the phases are differenti-
ated merely by what is invested with ultimate ethical authority: authentic
individuals or the *Volk* in 1927, Hitler in 1933, and transcendent Being in
Beiträge zur Philosophie (1936-1938) and after the Second World War.[53]

Philipse's charge of emptiness is not new. Already in 1948, the Marxist
philosopher Günter Stern Anders, a former student of Heidegger's, and
Hannah Arendt's husband from 1929 to 1937, charged Heidegger's
thought with "pseudo-concreteness," writing that "[i]f Heidegger
makes '*Können*' the fundamental category of 'Dasein,' he finds himself
in respectable society, although in a tradition which, by 'ontologifying'
liberty has renounced the idea of actually liberating man."[54] Adorno
also levels this accusation at Heidegger when he writes that the "freedom [promised by ontology] has largely remained an ideology...where
the thought of gaining freedom is twisted into unfreedom. Heidegger
promotes slave thinking."[55] Adorno's concern, shared by many others,
is that ontology is incapable of appreciating the *material conditions* that
impede emancipation, preferring to reduce emancipation to a merely
spiritual affair. Thus, ontology, so this line of criticism goes, is but a repetition of idealism. Caputo gives particular pathos to this concern:

> [Nowhere] in the call of Being is the cry of the victim to be heard,
> nowhere the plea for mercy, the summons for help. The silent peal of
> Being is deaf to the appeal of suffering. The assault upon the earth which
> turns the soil into an object of agricultural engineering is more primor-
> dial than the ravages of hunger, than ravaged bodies. The matter to be
> thought is not hunger and starvation but whether one works the land with
> hand and oxen instead of with motorized equipment. Hungry and under-
> nourished bodies do not figure in the account, do not come to presence;

[53] Herman Philipse, "Heidegger and Ethics," *Inquiry* 42, nos. 3–4 (1999): 439–474, 440.

[54] "On the Pseudo-Concreteness of Heidegger's Philosophy," Günther Stern (Anders) in *Philosophy and Phenomenological Research* 8, no. 3 (1948): 337–371, 352. For a similar critique, see Marjorie Grene, "Authenticity: An Existential Virtue," *Ethics* 62, no. 4 (1952): 266–274, 272.

[55] Adorno, *Negative Dialectics*, 89.

hunger is (*west*) not, it simply is (*ist*) [...] The thinker leaves no room at all for the victim in the history of Being's self-showing.[56]

Of course, one could counter, as Olafson has tried to do, that this is not so, or not necessarily so—that Heidegger's insistence on *Mitsein* (being-with) as equiprimordial with Dasein offers a firm rejoinder to this reading. And yet, as Zygmunt Bauman argues, such a reading is belied by the formal thinness of Heidegger's account:

> *Mitsein* is indeed the necessary condition of morality but not its sufficient condition. *Mitsein*, as Emmanuel Levinas quipped, may well mean no more than *Zusammenmarschieren* [marching together]. The fact that "we are all in the same boat," share space and time, meet face to face and hear about each other does not by itself make us moral beings.[57]

For each of these critics, Heidegger's thought fails to be an ethics because it fails to make our responsibility to concrete others nonnegotiable. Instead, what Heidegger's ontology offers, these critics claim, is at best a merely descriptive account of the status quo, and at worst an apology for it. George Pattison poignantly summarizes this view: "If the primary locus of authenticity is my relation to my own thrownness towards death the relation to the other can surely be no more than a secondary source of obligation, whether the other is teacher, neighbour, or God."[58]

The worry that ontology is ethically vacuous—that it provides no helpful criteria for distinguishing good and bad, valid and invalid, and that the enterprise of "thinking," however "originary," lacks

---

[56] Caputo, "Heidegger's Scandal: Thinking and the Essence of the Victim," in *The Heidegger Case: On Philosophy and Politics* (Philadelphia: Temple University Press, 1992), 265–281, 277. See also Caputo, *Demythologizing Heidegger* (Bloomington: Indiana University Press, 1993), 36. For similar criticisms of Heidegger's philosophy of technology as too idealistic, see Michael Zimmerman, *Heidegger's Confrontation with Modernity: Technology, Politics, Art* (Bloomington: Indiana University Press, 1991), 23, 179; Don Ihde, *Heidegger's Technologies: Postphenomenoloigcal Perspectives* (New York: Fordham University Press, 2010), 74–86; and Andrew Feenberg, *Questioning Technology* (London: Routledge, 1999).

[57] Zygmunt Bauman, "Ethics of Individuals," *The Canadian Journal of Sociology* 25, no. 1 (2000): 83; Levinas, *Entre Nous*, 116.

[58] George Pattison, *Heidegger and Death: A Critical Theological Essay* (Aldershot: Ashgate, 2013), 159.

any accountability—is shared by a range of commentators. As Jacques Taminaux asks,

> Is it possible to come to terms with the notion of value from a merely ontological viewpoint? Is it right to think that, in the problem of value, Being alone is an issue? After all, we can all experience that, in many discussions on values, what is at stake is human plurality and the way people judge human affairs. It does not seem that these topics have ever been a central concern in Heidegger's meditation.[59]

Werner Marx makes a similar point with regards to Heidegger's understanding of truth as unconcealment, arguing that Heidegger's radical conception of truth embroils his thought in moral relativism:

> Heidegger's coordination of the powers of error and sham with those of the luminous presents an extreme danger. The chief reason for this is that Heidegger—to put it in a traditional way—could give no rules for either the realm of theory or the realm of practice with regard to how to distinguish between a truth in which error and sham dominate and a truth which these "equal partners" have not disguised. Furthermore, in place of the moral commandments which—according to Heidegger—have evidently been overcome and dismissed, forethinking has arrived at no standards which can decide whether a specific interpretation or action is "good" or not.[60]

And,

> Heidegger does not speak of whether and how man can distinguish between good and the evil within the truth of Being, or whether he should seek, for example to do good and avoid evil. He forgoes the "setting-up of rules," since it is more essential 'for man to find his sojourn in the truth of Being.'[61]

---

[59] Jacques Taminaux, "Heidegger on Values," in *Heidegger Towards the Turn*, ed. James Risser (Albany: SUNY Press, 1999), 239.

[60] Werner Marx, *Heidegger and the Tradition*, trans. Theodore Kisiel (Evanston: Northwestern University Press, 1971), 248.

[61] Ibid., 249.

Thus, to summarize the criticisms that we have seen so far, Heidegger's thought—and perhaps ontology more generally—is at risk of being relativistic, formally empty, and indifferent to the "other." These are complex charges that need to be teased apart.

After all, for some readers, it is precisely Heidegger's refusal to ground ethical questioning in principled arguments that makes his thought compelling. Reiner Schürmann, for instance, suggests that an "avowal of ignorance" on all practical questions might be "integral to the body of writings which circulate, operate, put people to flight, or make them think—that is, which function—under the name of 'Heidegger.'"[62] Yet Schürmann also shows how this avowal of ignorance itself carries an ethical or metaethical charge:

> [Heidegger] raises the question of presencing in such a way that the question of acting is already answered; he raises it in such a way that action can no longer become a separate issue; in such a way that to seek an enduring standard for answering the question, "What is to be done?" is to search in the vacuum of the place deserted by the successive representations of an unshakeable ground; in such a way, finally, that the epochal constellations of presencing have always already prescribed not only the terms in which the question of action can and must be raised (ousiological, theological, transcendental, linguistic terms), but also the ground from which it can and must be answered (substance, God, cogito, discursive community) as well as the types of answers that can and must be adduced (hierarchy of virtues, hierarchy of laws—divine, natural, and human—hierarchy of imperatives, and hierarchy of discursive interests, that is, cognitive or emancipatory).[63]

For Schürmann, Heidegger's thought must be considered as a sustained attempt to think outside and beyond the *pros hen* logic of Aristotle, whereby all things derive their being and justification from a single source or first principle. Instead, Schürmann argues that Heidegger's project offers an "anarchic" and decentering move that makes space for recognizing a plurality of competing and incommensurable goods, while also recognizing the contingency of our attempts to privilege some of these goods over others. Heidegger's "avowal of ignorance,"

---

[62] Schürmann, *Heidegger on Being and Acting: From Principles to Anarchy* (Bloomington: Indiana University Press, 2003), 2–3.

[63] Ibid., 4.

for Schürmann, is thus not an ethical failing, but the mark of its import in a post-metaphysical age. As he explains, "[N]one has expressed the tragic in its modern form as has Heidegger."[64] "Heidegger shows how edification has proved hubristic and the platform it presupposed anything but solid."[65] Schürmann recognizes that Heidegger's conclusion will be unacceptable to many, and that those who are given over to a "manic denial of tragic truth" will have no choice but to "cry nihilism" when confronted by it; but this only testifies, for Schürmann, to its critical import, i.e., to its ability to offer an alternative to a thinking that conducts "business as usual."[66]

For Schürmann, Heidegger's critique of metaphysical ethics offers a sober reminder that our ethical decisions are essentially contestable, and therefore inexorably tragic. Citing the ancient story of Agamemnon, who is faced with the impossible choice between sacrificing his daughter, Iphigenia, and deserting his brother, Menelaus, Schürmann says that where Agamemnon goes astray is not in choosing to sacrifice his daughter—he would have had to do something objectionable no matter what—but in convincing himself and trying to convince others that his decision was unequivocally right. What Heidegger's thought calls into question, Schürmann contends, is the rightness of claiming a monopoly on rightness.[67]

Dennis Schmidt offers a similar, though less polemical version of Schürmann's argument, claiming that the ethical legacy of Heidegger's

---

[64] Schürmann, *Broken Hegemonies*, 535.

[65] Ibid., 562.

[66] Ibid., 535, 539, 562. For a critique of the purportedly nihilistic legacy of Heideggerian thought, see Richard Wolin, "Kant at Ground Zero: Philosophers Respond to September 11," in *The Frankfurt School Revisited: And Other Essays on Politics and Society* (London: Routledge, 2006).

[67] Schürmann, "Ultimate Double Binds," in *Heidegger Towards The Turn*, 243–268. For a similar argument, see also William E. Connolly, *Identity/Difference: Democratic Negotiations of Political Paradox* (Ithaca: Cornell University Press, 1991), 80. Connolly argues that the critiques of ethics put forward by Nietzsche, Foucault, and Heidegger, can be understood more positively as a call to what he terms "second-order ethicality." Second-order ethicality, Connolly claims, seeks to turn our attention to the violence wrought by first-order ethical systems through their enforcement of hard distinctions between the permissible and impermissible, good and evil, orthodoxy and heresy, or normalcy and abnormality. Charles Scott also argues a similar point when he writes that Heidegger, along with Nietzsche and Foucault, share "a common suspicion" "that what we ordinarily take to be a satisfaction and the good conceal suffering that we have an investment in maintaining because of who we have come to be." Scott, *The Question of Ethics*, 112.

ontology should be regarded not as a *rejection* of ethical norms and considerations, but as a call to approach them hermeneutically, rather than metaphysically. Schmidt writes,

> [T]he reach and legitimate claim of philosophy in the realm of ethical understanding is neither complete nor final. Philosophical hermeneutics understands that its final gesture must be to enact a return to factical life and the realities of ethical life as realities borne and suffered in the singular. This return is essential and it is at the heart of what constitutes hermeneutics as a practice.[68]

Thus, for both Schürmann and Schmidt, what others would call a philosophy of moral relativism can be more positively framed as a philosophy that makes us sensitive to the "realities" that must be "borne and suffered in the singular."[69]

As we can now see, the debate about Heidegger's ontology and ethics is permeated by a number of ambiguities and questions. One question is whether it is fair to say that ontology is ethically vacuous. Another is whether the charge of ethical vacuity, even if fair, should be taken as a count against ontology or precisely as a count in its favor. Charles Scott captures the heart of this philosophical dilemma:

> Heidegger's thought is…a field of conflict in relation to traditional ethics, not because he espouses new values, but because those ways of thought that have given rise to our ethics and moralities are already in question and his thinking preserves the question rather than advocating a solution.[70]

Thus, one of the questions that seems to be animating the debate about Heidegger and ethics is whether the kind of thinking that "preserves the question rather than advocating a solution" should be considered a boon or a threat to ethical thinking and ethical life.

Another set of ambiguities concerns whether the criticisms of Heidegger's ontology we have surveyed above should be taken as a

---

[68] Schmidt, "Sources of Ethical Life," 41.

[69] For a similar argument along these lines see François Dastur, "The Call of Conscience," in *Heidegger and Practical Philosophy*, 95.

[70] Charles E. Scott, "Heidegger and the Question of Ethics," *Research in Phenomenology* 18, no. 1 (1988): 28, 23–40.

rebuttal of ontology itself (as Levinas claims), or only of Heidegger's particular construction of it. If the latter, then the question remains what an ethical ontology might involve. If the former, we need to ask what sort of definition of ontology is being presumed, and whether this is a fair definition. Finally, we should ask whether the criticisms leveled against Heideggerian ontology can be formulated without presupposing a certain ontology themselves. And if they cannot, then perhaps an ethical critique of ontology will turn out to be itself a deeply ontological posture. These are questions and possibilities that we will examine in the next sections.

INTERLUDE: NAMING AS AN ETHICAL EVENT

So far we have seen that the question of whether and how ontology and ethics relate to each other turns on how these terms are defined, as well as on the kinds of expectations that are being placed on these definitions. But we should therefore take a step back and acknowledge that the question of ontology's relationship to ethics is also a question about language more generally. In thinking about the relationship between ontology and ethics, we must ask ourselves what constitutes the appropriate use of a word, as well as consider who, under what circumstances, gets to determine the parameters of appropriate use. Such considerations are, in turn, quite circularly, ontological and ethical. They are ontological because they ask us to consider what language *is*, and they are ethical because they ask us to consider the personal, interpersonal, and ecological stakes of how we ourselves inhabit language (a topic explored in greater depth in Chapter 4). Thus, part of deciding whether Heidegger's ontology (or just simply, ontology) can be construed as ethical depends upon whether we are willing to grant words such as "ontology" and "ethics"—and words, more generally—a semantic flexibility, or whether we think that they must refer to something very specific and definitive. Heidegger's own thought seems both to advocate for and to enact the former position. In *Being and Time*, for instance, Heidegger states,

> It is the business of philosophy to protect the *power of the most elemental words* in which Da-sein expresses itself from being flattened by the common understanding to the point of unintelligibility, which in turn functions as source for illusory problems.[71]

[71] SZ, 220/ BT, 202.

Here, Heidegger emphasizes that the "common understanding" of words—which is concerned with "flattening" their meaning, rather than "protect[ing their] power"—is to be resisted. In his essay on "The Origin of the Work of Art" Heidegger takes this point to an even further conclusion, claiming that the meaning of Being—or "Beyng" [*Seyn*] as he spells it—cannot be reductively captured or expressed in definitional or propositional terms:

> To desire to say directly, in one statement, what the essence of Beyng is, is already to misunderstand this essence. Beyng needs the *founding of Beyng* precisely because it can never be shown like something present at hand.[72]

Heidegger does not specify in this passage what "the founding of Beyng" refers to, but he does specify what it is *not*. It is *not* a mode of discussing Being that seeks to reduce its meaning to something that can be described as though it were "present at hand." By spelling Beyng with a "y" rather than with an "i," Heidegger, however, demonstrates that such a "founding of Beyng" may entail using a defamiliarized vocabulary to try to free the speaker and listener (or writer and reader) from their attachment to a word's ordinary meaning so as to open them up to an experience of a word's inherent polyvocality.[73]

From these brief passages we can conclude that Heidegger's thought invites its readers to engage with words on an unconventional level, and, rather than simply take the meaning of particular words as fixed, to open

---

[72] "Origin of the Work of Art: First Version," in *The Heidegger Reader*, 146.

[73] Further reasons for Heidegger's archaic use of *Seyn* may involve a desire, coming out of Schelling and Boehme, to indicate that Being (meaningfulness) depends upon an even more primordial, non-graspable abyss (*Ab-grund*) which we can encounter only obliquely, i.e., as a deformation of the familiar. Thus, by spelling Being in an unfamiliar way, Heidegger calls attention to the essential strangeness of Being's abyssal origins. Another possibility may be that because the archaic spelling of *Seyn* can be found in Hölderlin's poetry, Heidegger wishes to call attention to the futural/prophetic dimension of this word's meaning, as if to say that we are still not yet capable of understanding the word "Being" means. Finally, Heidegger may be trying to suggest that thinking should aspire to understand Being not as a category or an object for representation, but as a name for the *singular* (and self-displacing) occurrence of meaningfulness constituting each moment.

themselves up to a given word's multiplicity of meanings. This invitation, of course, does not yet resolve the questions and criticisms leveled at (Heidegger's) ontology, but it allows us to draw a few key conclusions about what it might mean to try to do so. The first is that we should not take "ontology" and "ethics" as reductively conceptual terms, but must instead consider them as words whose significance is far richer than any single definition of them can give. And the second, related conclusion is that the question of whether Heidegger's ontology (or ontology more generally) can be considered an ethical project is not something that can be answered as a matter of fact. Instead what it requires us to ask is whether it is *appropriate* to call it by the name of ethics. I am suggesting that it is, but it should be emphasized that in doing so, my aim is not to *refute* those who say otherwise, so much as to show that their evaluative conclusions needn't be taken as the last word. Such an approach is in keeping with Heidegger's claim that "Whoever engages in opposition loses what is essential, regardless of whether he is victorious or is defeated...."[74] It is also in keeping with Heidegger's claim that the aim of critique should ultimately be constructive, rather than simply pointing out where others went wrong. As he writes,

> Genuine critique is something other than criticizing in the sense of fault-finding, blaming, and complaining. Critique as 'to distinguish,' means to allow the different as such to be seen in its difference. What is different is only different in one respect. In this respect, we catch sight of what is the same beforehand regarding what different things belong together. This same[ness] must be brought into view in each distinction. In other words, true critique, as in this letting-be-seen [*Sehenlassen*], is something eminently positive.[75]

If we follow the implications of Heidegger's positive conception of critique, we come to the conclusion that locating the fractures-points and inconsistencies in a thinker's work does not amount to discrediting it so much as it helps us appreciate the extent to which they may also be our own. With this in mind, it becomes possible to reframe the debate about ontology and ethics not as a winner-take-all contest between

---

[74] Heidegger, *Country Path Conversations*, 33; GA 77, 51.
[75] *Zollikon Seminars*, 76–77; GA 89, 99.

"yays" and "nays," but as a productive conversation about the limits of both ontology and ethics. Finally, it is helpful in this context to remember Heidegger's claim in *Being and Time* that a way of understanding is only as great as its capacity to undergo a crisis.[76] Thus, whatever the limits and blindspots of ontological and ethical discourse, we should at the same time acknowledge that locating and coming to terms with them can itself be construed as an onto-ethical posture.

THE AMBIGUITY OF "CARE"

We began this chapter by examining Heidegger's ambivalence about regarding his thought in ethical terms. We saw that Heidegger sought to resist a number of the assumptions on which traditional conceptions of ethics rest. One was its conception of the human being as an egoic subject, and its characterization of ethical action in terms of effectiveness, will, and assertion—conceptions which diminish the fact that action can itself only arise in *response* to an already disclosed situation, and can only be taken up by a being characterized by being-in-the-world. Another was its assumption that ethics should be about formulating universally valid rules for behavior, rather than about learning, more basically "how to dwell." And a third was that it failed to consider that how we approach and frame ethical questions is itself of ethical significance in the sense that it has an impact on the kind of world we end up inhabiting. We also saw that in spite of these reservations, Heidegger still insisted that his thought could be considered an ethics in an originary sense. The question we now raise is whether such an originary approach to ethics must be read as solipsistic, or whether it can be read as offering a new way to understand our responsibility to others.

The textual source for both options can be found in Heidegger's concept of *care* ("*Sorge*"). In *Being and Time*, Heidegger claims that "care is the meaning of Being" as well as a "fundamental structure of Dasein." He even goes so far as to say that "Da-sein, ontologically understood, *is* care" (emphasis added).[77] These claims might lead one to read *Being and Time* as an "ethics of care." In understanding that we are beings who are fundamentally structured by care, this argument would go, we

---

[76] SZ, 9/ BT, 8.
[77] SZ, 57/ BT, 53.

come to clarify, affirm, and even intensify our commitment to caring for ourselves and others. Yet because Heidegger's definition of care is, at least in *Being and Time*, value-neutral, it would be a mistake—on exegetical grounds—to equate the care that he describes as the meaning of Being with what we typically think of as "care." In fact, since ontological care is *constitutive* of Dasein, there does not seem to be anything moral about it. I am just as "caring" in the ontological sense when I take care to torture someone as I am when I take care to feed someone, for in both cases, I am engaged in disclosing and enacting possibilities of being. It so happens that in one case, my care is oriented toward harming someone and in the other toward helping them, but in both cases, I am engaged in a project of discovering meaning/meaning-making. In addition, Heidegger insists that "care" in the ontological sense should not be understood as a subspecies of or synonym for "will, wish, predilection, [or] urge [*Wille, Wunsch, Hang, und Drang*]," since these modes of being are themselves derivative of it.[78] "Care," Heidegger explains, "is not a mere attitude of will and cannot at all be reckoned up out of the faculties of the soul."[79] Thus, whatever ethical resonances one would want to draw out of Heidegger's claim that we are fundamentally beings who care, it must also be admitted that these resonances remain only resonances.

At the same time, however, it would be equally narrow—on textual grounds—to conclude that ontological care is synonymous with egocentrism, since Heidegger precisely does not define Dasein as a *subject*, but instead defines Dasein as "being-*in-the-world*." Thus, even if we accept that Dasein is individuated by its ownmost relationship to its death, and by its ownmost sense of possibilities, we would still not have to accept that this "ownmostness" entails ethical indifference to "the other." In fact, Heidegger even suggests the opposite when he writes that "death individualizes, but only [...] in order to make Da-sein as being-with understanding the potentialities-of-being of the others."[80] In *The Fundamental Concepts of Metaphysics*, Heidegger argues that individuation enables one to become more intimate with and more receptive to those others with whom it shares its world:

---

[78] SZ, 182/ BT, 171.
[79] *Contributions to Philosophy*, 30; GA 65, 35.
[80] SZ, 265/ BT, 244.

In becoming finite [...] there ultimately occurs an *individuation* of man with respect to his Dasein. Individuation—this does not mean that man clings to his frail little ego that puffs itself up against something or other which it takes to be the world. This individuation is rather that *solitariness* in which each human being first of all enters into a nearness to what is essential in all things, a nearness to world.[81]

On this account, "individuation" must be understood as something that occurs in proportionality to one's capacity to enter into "a nearness" that is "essential in all things," and that is fundamentally shared with other beings. In the *Zollikon Seminars,* Heidegger makes it explicit that the aspiration toward authenticity, wholeness, or integrity is not an egoic affair, but one that is always opened to the world: "[We] must proceed on the 'path toward' ourselves. But this is no longer a path toward a merely isolated, principally singular 'I.'"[82] Or as he emphatically puts it in *Being and Time,*

We shall call the sight which is primarily and as a whole related to existence *transparency* [*Dursichtigkeit*]. We choose this term to designate [that] correctly understood "self knowledge" [...] is not a matter here of perceptually finding and gazing at a point which is the self, but of grasping and understanding the full disclosedness of being-in-the-world *throughout all* its essential constitutive factors. Existent beings glimpse "themselves" only when they have become transparent to themselves equiprimordially in their being with the world, in being together with others as the constitutive factors of their existence. Conversely, the opacity of Da-sein is not solely and primarily rooted in "egocentric" self-deception, but also in lack of knowledge about the world.[83]

Thus, "care" in the ontological sense is an ambiguous concept. Framed negatively, it suggests something that is so basic to who we are that it cannot possibly be considered a moral or ethical category in any thick sense, because it gives no uncontestable bottom-line axioms about "the good" or "the good life." Framed positively, however, it suggests that our being is *elementally* ethical, and that in every moment, we are engaged—even when we do not consciously know it—in projects whose

---

[81] Heidegger, *The Fundamental Concepts of Metaphysics,* 8.
[82] *Zollikon Seminars,* 110; GA 89, 144.
[83] SZ, 146/ BT, 137.

stakes are ethical, that is, which concern the quality of the world in which we live and the kind of people we are.

Heidegger himself acknowledges that his concept of "care" is ambiguous:

> The *perfectio* of human being—becoming what one can be in being free for one's ownmost possibilities (project)—is an "accomplishment" of "care." But, equiprimordially, care determines the fundamental mode of this being according to which it is delivered over (thrownness) to the world taken care of. The "ambiguity" of "care" means a *single* basic constitution in its essentially twofold structure of thrown project.[84]

In this passage we see that care is ambiguous because it is determined by both projection and throwness. On the one hand, care motivates us to formulate and pursue our ownmost possibilities. At the same time, however, care also discloses these possibilities within a context of "throwness" and a "world [to be] taken care of." In short, the ontological concept of care calls into question the dichotomy between ego and other, and instead shows Dasein to be a being whose being is dialogically constituted, being both a recipient of and a responder to its condition. Such a formal account cannot yield a science of values or norms, but it can show that Dasein, as an ontological being engaged in projects of meaning-making and world-disclosure, must also be a being engaged in "a world taken care of." Thus, even if, on one level, ontology is simply an understanding of *Being*, on another level, because Being is always the Being of beings, and not simply a Platonic realm that stands behind them, ontology must also involve an understanding of and relationship to *beings*. Ontology and ethics can therefore be said to belong together. And, as we have now seen, it is this belonging together of ontology and ethics that makes the status of ontology (or "originary ethics") so ambiguous. For, on the one hand, ontology can be positively understood as helping us come to terms with the existential infrastructure that motivates and enables us to care about the things that we do. On the other hand, ontology can be negatively understood as too broad or abstract to be of any practical relevance. Heidegger seems to endorse both of these interpretations in his "Letter on Humanism" when he writes,

---

[84]SZ, 199/ BT, 185.

Thinking [that ponders the truth of Being] is neither theoretical nor practical. It comes to pass before this distinction...Such thinking has no result.
It has no effect. It satisfies its essence in that it is.[85]

On the one hand, Heidegger admits that ontology is useless in the
sense that it has "no result." On the other hand, he similarly rejects the
idea that it is merely theoretical or abstract. In insisting that "thinking" comes to pass before the distinction between theory and practice,
Heidegger suggests that it has an ur-significance for both theory and
practice, even if this ur-significance is difficult to evaluate in metaphysical terms. Heidegger makes this point when he asks rhetorically, "Are
actions found only where one can specify results and consequences? Or
is there also action which does not bring consequences?"[86] And he also
makes it in his "Letter on Humanism," when he writes, "Thinking does
not become action only because some effect issues from it or because it is
applied. Thinking acts insofar as it thinks."[87] And,

Thinking is a deed. But a deed that also surpasses all *praxis*. Thinking tow-
ers above action and production, not through the grandeur of its achievement and not as a consequence of its effect, but through the humbleness
of its inconsequential accomplishment.[88]

With these passages Heidegger suggests that we should not regard thinking and action as strict opposites—since this would be to regard thinking
simply as a mental process and action as simply as physical process—but
instead we should understand thinking as a kind of action in the most
basic sense that it determines which aspects of our being-in-the-world
are salient.

Heidegger strongly articulates his contention that it is inappropriate
to gauge the value of thinking in terms of its results or consequences in
his *Zollikon Seminars*:

---

[85] Heidegger, "Letter on Humanism," 259.
[86] Heidegger, *Elucidations of Hölderlin's Poetry*, 135.
[87] "Letter on Humanism," 217.
[88] Ibid., 262

The most useful is the useless. But to experience the useless is the most difficult undertaking for [the] contemporary [human being]. Thereby, what is "useful" is understood as what can be applied practically, as what serves an immediate technical purpose, as what produces some effect, and as that with which I can operate economically and productively. Yet one must look upon the useful as "what makes someone wholesome" [*das Heilsame*], that is, what brings the human being to himself [*zu ihm selbst bringt*].[89]

In this passage, Heidegger suggests that while ontology may be considered useless by economic standards, i.e., is not something that can be valued on the marketplace, it is nevertheless "useful" in a far deeper sense, namely, that it can help us encounter ourselves in non-reductive, nonutilitarian terms, and in so doing help us become "wholesome."

What is the "value" of wholesomeness or authenticity when so many other more concrete problems imperil humanity, Levinasians and Marxists may rightfully ask? But the Heideggerian response is that the absence of wholesomeness or authenticity and the predominance of institutions predicated on domination and exploitation are deeply connected. If we cannot question the metaphysical premises of valuing itself, then we will remain caught in a paradigm that is harmful to all. As Heidegger explains,

[I]t is important to realize that precisely through the characterization of something as "a value" what is so valued is robbed of its worth. That is to say, by the assessment of something as a value what is valued is admitted only as an object for man's estimation. But what a thing is in its Being is not exhausted by its being an object, particularly when objectivity takes the form of value. Every valuing, even where it values positively, is a subjectivizing. It does not let beings: be. Rather, valuing lets beings: be valid—solely as the objects of its doing.[90]

---

[89] *Zollikon Seminars*, 159–160; GA 89, 204.

[90] Heidegger, "Letter on Humanism," 251. For a similar articulation of this point, see also Heidegger, "The Word of Nietzsche," in *The Question Concerning Technology*, 103–104. Note that Marx also makes a similar point to this effect when he writes, "In the expression 'value of labour', the concept of value is not only completely extinguished, but inverted, so that it becomes its contrary. It is an expression as imaginary as the value of the earth." See Karl Marx, *Capital, Volume One: A Critique of Political Economy*, trans. Ben Fowkes (London: Penguin, 1976), 677, 1037–1038.

Heidegger's position, which remains contestable, is that the imperative to defend something's worth in terms of its value is a function of a paradigm premised on subjectivism (the ideology that subjectivity alone determines what is true and good) and objectivism (the ideology that objectivity alone determines what is true and good). Both ideologies prevent us from engaging with beings in non-dualistic terms, i.e., "to let beings: be." Subjectivism fails to let beings be because it turns them into objects for the ego to consume or incorporate, while "objectivism" fails to let beings be by regarding them as somehow detached from or irrelevant to the self, and by regarding the self as nothing but an ego-like thing. Consequently, what is needed is a much more subtle capacity to move beyond a thinking premised on subject–object dualism, one that can affirm Dasein as *both* individuated from *and* opened toward others. Such thinking, I have been claiming, holds a critically ethical dimension even if the specific terms of this dimension remain ambiguous and contentious. Having offered a defense of ontological ethics, we are now in a better position to examine one of the more challenging criticisms leveled against it, namely, that an ontological perspective is actively hostile to everyday life and common sense—a worry that is provoked both by Heidegger's life politics, his opaque style, and his incendiary claims that philosophy should not be held to mundane standards.

"Merely Parables?"

A number of critics have accused Heidegger of promoting a philosophy that is pseudo-deep, employing pretentious jargon, tautological logic, and tortuous syntax to give his thought an undeserved authority. Adorno, for instance, calls Heidegger's thought "an aura without a light-giving star."[91] Hans Jonas calls Heidegger's "haunting language," "*kitschig*," and writes, "I shudder to think of what might happen when

---

[91] See Adorno, *Negative Dialectics*, 99. Adorno's concern also seems to animate the commentaries of John Caputo. In his early work, Caputo criticizes Heidegger for being pseudo-theological and not properly theological *enough*. See John D. Caputo, "Meister Eckhart and the Later Heidegger: The Mystical Element in Heidegger's Thought Part Two," *Journal of the History of Philosophy* 13, no. 1 (1975): 61–80, 77. Elsewhere, however, Caputo charges Heidegger not with being falsely religious, but with being *too pious*. See John D. Caputo, *Against Ethics: Contributions to a Poetics Of Obligation with Constant Reference to Deconstruction* (Bloomington: Indiana University Press, 1993), 227–232.

people begin to decide to be poets."[92] The implication of such accusations, in our context, is that talk of "ontology" and "Being" obstructs a
more sober analysis of our situation, and is therefore a distraction from
more pressing ethical and political concerns. Pierre Bourdieu epitomizes
this critique:

> One does not react to a sentence such as this: "the real dwelling plight
> lies in this that mortals ever search anew for the nature of dwelling, that
> they must ever learn to dwell," in the same way that one would react to
> a statement in ordinary language, such as this: "the housing shortage is
> getting worse," or even a statement in technical language, such as "On
> the Hausvogteiplatz, in one of the financial centres of Berlin, the price
> of building land per square metre rose from 115 Marks in 1865 to 344
> Mark in 1880..." As a formally constructed discourse, philosophical dis-
> course dictates the conditions of its own perception. The imposition of
> form, which keeps the layman at a respectable distance, protects the text
> from "trivialization"—as Heidegger calls it—by reserving it for an *internal
> reading*, in both senses, that of a reading confined within the bounds of
> the text itself, and, concomitantly, that of a reading reserved for the closed
> group of professional readers who accept as self-evident an "internalist"
> definition of reading...[93]

Bourdieu hits on a troubling irony about Heidegger's thought, for
he points out that the effect, even if not the intention, of Heidegger's
ontological posture is to immunize itself from the criticisms of the lay-
person, while forcing all who would seek to engage with it to enter it
on its own terms. Stanley Cavell, a much more sympathetic reader of
Heidegger, agrees, suggesting that to understand what Heidegger is saying, one must undergo a "*conversion* to his way of thinking" (emphasis added).[94] In light of Bourdieu's critique, it is worth asking why one
should embrace an ontological perspective at all. Of course, one could,
on Heideggerian grounds, reject such a question out of hand, claiming

---

[92] Jonas, *The Phenomenon of Life*, 256.

[93] Pierre Bourdieu, *The Political Ontology of Martin Heidegger*, trans. Peter Collier
(Cambridge: Polity, 1991), 88–89.

[94] See Cavell, "Politics—As Opposed to What?," in *The Politics of Interpretation*, ed.
W.J.T. Mitchell (Chicago: University of Chicago Press, 1983), 197. For another critique of
Heidegger along these lines, see Graham Harman, *Guerilla Metaphysics: Phenomenology and
the Carpentry of Things* (Peru, IL: Open Court, 2005), 111.

that our being is quite simply "to be ontological"—we are beings who can't help but care about what it means for us and others to be. Yet such a response would miss the deeper point of Bourdieu's concern, which is essentially, "Why should we care about the fact that we are beings who care?" Why idealize or aestheticize—or turn into a source of mystery—a situation that is perfectly simple, and perfectly analyzable within the disciplinary methods of a materialist sociology? Or to put it in Levinasian terms, why insist on "the mystery of Being" when "[t]he mystery of things is the source of all cruelty towards men"?[95]

To begin answering these questions, we can turn to Kafka's parable "On Parables," which offers a dramatic, tragicomic sketch of the impasse that motivates them:

> Many complain that the words of the wise are always merely parables and of no use in daily life, which is the only life we have. When the sage says: "Go over," he does not mean that we should cross over to some actual place, which we could do anyhow if the labor were worth it; he means some fabulous yonder, something unknown to us, something too that he cannot designate more precisely, and therefore cannot help us here in the very least. All these parables really set out to say merely that the incomprehensible is incomprehensible, and we know that already. But the cares we have to struggle with every day: that is a different matter.
>
> Concerning this a man once said: Why such reluctance? If you only followed the parables you yourselves would become parables and with that rid yourself of all your daily cares.
>
> Another said: I bet that is also a parable.
>
> The first said: You have won.
> The second said: But unfortunately only in parable.
> The first said: No, in reality: in parable you have lost.[96]

[95] Levinas, *Difficult Freedom: Essays on Judaism*, trans. Sean Hand (Baltimore: Johns Hopkins University Press), 232. Levinas similarly claims, in a clear polemic against Heidegger, that works of art are in danger of obstructing "sociality, the face, and speech." *Entre Nous*, 10.

[96] *Franz Kafka: The Complete Stories*, ed. Nachum Glatzer (New York: Schocken Books, 1971), 457.

"On Parables," presents a tension between a sagacious perspective that must remain cryptic and an "everyday" perspective that demands straightforward guidance. It suggests that these perspectives may be incommensurable, that one can "win" in one world while "losing" in the other. In what counts as reality for the everyday, "the words of the wise are *merely* parables." For the sage, however, the whole point is that wisdom must be sheltered in parable form. The way toward understanding is not to render esoteric truth exoteric, but to enter into an enigmatic logic and become a parable oneself.

From the everyday perspective, however, which demands that wisdom be submitted to the test of measurable utility or else dismissed as nonsense, this is a ludicrous—or *merely* parabolic—suggestion. Telling a man with everyday cares that the way toward deeper understanding is to enter the mysterious on its own terms is surely of no more help than telling him to "Go over." "On Parables," is thus itself a text whose wisdom remains questionable. The final line of "On Parables" suggests that parables are not just incidental loci of wisdom, but wisdom's essential residence, yet it offers no assurance that wisdom itself can meet the skeptic's everyday criteria. All parabolic wisdom can say in its own defense is that while it may always lose when measured against the everyday, on its own terms, it wins.[97] "On Parables" is thus tragicomic precisely because its very pathos is not obviously instructive. Instead, "On Parables" only invites the meta-question of whether it is itself of any use in everyday life, and the meta-meta question of whether it matters. Reading "On Parables," we can "go over" into it, becoming parables ourselves, or we

---

[97] If we read Kafka's figures such as Gregor Samsa and the hunger artist as beings who have "gone over," that is, as beings who live *between* the human and the nonhuman, the skeptic's question becomes even more compelling. Do not such characters instantiate, the skeptic wonders, what is so fear-inducing about metamorphosis (*Verwandlung*), namely, an irreversible self-estrangement? Perhaps, it is in this light that we might interpret Kafka's story "The Cares of a Family Man" (*Die Sorge Des Hausvaters*). Although the story is largely a description of a nonhuman, and nearly mute character named "Odradek" who has "no fixed abode," the title of the story suggests that the real drama of the story is not simply Odradek's impoverished condition, but the disturbance that Odradek's impenetrability brings upon the Family Man. The question raised by characters such as Odradek and Gregor Samsa is what the limits of Dasein are. Are these creatures non-Dasein simply because they lack the ontic features associated with average, everyday Dasein, or do they signify the essence of Dasein stripped down to its essential uncanniness?

can attempt to seek some everyday utility from it, but perhaps only by locking ourselves out of it.

"On Parables" also raises the question of whether and how wisdom can be kindled. If the unwise (or, in more hopeful terms, "the not yet wise") are those most likely to reject wisdom out of hand as nonsense or as a distraction from everyday life (note a hint of what Freud calls "kettle-logic"), how can the sage move them to listen differently?[98] While parables, koans, poems, and dense ontological treatises may paradoxically succeed in saying the unsayable, they often still fail to convey that this is profound rather than trivial, thought-worthy rather than bunk, or healing rather than debilitating. This is because, at least according to Kafka's story, while the wise welcome bewilderment and paradox, those whose primary concerns are almost exclusively mundane will find bewilderment to be a terrifying threat to their egocentric identity, that is, "to the only life we have." It is not enough, therefore, for the sage simply to expose existence as fundamentally bewildering. The sage must also show or try to show that bewilderment needn't be a cause for fear, that wisdom leads not away from the world but simply offers a reorientation to it. But how? How can she respond to the suspicion that *Seinsdenken* (thinking being), far from making us more compassionate toward others, only leads us to pass them over in favor of something more "essential"? These questions only gain force when we consider Heidegger's own responses to them:

> When one attempts to prove that...something does "come" of philosophy, one merely consists in the prejudice that one can evaluate philosophy according to everyday standards that one would otherwise employ to judge the utility of bicycles or the effectiveness of mineral baths.[99]

---

[98] Sigmund Freud, *Jokes and Their Relation to the Unconscious*, trans. James Strachey (New York: Norton, 1989), 72: "A. borrowed a copper kettle from B. and after he had returned it was sued by B. because the kettle now had a big hole in it which made it unusable. His defense was: 'First, I never borrowed a kettle from B. at all; secondly, the kettle had a hole in it already when I got it from him; and thirdly, I gave him back the kettle undamaged.'" In this case, the person of everyday cares complains: "First, wisdom is just pretentious nonsense; second, I'm too busy for wisdom; and thirdly, any wisdom that demands I rethink how I'm living must be pernicious." Freud's point is that were only one excuse given, it would be plausible, but since the excuses, taken together, are mutually contradictory, they only prove themselves fantastic.

[99] Heidegger, *Introduction to Metaphysics*, 13; GA 40, 9.

Or as he quotes Schelling in the epigraph to his 1936 lecture course on him, "It is a poor objection to a philosopher to say that he is incomprehensible."[100] Still, Heidegger's bursts of inflammatory and uncompromising rhetoric on the essential uselessness of ontology needn't provide us with the summary word on the matter. Consider, for instance, Heidegger's example of Heraclitus, for whom ontological ethics consists in welcoming strangers into his home and helping them, without hostility, to recognize the sublimity of the quotidian. Another reason we should not take Heidegger's words as summary is that the questions we have raised do not just implicate him, but difficult and mystical discourses more generally. Even Adorno, who, we have seen, is deeply suspicious of ontology, suggests that his own thought is arrested by the double bind of seeking to be both critical of everyday life and relevant to it. In an essay in 1966, he writes about the music critic's pedagogic dilemma between, on the one hand, seeking to interpret new works of music in such a way that they retain their "fangs," and on the other hand, seeking to interpret them in such a way as "to reach people."[101] How, Adorno asks, can we maintain a critical stance toward the status quo without consigning ourselves to "irrelevance"?[102] His answer is that we should regard "the intention of being understood and the hesitancy in this respect" as "equally integral."[103] This, Adorno suggests, will not get us out of the dilemma, but will at least "elevate it to the level of consciousness," and in doing that, will grant the *possibility* of "a music whose power compels the understanding of those who currently feel indifference or animosity."[104]

Adorno's answer is one that, I want to suggest, should be extended to our reception of ontological discourse. Rather than regard ontology simply as the enemy of ethics or some other "merely ontic" field of

---

[100] Heidegger, *Schelling's Treatise: On the Essence of Human Freedom*, trans. Joan Stambaugh (Athens: Ohio University Press, 1985), 9.

[101] Adorno, "Difficulties*," in *Essays on Music*, ed. Richard Leppert, trans. Susan H. Gillespie (Berkeley: University of California Press, 2002), 664.

[102] Ibid.

[103] Ibid.

[104] Ibid., 675. Note that Adorno's dilemma is simply an eloquent reformulation of the ancient tension between rhetoric and philosophy, i.e., between persuasion and truth. It is particularly ironic, then, that Adorno's thought often elicits many of the same criticisms that he casts on Heidegger's, namely, that it is jargon-heavy, useless, and fatalistic.

enquiry, we should regard ontology as helping us to navigate these fields in all of their complexity. There are plenty of important and urgent questions we need to be asking besides "the question of Being," but one of the advantages of ontology is its capacity to show that all other questions both presuppose and disclose an implicit position on this question. In this sense, the goodness or badness of ontology is not really up for debate. We exist, and qua existing, we are both thrown into and projecting toward an understanding of Being. As Heidegger puts it, "Every human attitude to something, every human stand in this or that sphere of beings, would rush away resistlessly into the void if the 'is' did not *speak*."[105] In another sense, however, the possibility of recognizing *this*, and so of gaining some transparency on the ontological structure of our situation, can help us inhabit our particular situation as historically situated mortals with greater awareness. Such awareness is not ethical in the narrow sense, but it enables us to broaden our conception of ethics so that, rather than being a simple, algorithmic pursuit of an unquestioned good, it turns the difficult and ever questionable task of *being* good into an ontological and existential project.

Conclusion

We have seen from a variety of angles that the ethical status of ontology is ambiguous. On the one hand, we saw that ontological discourse risks covering over material concerns and issues that deserve an ontic response. On the other hand, however, we saw that ontology can also help us navigate the tensions that constitute our ontic existence with greater awareness of and appreciation for their complexity and uniqueness. And we saw that while ontology cannot *solve* our ontic problems, it can help us engage with beings in a non-reductively instrumental way, thereby coming to a different way of framing many of these problems.

One passage that captures these ambiguities is Heidegger's riddling claim that "What is most thought provoking is that we are still not yet thinking" (*Das Bendenklichste ist: dass wir noch nicht denken*).[106] For here, Heidegger prescribes not a positive definition of "thinking," but rather an oblique indication that, if we were to begin thinking, we would

---

[105] *What Is Called Thinking?*, 174.
[106] GA 8, 6.

have to start by recognizing that we are "still not yet thinking." Such a vertiginous definition of thinking ties the meaning of thinking not to an identifiable act, but to an ever-deferred process of being on the path toward thinking, as if the more thoughtful one were, the more one would have to ponder how one was not yet thinking. If we read this passage suspiciously, then ontology or thinking is indeed a pseudo-deep, utopian project, as it is one that lacks any reachable or identifiable goal. If we read it more generously, however, then ontology or thinking appears as a devotional practice of and commitment to being ever *on the way*. On this reading, the negativity of thinking is precisely what makes it most significant to ethical life.

In this chapter, I have sought to show why there are strong reasons to maintain a suspicion of ontology, while also showing that there are critical reasons for interpreting ontology more generously, taking seriously Heidegger's claim that "[t]he poverty of reflection is the promise of a wealth whose treasures glow in the resplendence of that uselessness which can never be included in any reckoning."[107] The reason we need to take this claim seriously, according to Heidegger—the reason why it is precisely the poverty of reflection that offers a promise of wealth—is that it reminds us that our ontic means of showing value miss something that is ur-valuable: Being itself. In reminding us that it is Being, or more simply, meaningfulness, that is ur-valuable, ontology reminds us that our capacity and need to make and debate ethical choices is most basically rooted in an understanding of and care for Being. In so doing, it helps us affirm our condition as beings who are ineluctably called on *to be* and *to enact* our understanding, as limited, questionable, and open to revision as it is.

Thus, we are now in a better position to see that Levinas's criticisms of ontology, though trenchant, needn't be taken wholesale. In particular, Levinas's claim that the first question we should be asking is not "what is Being?" but rather, "[i]s it just to be?" presumes a dichotomy between these questions that we needn't accept.[108] Rather than consider the question of being as anterior to the call issuing from what Levinas names "the face of the other," we can consider them to be

[107] Heidegger, "Science and Reflection," in *The Question Concerning Technology*, 181.

[108] Levinas, *Outside the Subject*, trans. Michael B. Smith (London: Continuum, 2008), 72; *Ethics and Infinity. Conversations with Philippe Nemo*, trans. Richard A. Cohen (Pittsburgh: Duquesne University Press 1982), 120.

possibly congruent with each other. We might even hazard to say that "Being 'is' the face." While such a conclusion may seem to be exterior to Heidegger's thought, we should not overlook Heidegger's claim that "Being-here as an existing human being is always one and the same as being-there with you," a claim that indicates existential questions are always motivated by questions of coexistence.[109] Additionally, we should take seriously Levinas's admissions that "one cannot, in fact, ignore fundamental ontology and its problematic."[110] Or, as he once confessed in a lecture he gave in 1987 at the *Collège International de Philosophie* in Paris, "nothing has been able to destroy in my mind the conviction that the *Sein und Zeit* of 1927 cannot be annulled, no more than can the few other eternal books in the history of philosophy..."[111]

Thus, despite the significant differences in inflection between Levinas and Heidegger, and despite Levinas's official rhetoric to the contrary, it is possible, in principle, to regard care for "Being" and care for "the other" as mutually inclusive and mutually implicating ways of authentically responding to the human condition. While such a conclusion is not one that Heidegger himself makes directly, this chapter has sought to show that it is at least a plausible direction in which to take Heidegger's project. In particular, I have sought to call attention to Heidegger's insight that because our being is always being-in-the-world, and always complexly mediated, ontology offers important contributions to ethical discourse. We owe thanks to Levinas for criticizing the individualistic, egocentric reading of Heidegger, according to which the unfolding of truth occurs simply as a conversation between me and my surroundings, completely detached from any sense of intersubjective obligation. And we should therefore accept Levinas's insight that "[q]uestioning is not explained by astonishment only, but by the presence of him to whom it is addressed."[112] Yet we owe thanks to Heidegger for reminding us that the call of "the other" always occurs "in-the-world," and that therefore our ethical obligations cannot be abstracted from the concrete context of meaningfulness that makes them possible. As Heidegger writes,

[109] *Zollikon Seminars*, 108; GA 89, 141.
[110] Levinas, *Ethics and Infinity*, 43.
[111] *Entre Nous*, 208.
[112] *Totality and Infinity*, 96.

The basic condition for [the] possibility of the self's being a possible thou in being-with others is based on the circumstance that Dasein as the self that it is, is such that it exists as *being-in-the-world*. For 'thou' means 'you who are with me *in the world*' (emphasis added).[113]

Taking an ontological perspective such as the one described above, can, moreover, help us appreciate the crucial *differences* between the calls of the friend, the calls of the father and mother, the calls of children, the calls of the elderly, the calls of the student, the calls of the rebel, the calls of the beggar, the calls of the survivor, the calls of the perpetrator, and the calls of conscience, holding open a space where these calls can emerge in their plurality, rather than being subsumed under a mono-chromatic rubric of "alterity."[114] And even if, as Levinas suggests, each "other" presents us with the universal ur-commandment, "Thou shalt not kill,"[115] an ontological perspective can remind us that our capacity to hear and obey this commandment presupposes that we are already "thrown" into an understanding of what it means for us and others to be. Without this pre-given orientation, it would be impossible for us to appreciate the complexity of the other's needs and thus to be competent in responding to them. Response-ability, in other words, makes sense only as a modality of being-in-the-world. Moreover, the "face-to-face" encounter that Levinas celebrates is only possible for beings that have already *learned* to regard the presence of another human being as fundamentally different from the presence of other beings such as a loaf of bread, a caterpillar, the moon, a book, a washing machine, a river, or a computer screen.[116] This differentiation does not come to pass *before* an

---

[113] Heidegger, *The Basic Problems of Phenomenology*, trans. Albert Hofstadter (Bloomington: Indiana University Press, 1982), 297–298.

[114] The same point holds for why Buber's I-Thou/I-It binary, though existentially and pedagogically instructive, cannot be analytically satisfying.

[115] *Totality and Infinity*, 87; "Peace and Proximity," in *Basic Philosophical Writings*, ed. Aadrian T. Peperzak, Simon Critchley, and Robert Bernasconi (Bloomington: University of Indiana Press, 1996), 164, 161–170.

[116] On this point, see Clifford Geertz, "Deep Play: Notes on the Balinese Cockfight," in *The Interpretation of Cultures: Selected Essays* (New York: Basic Books, 1973), 412–417. Geertz describes how, when he and his wife first came to a Balinese village, they were simply disregarded by the villagers, as if they did not exist, and only upon passing through a particular rite of passage, did they earn the trust and thus the acknowledgment of the villagers.

2 ONTOLOGICAL ETHICS AS A RESTORATION OF QUESTIONABILITY 105

understanding of being, as Levinas claims, but is instead a clear sign that an understanding of being is always at work.

We can also thank Heidegger for showing us that ethics is not just an interpersonal affair, but concerns our *ethos*, that is, how we bear ourselves with and toward each and all the beings that comprise our environment. In other words, Heidegger helps us appreciate that ethics is always also ecology, and thus that ethics concerns not only how we bear ourselves toward other human beings, but also how we bear ourselves toward non-human others, a point that is understated in Levinas.

Thus, while we should appreciate Levinas' insistence on the "exteriority," or non-incorporability of the other, we must also appreciate that this cannot be the whole story. If it were, Levinas's thought would simply be the inverse of Cartesian solipsism, swapping one sovereign, the ego, with another, "the Other."[117] In defining ethics as a kind of sacrifice of the self for the sake of the other (evident in his use of terms such as "accusation" "being taken hostage" and "substitution"), Levinas would be leaving unquestioned the traditional, metaphysical conception of the self. On Heidegger's account, however, the very terms of the classical debate—between whether the "I" is grounded in the other or the other is grounded in the "I"—are considered derivative of a self or "clearing" that is antecedent to this distinction. To be sure, the self is always qualified by "mineness" (*Jemeinigkeit*), yet it is also always, "in-the-world"— "thrown" from and "projecting" toward and with others (*Mitsein*). And, although Heidegger does seem to give a certain primacy to *jemeinigkeit* in *Being and Time*, in his *Contributions to Philosophy*, he makes clear that selfhood cannot simply be conflated with mineness:

> *Selfhood* is more originary than I or thou or we. These are as such first gathered in the *self* and thereby become each respective 'self.' Conversely, the dispersal of the I, the thou, and the we, as well as their crumbling and massing together, are not simply human failures; they are the occurrence of the powerlessness to endure and know the *domain of what what is proper...*[118]

---

[117] For an extended argument on this point, see Roberto Esposito's avowedly Heideggerian, *Communitas: The Origin and Destiny of Community*, trans. Timothy Campbell (Stanford: Stanford University Press, 2010), 93–94.

[118] *Contributions to Philosophy*, 253–254; GA 65, 321.

In other words, as Paul Ricouer helpfully explains, we must make sure not to equate "the self" and "myself."[119] To be sure, the "I" is an integral dimension of the self, but it does not exhaust it. Once we appreciate this, however, then the severity of Levinas' complaint is diminished. As François Raffoul has argued, "the opposition between a responsibility to the other and a responsibility-to-self [is] moot."[120]

Heidegger's attempt to affirm the self without conflating it with egocentric subjectivity is evident in his claim that

> [o]nly where man is essentially already subject does there exist the possibility of his slipping into the aberration of subjectivism in the sense of individualism. But also, only where man *remains* subject does the positive struggle against individualism and for the community as the sphere of those goals that govern all achievement and usefulness have any meaning.[121]

In other words, Heidegger here suggests that it is only subjectiv*ism*—the misguided belief that the individual subject determines his reality from the ground up—that is at odds with social ethics, but not subjectivity as such. On the contrary, subjectivity, however precarious a phenomenon it may be, is integral to the enterprise of social ethics. As Heidegger writes, "one can only listen, if one involves oneself, with all of one's specificity."

Thus, it is too simplistic to oppose autonomy and heteronomy (or ontology and ethics) as if they were mutually exclusive. Instead, we do better to regard the tensions between "self-determination" and obligation, or between "self-reliance" and dependency as tensions that constitute the very meaning and challenge of selfhood as both an ontological and ethical enterprise. We can thereby begin to appreciate that ontological questioning—the practice of letting things emerge as questionable—far from simply being the precinct of the detached, irresponsible ego, always arises from an existence that is singularly and jointly situated in this tension. Thus, not only may ontological questioning reveal our

---

[119] Paul Ricouer, *Oneself as Another*, trans. Kathleen Blamey (Chicago: University of Chicago Press, 1992), 188.

[120] François Raffoul, *The Origins of Responsibility*, 254.

[121] "The Age of the World Picture," 133.

being as fundamentally being-with, and not only may it thereby expand the scope of our sense of responsibility, but it may even transform the way we understand and take responsibility for the terms of our responsibility itself (a topic explored further in the next chapter).

While our questions are always shaped by the context in which they are received, rearticulated, and addressed, and thus can be dismantled—that is, shown to depend upon assumptions that are historically contingent and that serve to conceal other questions—(e.g., "What economic, juridical, social, and political structures do they indirectly reinforce?" or "Who is fighting our wars, cleaning our bathrooms, and financing our projects, while we ask these questions?")—ontology reveals that the capacity and the need to question itself cannot be dismantled. In this sense, even if "being-in-the-world" is just as contingent as anything else that came into being and that will morph into something else, the *questionability* of "being-in-the-world" remains a necessity.

We can now see why "ontological ethics" resists the categories of "the good" or "the good life" endorsed by metaphysical conceptions of ethics. In advocating for an ideal that is untouched by the existential limits of temporality, history, language, and embodiment, metaphysical conceptions of ethics neglect to consider the very humanness that makes ethical life both possible and meaningful. From an ontological perspective, by contrast, we are able to see that our ethical aspirations must always be directed at and mediated by "being-in-the-world." Such aspirations will therefore have to seek not the dissolution of questions and the dispelling of bewilderment, but instead a capacity to let things reveal themselves as essentially questionable. In contrast to the Hegelian goal of an Absolute self-knowledge, the ontological perspective supported by Heidegger's thought enjoins us to consider the ineradicable unknowability and non-graspability of our condition. In enjoining us to let aspects of our perplexing condition remain perplexing, ontology opens up an ethics of engaged receptivity.

CHAPTER 3

"Dwelling Poetically" in a Metaphysical World

Today we are too easily inclined either to understand being responsible and being indebted moralistically as a lapse, or else to construe them in terms of effecting [...] The principle characteristic of being responsible [however] is [...] starting something on its way into arrival.[1]

In the last chapter, we saw how ontology—understood not as a theory about Being, but as a holistic and embodied engagement with the questionability of our own Being in both its singularity and commonness—can be construed as an ethical enterprise. We saw, in particular, how ontology helps us approach ethical questions as questions that concern not just moral behavior, but more broadly, the existential health and wholesomeness of how we "dwell" in the world. But an important question remains: how, given our position in a world that does not define ethics in this way, can we bear a world where a more holistic, non-metaphysical understanding of ethics holds sway?

Here, as in the last chapter, language falters. For it is difficult to speak of "dwelling" without reifying it, thereby mischaracterizing it as an ideal or a goal to be pursued by subjects. But if we were to talk about "dwelling" in such instrumentalist and dualistic terms, we would risk perpetuating a framework that such a concept is meant to resist. Thus, our question is sharpened: if "dwelling" is not, properly speaking, a goal or

---

[1] Heidegger, "The Question Concerning Technology," 9.

© The Author(s) 2018
Z. Atkins, *An Ethical and Theological Appropriation of Heidegger's Critique of Modernity*,
https://doi.org/10.1007/978-3-319-96917-6_3

a value and is not simply an identifiable project that an individual or an organized group (such as a nation, a political party, or a religious body) can perform or accomplish, how can we talk about it, and how—here again, the language is imprecise—can we discern when it is happening or not happening? Finally, we must ask what understanding ethics in terms of "dwelling" means for how we conceive of agency and responsibility, especially given that many critics accuse Heidegger of fatalism.[2]

An answer to these questions, this chapter shows, can be found in Heidegger's claims, advanced in his essay on Hölderlin "...Poetically Man Dwells..." that "poetry and dwelling belong together, each calling for the other," and that "dwelling occurs only when poetry comes to pass and is present."[3] Understanding the connection between dwelling and poetry—understanding, in other words, how the question of Being can also be parsed as a question of how we can "dwell poetically"—not only steers us through the Scylla of subjectivism and the Charybdis of fatalism, but also helps us clarify a potentially religious and devotional dimension of ontology (a topic developed in subsequent chapters). For now, we can simply note that for Heidegger there is a direct connection between poetry and what he calls "the holy," and between "the holy" and our capacity to encounter God. As Heidegger writes in his essay "What Is Metaphysics?", "The thinker says Being. The poet names the holy" (*Der Denker sagt das Sein. Der dichter nennt das Heilige.*).[4] And "The holy," Heidegger writes in his "Letter on Humanism," "is the essential sphere of divinity, which in turn alone affords a dimension for the gods and for God..."[5]

Before we further analyze the relationship between dwelling and poetry and between poetry and the holy, however, let us return to our original question: how can we come to "dwell" when our every-day language and social institutions rely on and reinforce metaphysical

---

[2]For fatalistic readings see Richard Wolin, *The Politics of Being*, 137–171; Karsten Harries, "Heidegger as a Political Thinker," *The Review of Metaphysics* 29, no. 4 (1976): 642–669; and Jürgen Habermas, "The Undermining of Western Rationalism Through the Critique of Modern Metaphysics: Martin Heidegger," in *The Philosophical Discourse of Modernity. Twelve Lectures*, trans. Frederick Lawrence (Cambridge: MIT Press, 1990), 138–152.

[3]"Poetically Man Dwells," 225.

[4]Heidegger, "What is Metaphysics?" trans. R.F.C. Hull and Alan Crick, in *Existence and Being* (Chicago: Henry Regnery and Co., 1988), 360; GA 9, 312.

[5]Heidegger, "Letter on Humanism," 242.

definitions of truth, value, and being? To answer this question we need to appreciate that Heidegger endorses two apparently divergent narratives about the source of our alienation from Being. In the following sections, I argue that both narratives are true simultaneously and that understanding this is itself critical to the ontological health of our being-in-the-world, as it allows us to affirm the importance of human responsibility and agency without exaggerating or misunderstanding it. In accepting the truth of both narratives, we can embrace the importance of both activity *and* passivity, pragmatism *and* yearning, "works" *and* "faith," and, rather than opposing them, appreciate their fundamental entwinement.

In doing so, we can also affirm both Plato's belief in the importance of contemplation and Marx's belief in the importance of social action, while recognizing the essential limits of each approach. Marx was right to enjoin philosophers not just to interpret the world, but to change it.[6] At the same time, however, Heidegger helps us consider that Marx's dichotomy between "changing the world" and "interpreting it" is too simplistic. For in defining "the world" as an existential structure of "Dasein," Heidegger indicates that the challenge of transforming the world concerns as much an economy of *meaning* as it does an economy of goods and services, labor and production.[7] Since, as Heidegger writes, "[the] designation 'Dasein' for the distinctive entity so named does not signify a *what*...[but rather] a *way to be*," we err if we think that a total understanding of Dasein can be reached through scientific or social scientific analysis.[8] As Heidegger writes explicitly, "the being of Da-sein is not to be deduced from an idea of human being."[9] Thus, ontology helps us recognize that human needs are always oriented around questions of meaning and meaningfulness, and are therefore open to question

---

[6]See Marx's eleventh book on Feuerbach (1845) in Karl Marx, *The German Ideology* (Amherst, NY: Prometheus Books, 1998), 574.

[7]In Heidegger's 1969 interview on German public television, http://www.youtube.com/watch?v=jQsQOqa0UVc (accessed August 12, 2013), he makes this critique of Marx's eleventh book on Feuerbach (1845) explicit. For Heidegger's more extended critiques of Marx, see "Letter on Humanism," 225; *What Is Called Thinking?*, 24–25.

[8]Heidegger, *History of the Concept of Time: Prolegomena*, trans. Theodore Kisiel (Bloomington and Indianapolis: Indiana University Press, 1992), 153.

[9]SZ, 182/ BT, 170.

and interpretation, even when they are as basic as the need for food, clothing, and shelter. Thus, although Heidegger, as I interpret him, sides with Marx over Plato, in rejecting the ontological priority of an out-of-cave-experience that would shine a special light on life inside the cave, Heidegger diverges from Marx and sides with Plato in his contention that thinking's essential worth cannot be submitted for final analysis to materialist evaluation.[10] As Heidegger writes in *Being and Time*, "Life has its own kind of being, but it is essentially accessible only in Da-sein." "Dasein," meanwhile, "should never be defined ontologically by regarding it as life—(ontologically undetermined) and then as something else on top of that."[11] Consequently, "the question of Being," cannot simply be dismissed as "an opiate," as Marx might have claimed.[12] Nor, however, should it be understood as a question that is indifferent to the ontic circumstances of our everyday being-in-the-world and the obligations that arise from them. As Mary Jane Rubenstein puts it,

> Heidegger's great insight is that truth does not reside in the brilliance of the Forms, but rather in the transitions from the cave to the sunlight, and from the sunlight back down to the cave. This is to say that truth and shadow open *through* one another, or to push Heidegger a bit further [...] cave and [...] sunlight are not two separate spaces at all. They are, rather, different modes of seeing the *same world*.[13]

Or as Eugene Gendlin helpfully articulates it:

> It needs to be clear that, although we distinguished the philosophical and ontological level from the ontic (for example, psychology [or sociology]), the two are about the same world, the same things, the same beings. One

---

[10]For an incisive essay on anti-Platonism in the thought of Marx, Kierkegaard, and Nietzsche, see Hannah Arendt, "Tradition and the Modern Age," in *Between Past and Future* (New York: Penguin, 2006), 17–40.

[11]SZ, 50/ BT, 46.

[12]George Lukacs once described Heidegger's project as a "carnival of fetishized interiority." Quoted in Jean-Paul Sartre, *The Problem of Method*, trans. Hazel E. Barnes (London: Methuen & Co., 1963), 52.

[13]See Mary Jane Rubenstein, "Thinking Otherwise," in *The Immanent Frame*, December 3, 2010, http://blogs.ssrc.org/tif/2010/12/03/thinking-otherwise/ (accessed June 7, 2013); see also *Strange Wonder*, 49–52.

is an account of the basic structure of the other. If they were not about the same beings, there would have to be a separate realm of beings, just for philosophy to be about![14]

In other words, as Rubenstein and Gendlin show, ontology is best understood not as a single, explanatory narrative of our condition (be it Platonist or Marxist), but as a way of making space for a variety of narratives about our condition to elucidate one another. Thus, rather than simply oppose ontology to other discourses, we should see ontology as a practice of moving between different discourses with an appreciation both for what they reveal and for what they conceal.

RESPONSIBILITY AND THE HISTORY OF BEING

In his later writings, Heidegger offers two seemingly contradictory accounts of what he calls "the history of Being" (*Seinsgeschichte*), that is, the history of how each age understood "what is." On the one hand, Heidegger says the history of Being can be characterized as a history of "forgetting Being" (*Seinsvergessenheit*), and on the other hand, he says it can be characterized as a history of "abandonment by Being" (*Seinsverlassenheit*).[15] If we emphasize the first approach, we may come to the conclusion that simply by remembering or un-forgetting Being, we can bear a world that is more open, generous, and just. And this seems to be the driving narrative of *Being and Time*, which proposes that by dismantling, or more literally "unbuilding" (*Abbauen*) the philosophical tradition running from Plato and Aristotle up through Descartes and Hegel, one may recover the meaning of Being that they overlooked. But if we emphasize the second approach, we may come to the conclusion that the inherited, structural limits of our world severely hinder our capacity to bring about ontological change either individually or collectively. Furthermore, we may conclude that our very belief that ontological problems can be solved, let alone solved by greater human agency, is itself part of the problem. As Heidegger puts it in "What Are Poets For?"

---

[14]See Eugene T. Gendlin, "*Befindlichkeit*: Heidegger and the Philosophy of Psychology," *Review of Existential Psychology & Psychiatry* 16, nos. 1–3 (1978–79): 43–71, http://www.focusing.org/gendlin_befindlichkeit.html (accessed March 20, 2013).

[15]Heidegger, *Contributions to Philosophy*, 138, 206; GA 65, 175, 261–262; Heidegger, *Nietzsche: Volume IV*, 215–216; GA 6.2, 355.

[Human] willing [turns] everything, beforehand and thus subsequently, irresistibly into material for self-assertive production. The earth and its atmosphere become raw material. Man becomes human material, which is disposed of with a view to proposed goals.[16]

On this account, even when our goals and desires are benign, the risk remains that the very terms by which we frame our problems only serve to entrench us further in them. The tragedy, according to this narrative, is that the more agency we attempt to exercise, the more we end up objectifying ourselves, thereby turning ourselves into "human material," and objectifying our surroundings, thereby turning the earth into "raw material."

Heidegger makes this point more explicitly when he suggests that the forgetfulness of Being characteristic of modernity is, in fact, a double forgetfulness, as it also includes an enforced forgetfulness of the very fact of its forgetting. As he writes,

Enframing [*Gestell*] disguises even this, its disguising, just as the forgetting of something forgets itself and is drawn away in the wake of forgetful oblivion. The coming-to-pass of oblivion not only lets fall from remembrance into concealment; but that falling itself falls simultaneously from remembrance into concealment, which itself also falls way in that falling.[17]

Or as Heidegger puts it even more succinctly, "the destitute time is no longer able even to experience its own destitution."[18] These observations lead Heidegger to claim repeatedly that "our greatest and most concealed plight is our lack [of our sense] of plight" (*"die Notlosigkeit die*

---

[16]Heidegger, "What Are Poets For?," in *Poetry, Language, and Thought*, 111.

[17]Heidegger, "The Turning," in *The Question Concerning Technology*, 46.

[18]Heidegger, "What Are Poets For?," 91. It is worth noting the resemblance between Heidegger's claims and that of the Hasidic rabbi, Rav Hanokh Heynekh HaKohen Levin (1798–1870), who, according to Martin Buber, taught that "the real exile of [the Israelites] in Egypt was that they had learned to endure it." Buber, *Tales of the Hasidim: The Late Masters*, trans. Olga Marx (New York: Schocken, 1961), 315. Taken together, these passages suggest that one of the most calamitous effects of an oppressive system is the *resignation* it instills such that it becomes difficult for the oppressed even to recognize their conditions *as* oppressive. For a discussion of this problem in the context of philosophy of education, see Paulo Freire, *Pedagogy of the Oppressed*, trans. Myra Bergman Ramos (New York: Continuum, 2005), 54–55.

höchste und verborgenste Not ist").[19] The implications of these sentiments is that ameliorating our situation requires not simply that we remember Being, but that, more critically, we remember how to remember Being. The difficulty, of course, is that it is precisely our double forgetfulness that makes the meaning of such a task so elusive. How can we remember something when we have forgotten both how to remember and what to remember? Moreover, how can the kind of remembering that we are needed for succeed if the very terms on which we would conduct it are shot through by this double amnesia?

In arguing that our greatest plight is our inability to perceive our plight for what it is, Heidegger suggests that the path toward recognizing and reversing this condition cannot simply be brought about through a personal, mental operation. As Heidegger writes, "Transformation [...] cannot be established as readily as a ship can alter its course, and even less can it be established as the consequence of an accumulation of the results of philosophical research."[20] Or again,

> The step back from the one thinking to the other is no mere shift of attitude. It can never be any such thing for this reason alone: that all attitudes, including the ways in which they shift, remain committed to the precincts of representational thinking...A mere shift of attitude is powerless to bring about the advent of the thing as thing...[21]

Heidegger's point here is that the deleterious effects of what he calls "representational thinking" cannot simply be combated by the introduction of more representational thinking. This is why the remembering of Being requires something far deeper and more elusive than just a new theory *about Being*, as we have already seen. As Heidegger says explicitly, "The step back [from representational thinking]...departs from the sphere of mere attitudes."[22] It also helps us appreciate why, for all the

---

[19]"Overcoming Metaphysics," 102; GA 7, 89; *Contributions to Philosophy*, 11; and "Building Dwelling Thinking," 159. Heidegger' claim is particularly salient in the German, since *Not* can also translate as "need," making the phrase mean, "our greatest and most concealed need is our lack of [a sense of] need." See Chapters 5 and 6 for a greater exploration of ontological need.

[20]*On the Way to Language*, 42.

[21]"The Thing," 179.

[22]Ibid.

surface commonalities between Heidegger's thought and some of the teachings of the "mindfulness" movement—whether of the pop-Buddhist variety à la Alan Watts, Ram Dass, Eckhart Tolle, and others, or whether of the cognitive-based therapy variety endorsed by the NHS as a clinical way to treat stress and depression—Heidegger cannot simply be read as advocating "meditation" as the *solution* to our plight.[23] The reason, quite simply, is that if our plight goes as deep as Heidegger contends that it does, then we are in no position to know whether our meditation practice is "authentic" or whether it isn't simply another practice through which we perpetuate our forgetfulness of Being.[24] In "The Question Concerning Technology," Heidegger concretizes this point by suggesting that "The forester who, in the wood, measures the felled timber and to all appearances walks the same forest path in the same way as did his grandfather is today commanded by profit-making in the lumber industry, whether he knows it or not."[25] Heidegger goes on to explain why:

[23]The temptation to read Heidegger's thought as a philosophy of "mindfulness" is evident in the 2006 translation of Heidegger's *Besinnung*, a collection of posthumously published writings written between 1936 and 1944, as *Mindfulness*. See Heidegger, *Mindfulness*, trans. Parvis Emad and Thomas Kalary (London: Continuum, 2006). My reservation about using the word "mindfulness" to describe ontology, however, has to do with the fact that in popular culture "mindfulness" has become an industry in which what is sold under this name is largely a "technique" for self-, i.e., ego-improvement. Moreover, I am concerned that the word "mindfulness" connotes a certain dualism between "what's in here" (mind) and "what's out there" (world) that Heidegger's ontology questions. The popular conception of "mindfulness," moreover, as a practice of observing one's own thoughts, risks privileging the interior experience of the person "practicing mindfulness" over and above anything social, ethical, or political. In so doing, it conflates feeling good with doing good. For important critiques of this tendency, see Christopher Lasch, *The Culture of Narcissism: American Life in an Age of Diminished Expectations* (New York: Norton, 1978); Richard Sennett, *The Fall of Public Man* (Cambridge: Cambridge University Press, 1977).

[24]For an excellent essay on the classic error of spiritual seekers, who, in their search for "Enlightenment," end up commodifying, instrumentalizing, and reifying it, see Chögyam Trungpa, *Cutting Through Spiritual Materialism* (Boston: Shambhala Press, 2002). For a work that deconstructs the concept of "Enlightenment" (*satori*) altogether, see Shunruyi Suzuki, *Zen Mind: Beginner's Mind: Informal Talks on Zen Meditation and Practice* (Boston: Shambhala, 2011); for a work that reads phenomenology as a practice of perpetual beginnership, see John Sallis, *Phenomenology and the Return to Beginnings* (Pittsburgh: Dusquesne University Press, 1973).

[25]"The Question Concerning Technology," 18.

He is made subordinate to the orderability of cellulose, which for its part is challenged forth by the need for paper, which is then delivered to newspapers and illustrated magazines. The latter, in their turn, set public opinion to swallowing what is printed, so that a set configuration of opinion becomes available on demand.[26]

In other words, the forester finds himself caught in a complex system—Heidegger calls it "Enframing" (*Gestell*)—whose imperatives he cannot but obey, despite his own best intentions. In suggesting that the forester is subject to "Enframing" regardless of whether he knows anything about it, Heidegger reinforces his more general claim that the forgetting of Being is not simply something that we participate in by choice, but a more global affliction endemic to modernity. Furthermore, in specifying that "'Enframing' does not mean...a tool or any kind of apparatus," but rather "a way of revealing that challenges forth," Heidegger shows why it is inappropriate to think that one can soften its hold simply by changing one's behavior. As he writes, "Everywhere we remain unfree and chained to [the essence of] technology, whether we passionately affirm or deny it."[27] Heidegger's point in each of these cited passages seems to be that our alienation from Being is structural, and that therefore what is needed to turn this situation around is an operation that does not simply perpetuate the conditions it seeks to ameliorate. And, as Patricia Huntington helpfully argues, this is why Heidegger's criticisms of metaphysics are best understood not just as criticisms of systematic thought, but of Nietzschean perspectivalism as well.[28] Both views fail "to deliver radical freedom," Huntington shows, because they perpetuate a mentalist and egocentric way of being-in-the-world, rather than moving us to be in the world in a non-self-centered, non-calculative way.[29]

In a late seminar, Heidegger clarifies that before can we come to an authentic understanding of Being, we need to come to a different understanding of what thinking itself can accomplish: "To believe thinking capable of changing the place of man would still conceive of it on

[26]Ibid.

[27]Ibid., 4.

[28]Patricia Huntington, "Stealing the Fire of Creativity: Heidegger's Challenge to Intellectuals," in *Feminist Interpretations of Martin Heidegger*, ed. Nancy J. Holland and Patricia Huntington (University Park: Penn State University Press, 2001), 351–376, 356.

[29]Ibid., 357.

the model of production. Therefore? Therefore, let us say cautiously that thinking begins to prepare the conditions for such an entry."[30] Or as he puts it in his *Contributions to Philosophy*, "The seeking is itself the goal. And that means 'goals' are still too much in the forefront and are still placing themselves before beyng—and covering over what is necessary."[31] In these passages, Heidegger intimates that the traditional dichotomy between problem and solution does not obtain when it comes to thinking about our plight and how we might appropriately respond to it. More than this, Heidegger suggests that our very desire to draw such a strict dichotomy between problem and solution may itself be a symptom of our metaphysical entanglement. Instead, we must understand thinking as akin to preparation rather than achievement.

Heidegger's most famous claim on the preparatory nature of thinking, and one that is often taken to be proof of his fatalism, is his comment in *Der Spiegel* that:

> Philosophy will not be able to effect any immediate transformation of the present condition of the world. This is not only true of philosophy, but of all human reflection and striving. Only a god can still save us. I see the only possibility of salvation in the process of preparing a readiness, through thinking and poetizing, for the appearance of the god or for the absence of the god in the decline.[32]

---

[30]Heidegger, *Four Seminars*, 75; GA 15, 128.

[31]*Contributions*, 16; GA 65, 18.

[32]"*Der Spiegel* Interview," *The Heidegger Reader*, 326. Heidegger's claim that philosophy consists in "preparing a readiness" is ultimately not far off from his earlier characterization of authenticity in *Being and Time* as a posture of "*anticipatory* resoluteness," (*Vorlaufende Entschlossenheit*) i.e., of resoluteness to be underway, in process, incomplete, partial. In his commentary on Hölderlin's poem, "Der Ister," Heidegger figures this stance as a poetic one, writing, "What is fittingly destined for us sends its destining in one way and another and *always remains in coming*. In such coming, however, it can be thought only in being taken up and preserved *as what is coming*" (my emphases). *Der Ister*, 128; GA 53, 159–160. Heidegger's claim that readiness and resoluteness are inseparable is also not far from the understanding enacted in the Zen Buddhist ritual practice of tea, according to which, the preparation of the tea is considered to be just as significant as the actual drinking of it. For it is only through the preparation of the tea that one can drink the tea *in its truth*, and thereby enjoy *the truth of tea*. On the explicit influence of Zen on Heidegger, see William Barrett, "Zen For the West," in *Zen Buddhism: Selected Writings of D.T. Suzuki*, ed. William Barrett (New York: Image Books, 1996), xii–xiii.

Leaving open what Heidegger means by "Only a god can still save us," it is possible, I argue, to read this passage not as a refutation of our responsibility for remembering Being, but instead as a reframing of what such responsibility involves. For we should note that while Heidegger here argues that "salvation" cannot come from "human reflection and striving," he also indicates that "the only possibility of salvation" is "in the process of preparing a readiness, through thinking and poetizing..." Thus, it is too simple to say that we can or should do nothing about our alienation from Being and its accompanying malaise. Instead, what is needed is a way of responding to our condition, named here as "thinking and poetizing," that can create the conditions for the possibility of ontological transformation.

Heidegger intimates such a point in his essay, "The Thing," when he contends that we are not merely at the whim of our condition, but have a qualifiedly active role to play in healing it:

> Things do not appear *by means of* human making. But neither do they appear without the vigilance of mortals. The first step toward such vigilance is the step back from the thinking that merely represents—that is, explains—to the thinking that responds and recalls.

Here, Heidegger suggests that even if "things"—those entities which bring us into an intimate sense of the mystery and ubiquity of Being (meaningfulness), and thereby gather us into a greater sense of concord with everything else that constitutes our world—do not depend for their being on human *making*, their capacity to operate as the beings that they are does depend in some way on human vigilance, and in particular, on human vigilance *qua* mortal. In other words, while the power to gather a world belongs to things themselves, and not simply to an individual or collective human will, their power would not be operative without human attentiveness and participation, essentially finite as it is.

Heidegger makes a similar point in his "Question Concerning Technology," when he admits that although "man is challenged more originally than are the energies of nature...he never is transformed into mere standing-reserve (*Bestand*)."[33] By "standing-reserve" Heidegger is referring to those beings that *are* in the mode of their potentiality to be expeditiously set to use. His examples are extracted coal reserves and

---

[33]"The Question Concerning Technology," 18.

an airplane sitting on a runway, but to make his point more contemporarily accessible, we could list gas stations, "on demand" television, or the countless books, garments, and toys sitting on the shelves of shipping warehouses in the so-called "middle of nowhere." For although our being is always determined by the same imperatives of efficiency and order that drive these institutions, we ourselves cannot simply be understood reductively in the same terms. Of course, one can take the economic view of human beings as nothing more than laborers whose sole function is to produce goods and services that make the system of which they are a part run more and more efficiently, but Heidegger claims that this view cannot exhaust what we essentially are, since we are also beings fundamentally engaged in "revealing." And it is the fact that we are always already engaged in revealing that grants us the possibility of remembering Being and remembering who we are. As Heidegger writes, "Wherever man opens his eyes and ears, unlocks his heart, and gives himself over to meditating and striving, shaping and working, entreating and thanking, he finds himself everywhere already brought into the unconcealed."[34] Thus, Heidegger explains that while *Ge-stell* can be read pejoratively as meaning "challenging" [*Herausfordern*] it can also be interpreted more benignly, according to its etymological connection to "*Her-stellen*" (producing) and "*Dar-stellen*" (presenting), "which, in the sense of *poiesis*, lets what presences come forth into unconcealment." And thus, while Heidegger calls "Enframing" "the extreme danger," he also claims that it can be understood at the same time as a "saving power."[35] That Heidegger draws this conclusion from his reading of Hölderlin's poetry, that is, from a human artifact, is further evidence that for Heidegger, human beings have a role to play in freeing this saving power, even if the terms of their role remain difficult to fully define.[36]

It is true that in his later works, Heidegger places a greater emphasis on the abandonment narrative than the forgetting narrative, arguing that the latter is derivative of the former—"*die Seinsverlassenheit ist der Grund des Seinsvergessenheit*"[37] ("the oblivion of Being is the ground

---

[34]Ibid., 19.

[35]Ibid., 28.

[36]That both "the danger" and the "saving power" are *named*, and in particular, named by the poet, should give us a clue as to the onto-ethical importance of how we understand and inhabit language.

[37]*Contributions to Philosophy*, 90; GA 65, 114.

of the forgetting of Being")—and thus would seem to be privileging passivity over activity as the proper response to our condition. And in many passages, it is indeed difficult to see how Heidegger leaves any room for human agency whatsoever. Take for instance this passage from Heidegger's lectures on Nietzsche:

> To *want* to overcome nihilism…and to *overcome* it would mean that man of himself advances against Being itself in its default. But who or what would be powerful enough to attack Being itself, no matter from what perspective or with what intent, and to bring it under the sway of man? An overcoming of Being itself not only can never be accomplished—the very attempt would revert to a desire to unhinge the essence of man.[38]

Yet upon closer scrutiny, it is possible to read this passage not as a refutation of agency as such, but instead as an exhortation to appreciate the extent to which our agency can arise only in a situation into which it is already "thrown," and thus to consider that genuine agency does not mean unbridled and undirected freedom, but instead the ability to affirm as one's own (*eigen*), or to "appropriate" (*aneignen*), elements of one's being that are initially not one's own (*uneigen*). As Heidegger writes, "The appropriation of one's own *is* only as the encounter and guest-like dialogue with the foreign."[39] Or as he puts it even more forcefully, "Freedom has nothing to do with causality. Freedom [means] to be free and open for being claimed by something."[40] These passages indicate that even if human agency cannot manufacture its own conditions, we needn't deny it altogether. In fact, just the opposite: the more capable we are of acknowledging the essential limitations of our agency, the more capable we may be of clarifying the terms of our responsibility. Thus, when Heidegger declares that "even [an] openness to Being, which thinking can prepare, is of itself helpless to save man," and "a real openness in his relatedness to Being is a necessary though not sufficient condition for saving him," we needn't read these passages as fatalistic.[41] Instead, we can regard them as injunctions to acknowledge the essential limits of our agency.

[38] *Nietzsche IV*, 223; GA 6.2, 365–366.
[39] *Der Ister*, 142; GA 53, 177–178.
[40] *Zollikon Seminars*, 217; GA 89, 272.
[41] *What Is Called Thinking?*, 88.

Such a reading is further substantiated by Heidegger's own explicit claim at the end of his essay "Overcoming Metaphysics":

> Even the immense suffering which surrounds the earth is unable to waken a transformation, because it is only experienced as suffering, as passive, and thus as the opposite state of action, and thus experienced together with action in the same realm of being of the will to will.[42]

Here, Heidegger contends that the dichotomy between activity and passivity is a false one. More than this, he suggests that fatalism is simply subjectivism in disguise. Thus, it is best to read Heidegger's criticisms of subjectivism not as a critique of individual responsibility, but as a call to understand the nature of such responsibility in a more nuanced way.

In his philosophical dialogue "*Anxibasie*: A Triadic Conversation on a Country Path between a Scientist, a Scholar, and a Guide," Heidegger articulates the question of what it means to live non-subjectivistically and non-fatalistically as a question of how we can enter into a posture of "releasement" (*Gelassenheit*), a word he adopts from the German mystic, Meister Eckhart. There, Heidegger suggests that the difficulties that confront us in properly talking about "releasement" correspond to the difficulties that confront us in "trying to be" released, as if it were a project like any other:

> SCHOLAR: Insofar as we can at least disaccustom [*entwohnen*] ourselves to willing, we contribute to the awakening of releasement [*Erwachen der Gelassenheit*].
> GUIDE: Or rather to the remaining-awake for releasement [*Wachbleiben für die Gelassenheit*].
> SCHOLAR: why not, to the awakening?
> GUIDE: Because we do not awaken releasement in ourselves from out of ourselves.
> SCIENTIST: So releasement is effected from somewhere else [*anderswoher bewirkt*]?
> GUIDE: Not effected, but rather allowed [*Nicht bewirkt, sondern zugelassen*].
> SCHOLAR: Although I don't yet know what the word releasement means, I do have a vague sense that it awakens when our essence is

---

[42]"Overcoming Metaphysics," 110.

allowed [*zugelassen ist*] to let itself engage [*sich einzugelassen*] in that which is not a willing.

SCIENTIST: You talk everywhere of a letting, such that the impression arises that what is meant is a kind of passivity. At the same time, I believe I understand it is in no way a matter of impotently letting things slide and drift along [*keineswegs ein um kraftloses Gleiten-und-Treiben-lassen der Dinge handelt*].

SCHOLAR: Perhaps concealing itself in releasement is a higher activity than that found in all the machinations [*Machenschaften*] of the realms of humankind.

SCHOLAR: Only this higher activity is in fact not an activity.

SCIENTIST: Then releasement lies [*liegt*]—if we may still speak of a lying here—outside the distinction between activity and passivity [*auserhalb der Unterschiedung von Aktivität und Passivität*].[43]

We will come to the paradox of "releasement" described above more fully in the next chapter. For now, we need simply note that though releasement involves a posture of surrender—i.e., of letting go, or letting be, or loosening—it is also fundamentally a posture of *Dasein*. As such, it is not a matter of leaving oneself behind and dissolving into some hypostasized, universal void, but of a particular and particularized engagement of being-in-the-world.

BETWEEN INCAPACITY AND DESTINY

Having seen that Heidegger needn't be read as a fatalist, we may now venture an interpretation of his dense suggestion, made in his lectures on Nietzsche, that "Being" and "the staying away of Being" belong essentially together.[44] One way to interpret this claim is to say that our *capacity* to be claimed by something cannot be disentangled from our *incapacity* to fully and finally respond to all the claims made upon us. The positive phenomenon of choice always occurs within a horizon of negativity, that is, against a backdrop of countless other implicit choices "*not* to do" other things. Therefore being who we are and becoming who we are are interlinked in every moment by the necessity of having to choose to enact certain possibilities and not others. On the one hand, the kinds of choices we make (and don't make) reflect our

---

[43] *Country Path Conversations*, 70; GA 77, 108–109.

[44] *Nietzsche IV*, 223; GA 6.2, 365–366.

self-understanding. On the other hand, however, the kinds of choices we make and (and don't make) also *change* our self-understanding. Consequently, our being is, in Heidegger's terms, "ec-static," at once self-possessed and self-dispossessed, active and passive, determined and open. As Heidegger puts it in *Being and Time*:

> The ecstatic unity of temporality—that is, the unity of the "outside-it-self" in the raptures of the future, the having-been, and the present—is the condition of the possibility that there can be a being that exists as its "There."[45]

Here, Heidegger hits on the paradox of our condition as beings whose unity is constituted precisely as a disunity: Dasein is who it is only by being "outside-itself." Recall from the previous chapter how crucial this paradoxical understanding of Dasein as an ecstatic unity was to Heidegger's discussion of ethics:

> If the name "ethics," in keeping with the basic meaning of the word *ethos*, should now say that "ethics" ponders the abode [*Aufenthalt*] of man, then that thinking which thinks the truth of Being as the primordial element of man, *as one who ek-sists* (emphasis added), is in itself the originary ethics [*Ursprüngliche Ethik*].[46]

The reason why understanding the human being as one who "ek-sists" is so important, we can now see, is that such a definition says what dualistic language cannot, namely, that we are both already who we are, and perpetually not yet who we are. We can also see why both the narrative of forgetting Being and the narrative of abandonment by Being are true: on the one hand, we are beings who are permanently alienated from our Being, and on this level, we are incapacitated from doing anything about it. On the other hand, however, our essential alienation or incapacity also offers us a positive opportunity, namely, the ability to engage in unconcealment.

The conclusion that our essential limitations give shape to, but do not overdetermine our responsibility is further supported by the fact that although Heidegger defines "Enframing" in quasi-mythological terms as

---

[45]SZ, 351/ BT, 321.
[46]"Letter on Humanism," 258; GA 9, 356–357.

a "destining holding-sway," he also writes that "destining is never a fate that compels."[47] It is also supported by Heidegger's suggestion in *Being and Time*, that "Destiny" (*Geschick*) is not a synonym for individual or collective predestination, but a term for something whose "power... [can] become free...[for us] only in communication [*Mitteilung*] and struggle [*Kampf*]."[48] In other words, to speak of destiny is to affirm that our existence has a purpose—and that we have a charge to interpret and carry it out, even if the terms in which we do so are essentially contestable, partial, and incomplete.

That we can never completely realize our responsibility can, of course, put an immense strain on us, and this, in turn, can lead us to deny our responsibility altogether. But as I have been arguing in my reading of Heidegger's two narratives, if we can acknowledge—or aspire to acknowledge—the structural challenges of our condition, we can become more competent at accepting our essential limitations and perhaps, by extension, the essential limitations of others. And while acknowledgment and acceptance are no substitute for action, they can at least help us to act with greater sensitivity to the *significance* of our deeds and to carry ourselves in ways that honor our deepest concerns. Thus, rather than see the structural limits on our capacity to remember Being in simply negative terms, we can also see them more positively as conditions that give shape to our singular responsibility for Being.

FREEDOM FOR HISTORY

Heidegger's delicate attempt to navigate between subjectivism and fatalism is further evident in his idiosyncratic definition of freedom. "Freedom," Heidegger writes must be understood not as the absence of constraint, but instead as "the realm of the destining that at any given time starts a revealing upon its way."[49] In defining freedom not as an attribute of subjectivity, but instead as a "realm" in which we participate, Heidegger suggests that we become free not by casting off our history or

---

[47]"The Question Concerning Technology," 25.

[48]SZ, 285/ BT, 352. Stambaugh translates "Kampf" as "battle," clearly bringing out the ominous, martial resonance of this passage. I prefer to translate "Kampf" here as "struggle," not to foreclose this other translation, but simply so that it does not distract us from appreciating the ways in which one can "struggle" without resorting to physical force.

[49]"The Question Concerning Technology," 25.

thrownness, but by coming to terms with it. Heidegger's insistence that the freedom of the present can never be dissociated from the past, but is always only a freedom to respond to the open demands it casts upon us, resembles Walter Benjamin's remark that "[l]ike every generation that preceded us, we have been endowed with a *weak* Messianic power, a power to which the past has a claim" (Benjamin's emphasis).[50] For Benjamin, our freedom is *weak*, because it is conditioned, tethered to registers we ourselves did not elect. Yet it is also messianic, because the very claims of the past that make it impossible to stand outside of history enable and enjoin us to hearken to the singular possibilities opened up in the present moment. Consequently, we enter into what Benjamin calls "now-time" (*Jetztzeit*)—a radical hope that each moment, and thus, *this very moment,* could be "the strait gate through which the messiah might enter"—not by departing into the ethereal and ahistorical, but by attending sensitively and acutely to our particular, historical situation.[51] Similarly, Heidegger claims that we enter "into the realm of the upsurgence of healing" only through a "thinking that conducts (our) historical ek-sistence."[52]

At the same time, Heidegger's comments on Hölderlin's poem, "Der Ister," make clear that sensitivity to our historical inheritance also always involves sensitivity to the futural possibilities opened by our inheritance and cannot simply be reckoned according to historiographical method. As Heidegger writes, the "Now" in the opening line of Hölderlin's poem, "Der Ister," "Now come, fire" (*Jetzt komme, Feuer*),

> Will never...be grasped "historiographically," for instance by attempting to establish the historical dates of well-known historical events and trying to relate the "Now" of the poem to these points in time by means of calculation, [since it] appears to speak from a present into the future...The "Now" names an appropriative event [*Ereignis*].[53]

In "The Origin of the Work of Art," Heidegger makes this point even more strongly, "History...means not a sequence in time of events...but the transporting of a people into its appointed task as entry into that

[50]Benjamin, *Illuminations,* 254.

[51]Ibid., 261, 264.

[52]Heidegger, "Letter on Humanism," 260.

[53]*Der Ister,* 9; GA 53, 8–9.

people's endowment."[54] That Heidegger penned these words three years after the Nazis seized power is alarming, but not a reason to dismiss his larger point, which, we have seen, is also shared by Walter Benjamin, namely that *to be* is to stand in an existential relationship to one's inherited past.[55] Heidegger made this point already in *Being and Time* when he wrote,

> History is neither the connectedness of movements in the alteration of objects, nor the free-floating succession of experiences of 'subjects'...The book of the historicity of Da-sein does not say that the worldless subject is historical, but that what is historical is the being that exists as being-in-the-world. *The occurrence of history is the occurrence of being-in-the-world.*[56]

As such, "history" must be understood not simply a set of facts about the past, but as a set of possibilities of understanding into which the present is thrust. As Heidegger writes, "only because humans *are* historical...can they 'have' history."[57] One consequence of understanding history in such ecstatic terms is that we cannot regard the structural limits of historical inheritance as the final word on what is possible. Since the meaning of the past is not fixed, but depends upon how it is received in the present, which is in turn dependent upon how the present is opened in anticipation by and toward the future, it is inappropriate to regard the present moment simply as an effect of the moments that preceded it. Instead, as Heidegger had already argued in *Being and Time*, we must understand the meaning of "the moment" most basically as an existential of Dasein. As Heidegger writes:

[54]"The Origin of the Work of Art," 201–202.

[55]For a literary illustration of this point, see P.D. James, *The Children of Men* (London: Penguin, 1994). For historiographic study of how the existential understanding of time developed in Jewish history, see Yosef Hayim Yerushalmi, *Zakhor: Jewish History and Jewish Memory* (New York: Schocken, 1989). Finally, for a critical precursor of the anti-historicist, or counter-historicist streaks in Heidegger and Benjamin, see Friedrich Nietzsche, *On the Advantage and Disadvantage of History for Life*, trans. Peter Preuss (Indianapolis: Hackett, 1980), who lambasts historicism as an "idolatry of the factual" (*Götzedienste des Tatsächlichen*), 47.

[56]SZ, 388/ BT, 355.

[57]*Der Ister*, 127; GA 53, 158–159. For similar articulations of this point, see also *Der Ister*, 9; GA 53, 9; *Introduction to Metaphysics*, 189; GA 40, 144; *Four Seminars*, 9; GA 15, 21–23; *On the Way to Language*, 31, 54.

We call the *present* that is held in authentic temporality, and is thus *authentic*, the *Moment* [*Augenblick*]. This term must be understood in the active sense as an ecstasy. It means the resolute raptness of Da-sein, which is yet *held* in resoluteness, in what is encountered as possibilities and circumstances to be taken care of in the situation. The phenomenon of the Moment can *in principle not* be clarified in terms of the *now*. The now is a temporal phenomenon that belongs to time as within-time-ness: the now "in which" something comes into being passes away, or is objectively present.

What Heidegger's theory of "the moment" means in the context of our discussion of the Heidegger's two narratives about the history of Being is that although we are beings who are inevitably byproducts of history, and to such an extent that we can never step outside our history and look at ourselves from the "outside-in," we are at the same time beings for whom the significance of the past remains something for which we remain literally response-able, that is, compelled by our situation, to disclose, interpret, and enact in new ways. Thus, ontology reveals that although there is a sense in which an authentic encounter with Being will forever elude us, there is another sense in which we remain ever capable of and ever responsible for such an encounter.

Heidegger expresses this paradox in his lecture course on Parmenides when he affirms that "to think Being is very simple," even as it also remains "the most arduous [task]."[58] Or as he writes in his essay on "The Word of Nietzsche," "What is given to thinking to think is not some deeply hidden underlying meaning, but rather something lying near, that which lies nearest, [yet] which, because it is only this, we have therefore constantly already passed over."[59] In *Being and Time*, Heidegger describes the paradox of our simultaneous intimacy with and alienation from Being as a chiasmic lighting-effect, whereby "Everything looks as if it were genuinely understood, grasped, and spoken whereas

---

[58]Heidegger, *Parmenides*, trans. André Schuwer and Richard Rojcewicz (Bloomington: Indiana University Press, 1998), 149; GA 54, 222. A parallel sentiment can be found in Adorno's claim that "the task of thought" is both "the simplest of all things" and "the utterly impossible thing." Adorno, *Minima Moralia: Reflections From a Damaged Life*, trans. E.F.N. Jephcott (London: Verso, 2006), 247.

[59]Heidegger, "The Word of Nietzsche," 111.

basically it is not, or it does not look that way, yet basically it is."[60] In both remarks, Heidegger portrays human understanding as essentially partial. And, echoing Hegel's claim that "The well-known is not known, precisely because it is well-known" (*Das Bekannte überhaupt ist darum, weil es bekannt ist, nicht erkannt*)," Heidegger suggests that how we comport ourselves toward what we seek to know is decisive for the kind of knowledge we will come to have of it.[61] In cases where we take the meaning of something for granted, for instance, we block ourselves from experiencing it in its complexity and marvelousness. Meanwhile, in cases where we are disoriented, our very lack of wherewithal may help us notice things we would otherwise miss.

Heidegger describes a similar paradox in his commentary on Hölderlin's poem, "Der Ister," writing that being at home and journeying abroad are not opposites, but mutually inclusive: "Being a locality, being the essential locale of the homely, is a journeying into that which is not directly bestowed upon one's own essence but must be learned in journeying. Yet journeying is at the same time and necessarily locality, a thoughtful, anticipatory relation to the homely..."[62]

In characterizing our capacity to relate to Being in such chiastic terms, Heidegger offers two important points. The first is that although we are perpetually estranged from Being, our estrangement is never so deep as to be irreparable. Even when we are forgetful of Being, our forgetfulness bears an ineliminable ontological residue, and simply by being able to acknowledge *this*, we are already on the way to ontological wholeness. As Heidegger writes, "as soon as man *gives thought* to his homelessness, it is a misery no longer."[63] The second is that our estrangement from Being, though in many ways a source of great psychological, ethical, and ecological malaise, is, in another sense, a positive dimension of who we are. As such, we mischaracterize it when we treat it as a problem to be solved. As I will now show, the ability to live with an embodied understanding of this paradox is best characterized as "poetic."

[60]BT, 162/ SZ, 174.
[61]Hegel, *Phenomenology of Spirit*, trans. A.V. Miller (Oxford: Clarendon Press, 1977), 19.
[62]*Der Ister*, 142.
[63]"Building Dwelling Thinking," 159.

"...POETICALLY MAN DWELLS..."

Commenting on Hölderlin's phrase, "...poetically man dwells..." ("*dich-terisch wohnet der Mensch*"), Heidegger explains that for Hölderlin,

> the poetic is [not] merely an ornament and bonus added to dwelling. Nor does the poetic character of dwelling mean merely that the poetic turns up in some way or other in all dwelling. Rather, the phrase "poetically man dwells" says: poetry first causes dwelling to be dwelling. Poetry is what really lets us dwell.[64]

But what is poetry? And why does poetry let us dwell? In his essay "Language," Heidegger argues that we must understand poetry not as a linguistic technique or an aesthetic craft, but as a basic element of our being-in-the-world. As he writes, "Poetry proper is never merely a higher mode (*melos*) of everyday language. It is rather the reverse: everyday language is a forgotten and therefore used-up poem, from which there hardly resounds a call any longer."[65] And, in "The Origin of the Work of Art," Heidegger writes, "Language itself is poetry in the essential sense."[66] "Poesy" (or poetry in the ordinary sense of the term), Heidegger explains, "takes place in language [only] because language preserves the original nature of poetry."[67] "Language," in turn, Heidegger writes elsewhere, "is not merely a tool which man possesses alongside many others; rather, language first grants the possibility of standing in the midst of the openness of beings."[68]

Thus, "poetry," for Heidegger, is not to be understood as one mode of expression among others, but as the most basic way in which and through which things reveal themselves to us, that is, open up and transform our awareness of a given situation's meaningfulness. In this expansive sense of poetry, poetry is less something that we *do*, than the condition for the possibility of any occurrence of meaningfulness at all. Our dwelling is poetic, in one sense, then, not through any of our own efforts, but simply because to be is to be a revealer of and a responder to

---

[64]Ibid., 213.
[65]"What Are Poets For?", 125.
[66]"The Origin of the Work of Art," in *Poetry, Language, and Thought*, 72.
[67]Ibid.
[68]*Elucidations of Hölderlin's Poetry*, 55–56.

meaningfulness. On this conception, "poetry," is simply a synonym for "unconcealment," something that is always already occurring, regardless of *how* it is occurring: poetry occurs as much when a person recites Hölderlin as when she orders chemical waste to be dumped into the ocean, or wears clothing that has been made in a sweat-shop.

At the same time, however, Heidegger also contends that our particular engagements in unconcealment can be more or less authentic, and that "poetry is authentic or inauthentic according to the degree to [which we can enter into an appropriate relation] to that which has a liking for [us] and therefore needs [our] presence."[69] Bracketing what Heidegger means by "that which has a liking for [us] and therefore needs [our] presence," we can say that on this account, "dwelling poetically," is not only something constitutive of who we are but also something from which we are estranged and toward which we must aspire. For note that in Heidegger's claim, "The poetic is the basic capacity for human dwelling," the operative word is "capacity," not fulfillment. In other words, "poetic dwelling" is best understood less as a goal or destination than as a promise of authenticity or wholeness, which, though ever present, is also ever elusive.

On this second conception, poetry is a careful practice of attention that we must continuously take up, and from which we are always held at a distance. This latter conception of poetry is consistent with Heidegger's remark in his essay on "The Language of Johann Peter Hebel" (1955) that "true and high poetry only ever accomplishes one thing: it makes the inconspicuous shine" (*Die wahre und hohe Dichtung vollbringt immer nur das eine: sie bringt das Unscheinbare zum Scheinen*).[70] For if poetry means making the inconspicuous shine, then it is something we cannot but fail at, the inconspicuous being, by definition, what eludes our focus. Unless, of course, "the inconspicuous" that poetry makes shine is not an inconspicuous *thing*, but the play of revelation and concealment itself. In this sense, even though poetry cannot make all inconspicuous things conspicuous, it can at least make the structures and patterns of our care and attention themselves conspicuous. Poetry, in this sense, would involve making manifest the absence that is a basic feature of presence, but which we often miss. In doing so, poetry

---

[69]"...Poetically Man Dwells...," 226.

[70]*The Heidegger Reader*, 295; GA 13, 123. A more literal, though more awkward translation would be: "It brings the unmanifest to manifestation."

would not make this absence disappear, but it would help us recognize its positive qualities. Consequently, it might help us see "the forgetting of Being," or "the abandonment by Being," not only as impediments to our capacity to "dwell," but also as part and parcel of what it means for us to dwell. As such, poetry would not lift us out of the world, or offer us a way out of modern metaphysics, but it would enable us to be in the world and to inhabit institutions determined by the logic of modern metaphysics, in a freer way. Such a conclusion is warranted by Heidegger's emphatic point that, for Höldelrin, "poetic dwelling" does not occur somewhere outside of time and space, but "on this earth," that is, according to the specificity of our condition. As Heidegger writes, "Poetry does not fly above and surmount the earth in order to escape it and hover over it. Poetry is what first brings man onto the earth, making him belong to it, and thus brings him into dwelling."[71]

As should now be evident, the fact that poetry is both an elemental feature of being-in-the-world, and a rare and evanescent practice of attending to what forever hides from attention, means that "poetic dwelling," is an ambiguous term. Yet as we saw above, the ambiguity of this term is appropriately suited to the ambiguity of our condition as both estranged from Being and immersed in Being. As such, it offers a helpful way to name us as beings who are responsible for remembering Being, even as it also indicates the almost Sisyphean difficulty of ever "doing" so.

Articulating our condition/vocation/challenge as one of "poetic dwelling" also carries the advantage of opening the ethical field to concern not just what we do, but how we disclose meaning more generally.[72] It indicates that how we listen, speak, and disclose meaning more generally, bears essentially on the kind of world we end up inhabiting (a point explored in greater detail in the next chapter). Finally, to the extent that "poetic dwelling" names an ethical challenge, it signifies that our world will be a more wholesome place only to the extent that we

---

[71]"...Poetically Man Dwells...," 216.

[72]A careful reader may wonder if it is not too hasty to call a condition a vocation, and may rightly wonder, in the spirit of Leonard Cohen, if the real question is not whether ontology can be described as a vocation, but rather, "Who shall I say is calling?" These are questions we will address further in Chapter 5. For now we might simply note that the language of calling is not exterior to Heidegger's thought. As he writes, "Being [...] is a call to man and is not without man." "The Origin of the Work of Art," 211.

are capable of acknowledging that what eludes our conceptual and representational grasp is nevertheless an integral dimension of our world. As Heidegger writes,

> Every spoken word stems in a variety of ways from the unspoken, whether this be something not yet spoken, or whether it be what must remain unspoken in the sense that it is beyond the reach of speaking.[73]

The consequences of appreciating that all articulations of meaningfulness have their source in the unspoken, we will see in the coming chapters, are both ethical and theological, for they allow us to converse with others with greater sensitivity both to what is being said and to what is not being said. In the next chapter, we examine the implications of understanding our condition/vocation/challenge as one of "poetic dwelling" for what Heidegger calls "the task of thinking."

---

[73] *On the Way to Language*, 120.

CHAPTER 4

"The Task of Thinking": The Fecundity of Listening

> The thinking whose thoughts not only do not calculate but are absolutely determined by what is other than beings might be called essential thinking. Instead of calculating beings by means of beings, it expends itself in Being for the truth of Being.[1]

> All reflective thinking is poetic, and all poetry in turn is a kind of thinking.[2]

In the previous chapter, we saw that the structural challenges to our capacity to remember Being do not rule out our responsibility for such remembrance. Instead, they prompt us to take up the task of remembering Being in a way that is "poetic." We also saw that Heidegger's conception of "poetry" is both expansive and elusive. On the one hand, poetry was shown to be synonymous with disclosure or unconcealment, and therefore a constitutive feature of who we are. On the other hand, however, poetry was shown to be a practice of acknowledging the inexorable structures of absence that accompany all events of disclosure, and therefore something from which we are always at a distance. Consequently, "poetic dwelling" was shown to refer to a mode

---

[1] "What is Metaphysics?," in *Existence and Being*, 357–358; "Das Denken, dessen Gedanken nicht nur nicht rechnen, sondern überhaupt aus dem Anderen des Seienden bestimmt sind, heiße das wesentliche Denken. Statt mit dem Seienden auf das Seiende zu rechnen, verschwendet es sich im Sein für die Wahrheit des Seins." GA 9, 309.

[2] *On the Way to Language*, 136.

© The Author(s) 2018
Z. Atkins, *An Ethical and Theological Appropriation
of Heidegger's Critique of Modernity*,
https://doi.org/10.1007/978-3-319-96917-6_4

of being-in-the-world that is neither subjectivist nor fatalistic, and neither domineering nor passive, but instead, actively responsive. The question of this chapter is what consequences these insights hold for how we understand the task of thinking. What does it mean to *think* poetically? And how can poetic thinking help us engage more authentically with "the other," be it another person or God? If the previous chapters offered a defense of the import and *possibility* of ontology as an ethical and poetic enterprise, the coming chapters seek to highlight more concretely the ways that we might enact that possibility in everyday life.

As this chapter will show, poetic thinking is guided by an understanding that language is not simply a means for subjective expression or objective description, but is, as Heidegger put it, "the house of Being," which is to say, the place where the meaning and stakes of our essential questionability are ongoingly challenged, reinterpreted, and enacted.[3] As such, the task of thinking, this chapter will show, is not simply to discover true propositions, but, more critically, to hold open a space for language to be encountered *as* language. Understanding the task of thinking as the task of engaging with language in a noninstrumentalist and non-calculative way, this chapter will also show, can help us appreciate the affinities between thinking and listening. And, in exposing these affinities, it can show us how listening (understood existentially and ontologically) is a crucial way that we can "think" in a poetic way. As such, they offer the beginnings of a positive ethical and theological response to our modern metaphysical condition.

THE LIMITS OF METAPHYSICAL THINKING

To understand what the task of thinking demands, we can begin by considering what thinking, as Heidegger articulates it, is *not*. In the "Letter on Humanism," Heidegger explains that thinking should not be understood as a strictly theoretical or scientific enterprise:

> The characterization of thinking as *theoria* and the determination of knowing as "theoretical" behavior occur already within the "technical" interpretation of thinking. Such characterization is a reactive attempt to rescue thinking and preserve its autonomy over against acting and doing. Since then "philosophy" has been in the constant predicament of having to

[3] "What Are Poets For?," 129.

justify its existence before the "sciences." It believes it can do that most effectively by elevating itself to the rank of a science. But such an effort is the abandonment of the essence of thinking. Philosophy is hounded by the fear that it loses prestige and validity if it is not a science. Not to be a science is taken as a failing that is equivalent to being unscientific.[4]

The interpretation of "thinking" either as a theory or as a scientific method, Heidegger claims, is symptomatic of a set of prejudices that "thinking" itself is meant to question. As he explains,

> The rigor of thinking, in contrast to that of the sciences, does not consist merely in an artificial, that is, technical-theoretical exactness of concepts. It lies in the fact that [its] speaking remains purely in the element of Being and lets the simplicity of its manifold dimensions rule.[5]

Thus, according to Heidegger, thinking should be less concerned with drafting categories and concepts than with learning to speak in a non-categorical and nonconceptual way, that is, in a way that can preserve both a sense of "Being's simplicity" and its "manifold dimensions." In other words, thinking must be understood as a posture of openness to Being, rather than as a technique for grasping Being. Consequently, Heidegger warns that to judge such a way of thinking according to scientific and rationalistic standards is like "trying to evaluate the powers of a fish by seeing how long it can live on dry land."[6] If we follow this metaphor through, Heidegger is intimating that the element in which thinking is at home is one that is radically different from the element in which scientific rationality thrives.

Heidegger's most polemical articulation of the fundamental difference between thinking that is authentic, i.e., intimately engaged with the mystery of Being, and thinking that is only technical, is his claim that "[s]cience doesn't think" (*"die Wissenschaft denkt nicht"*).[7] Note, though, that with this claim, Heidegger is not saying that scientific discourse is wrong, false, or incorrect, but only that it is incapable of appreciating the enigma of Being itself. Moreover, "science doesn't think"

[4] "Letter on Humanism," 218–219.
[5] Ibid., 219.
[6] Ibid.
[7] GA 8, 9.

does not say that we should abandon scientific discourse altogether or that we should reject wholesale institutions that run on an unquestioning conflation of truth with data, or their concomitant philosophical anthropology, the human being as "data-point," but simply asks us to recognize that scientific discourses cannot exhaust what can or should be thought. In particular, "science doesn't think" offers a reminder that the terms and assumptions on which scientific disciplines rely are not self-evident or static, but rather the result of complex hermeneutic and historical processes. It says that science is a way of unconcealing "what is," but a way that has already decided in advance what kinds of discoveries are legitimate and illegitimate, valid and invalid. In particular, it is a way of revealing "what is" that takes the measurable as what is most real. And while there is nothing wrong with this decision within particular circumstances, if we forget *to think*, that is, if we forget to consider "the clearing" in which the terms of our measurements are conducted, we risk reducing ourselves to automata and our world to what can be standardized. As Heidegger warns, "Measuring is only possible when the thing is thought of as an object, that is, when it is represented in its objectivity."[8] Thus, if we cannot *think*, in the expansive sense, we are at risk of turning ourselves, others, and our planet into objects whose sole purpose is to be analyzed, set to use, consumed, or exchanged in an effort to increase and secure our power. As Heidegger explains, there is a strong correlation between metaphysical thinking and the reduction of the world to a vicious cycle of production, consumption, and militarization:

> The consumption of beings is as such and in its course determined by armament in the metaphysical sense, through which man himself the "master" of what is "elemental." The consumption includes the ordered use of beings which become the opportunity and the material for feats and their escalation. This use is employed for the utility of armament.[9]

Thus, it is clear that non-metaphysical thinking is a radical human and planetary need, and not simply one good amongst others. The same goes for our capacity to recognize ourselves as Dasein, that is, as beings capable of and responsible for thinking. Meanwhile, if we forget that we are Dasein, and regard ourselves according to a false binary as either subjects

[8] *Zollikon Seminars*, 98; GA 89, 128.
[9] "Overcoming Metaphysics," 103.

or objects, we turn our world into a place that is efficiently ordered, but in which there is no freedom and no responsibility. As Heidegger warns, "[When] reality consists in the uniformity of calculable reckoning, man, too must enter monotonous uniformity in order to keep up with what is real."[10] Heidegger calls such a set-up an "unworld" (*Unwelt*).[11] Thus, Heidegger's claim that "science doesn't think," might also be interpolated as, "science can't understand what the world would be if we approached every aspect of life in exclusively scientific, i.e., techno-rational terms."

We can now see even more clearly something that was only hinted at in Chapter 2, namely that "authenticity" (enacting and embodying a sense of one's being as Dasein) and ethical and ecological responsibility belong together, a conclusion that is further supported by Heidegger's claim that "[r]eleasement towards things [*Gelaseenheit zu den Dinge*] and openness to the mystery [*Offenheit für die Geheimnis*] belong together."[12] More will have to be said, of course, about what "release-ment towards things" involves, especially at an interpersonal level, but the point to be emphasized for now is that openness to mystery—or appreciation of the enigma of Being—is not simply a "feeling" or an interior "experience," but a way of engaging with the other. Meanwhile, self-objectification (subjectivism) other-objectification (objectivism), also belong together. As Heidegger writes, "perhaps our double ignorance about the truth and about ourselves is itself one and the same."[13] And, "subhumanity and superhumanity are the same."[14] Consequently, we can see that thinking, in the expansive sense, is not a method or a discipline that has objective aims, but a way of being that is guided by an aware-ness of the truth of Being as that which eludes representation, concep-tualization, and standard verification. As Heidegger writes, "Thinking is not knowing, but perhaps it is more essential than knowing, because it is closer to Being in that closeness which is concealed from afar."[15]

---

[10] "Overcoming Metaphysics," 108.

[11] Ibid.

[12] *Discourse on Thinking*, 55.

[13] Heidegger, *Parmenides*, 162.

[14] "Overcoming Metaphysics," 103.

[15] *Parmenides*, 162. Compare to Hegel, who writes, "To help bring philosophy closer to the form of science, to the goal where it can lay aside the title 'love of knowing' and be actual knowing—that is what I have set myself to do." *The Phenomenology of Spirit*, 3.

Heidegger's conception of thinking as a mode of resistance to the hegemony of metaphysical thinking is strikingly shared by Adorno, an irony of history, but one that demonstrates that "thinking" should not simply be conflated with an ontic political position or agenda, either of the right or the left. As Adorno writes, "If thought is not measured by the extremity that eludes the concept, it is from the outset in the nature of [the] musical accompaniment with which the SS liked to drown out the screams of its victims."[16] In other words, putting Heidegger and Adorno together, metaphysical understanding obtains a "clear and distinct" vision of things (Descartes) only by casting a blind eye to a more original and abyssal luminosity, varyingly named "the clearing," (*die Lichtung*) and "the Nothing" (*das Nichts*).[17] And in privileging conceptual clarity over "the extremity that eludes the concept"—in denying both the abyssal luminosity that resists systematic co-option as well as the denial itself—it sets up an inhumane hierarchy, one that privileges an

---

[16] Adorno, *Negative Dialectics*, 365. Although Adorno famously said that Heidegger's thought is "fascist to its innermost core," Habermas notes that "Adorno is in the end very similar to Heidegger as regards his position on the theoretical claims of objectivating thought and of reflection…" Habermas, *Theory of Communicative Action*, 385; see also Rüdiger Safranski, *Martin Heidegger: Between Good and Evil*, trans. Edwald Osers (Cambridge, MA: Harvard University Press, 2002), 412–413. Safranski quotes Adorno as saying in a letter to Horkheimer that Heidegger was "in a way…not all that different from us." For a more extended analysis of the elective affinities between Heidegger and Adorno, see Jan Rosiek, *Maintaining the Sublime: Heidegger and Adorno* (Bern: Peter Lang, 2000). For an excellent essay on Heidegger's and Adorno's shared belief in the radical, if ambiguous potential of works of art, see Krzysztof Ziarek, "Beyond Critique? Art and Power," in *Adorno and Heidegger: Philosophical Questions*, ed. Iain Macdonald and Krzysztof Ziarek (Stanford: Stanford University Press, 2008), 105–123. Finally, as another way to consider the parallels between Heidegger and Adorno, one might examine Zygmunt Bauman's description of *Negative Dialectics* as a tome one how to be "human in a world inhospitable to humanity." Bauman, *Liquid Modernity* (Cambridge: Polity, 2000), 41.

[17] These terms are ubiquitous in Heidegger's work, though Heidegger's most sustained discussion of "the Nothing" occurs in his 1929 lecture, "What is Metaphysics?" What makes these terms difficult to comprehend is that, like "Being," neither refers to an entity. Rather, they refer to the condition of possibility for beings to come to disclosure. As Heidegger "For thinking, which is always essentially thinking about something, must act in a way contrary to its own essence when it thinks of the nothing." "What is Metaphysics?," 97. See also "Letter on Humanism," 261, where Heidegger writes, "because it thinks Being, thinking thinks the nothing," and GA 71, 208, where he writes, "[t]he emptiness of the clearing is the initializing nothing." ("Diese Leere der Lichtung ist das anfängliche Nichts.")

epistemology founded on the principle of indubitability over an ontology founded on an irreducible exposure to the other. Thus, it is the task of thinking, in part, not to normalize or explain away those phenomena which elude thinking, but instead to make room for them to remain difficult.

THINKING-IN-THE-WORLD

Given that we have obliquely determined why thinking is needed, as well as what thinking is not, the question becomes: how do we think in a world whose infrastructure is ordered by the repression of thinking in favor of standardization, efficiency, security, and order? In *Being and Time*, Heidegger indicates that we cannot and should not simply leave these aspects of the world behind in favor of some kind of hermitage of inwardness, for doing so would not make us any less social beings. Moreover, in retreating from society we would be doing so in a way that remains dictated by it. As Heidegger writes in *Being and Time*, "We... withdraw from the 'great mass' the way they [*das Man*] withdraw."[18] And, as he puts it even more forcefully, in his later essay "The Turning" (1955):

> All attempts to reckon existing reality morphologically, psychologically, in terms of decline and loss, in terms of fate, catastrophe, and destruction, are merely technological behavior. That behavior operates through the device of the enumerating of symptoms whose standing-reserve can be increased to infinity and always varied anew.[19]

In other words, condemning the system, or attempting to leave it behind altogether, are not only hypocritical gestures in that they are inextricably bound up with the system they reject, but they are also self-undermining in effect; wholesale rejection of the system—whatever that would mean—only contributes to reinforcing a sense of its inevitability. Moreover, in thinking that we could ever simply exclude ourselves from the grip of some order, we would only be playing into the myth of subjectivism, the idea that we, as individuals, are somehow above and beyond the fray of "the crowd." But as many have shown, the idea that

---

[18] SZ, 127/ BT, 119.
[19] "The Turning," 48.

one can be "alternative" or "countercultural" is itself part of the ideology of consumerism.[20] Heidegger articulates the *Gestalt* of this point repeatedly:

> All counter-movements and counter-forces are essentially codetermined by that which they are counter to, although in the form of an inversion. Therefore a counter-movement never suffices for an essential transformation of history.[21]
>
> Negation only throws the negator off the path.[22]

Adorno describes it even more sharply, as a scenario of "damned if we do, damned if we don't":

> Whoever pleads for the maintenance of this radically culpable and shabby culture becomes its accomplice, while the man who says no to culture is directly furthering the barbarism which our culture showed itself to be.[23]

In *Minima Moralia*, Adorno shows that this conundrum is as much a philosophical conundrum as it is a sociological one:

> The departmentalization of mind [*Geist*] is a means of abolishing mind where it is not exercised *ex officio*, under contract. It performs this task all the more reliably, since anyone who repudiates the division of labor— if only by taking pleasure in his work—makes himself vulnerable by its standards in ways inseparable from his superiority. Thus is order ensured: some have to play the game because they cannot otherwise live and those who could live otherwise are kept out because they do not want to play the game. It is as if the class from which independent intellectuals have

---

[20] For an excellent articulation of how the very idea of a counter-cultural, antinomian aesthetic has become indistinguishable from mainstream consumer-culture, see David Foster Wallace, "E Unibus Pluram: Television and U.S. Fiction," *Review of Contemporary Fiction* 13, no. 2 (1993): 151–194.

[21] Heidegger, *Contributions to Philosophy*, 146; GA 65, 186–187.

[22] "The Age of the World Picture," 138.

[23] Adorno, *Negative Dialectics*, 367. For an excellent articulation how the very idea of a counter-cultural, antinomian aesthetic has become indistinguishable from mainstream consumer-culture, see David Foster Wallace, "E Unibus Pluram: Television and U.S. Fiction," *Review of Contemporary Fiction* 13, no. 2 (1993): 151–194.

defected takes its revenge, by pressing its demands home in the very domain where the deserter seeks refuge.[24]

Here, Adorno shows that the intellectual or "the thinker," in the professional sense, is caught in the same system of "Enframing" that, as we saw in the last chapter, binds the forester. For when thinking has itself become an industry, and thought or scholarship has become a good that is traded in "the marketplace of ideas," it becomes "departmentalized" regardless of the thinker's own best intentions. As such, thinkers in the modern world must become specialists, who work "under contract," or else dilettantes, who achieve some personal intellectual freedom, but by rendering their discourses irrelevant to public and political life. And here, the limits and risks of Heidegger's thought are acutely apparent, as we can wonder if it doesn't simply exchange Marie Antoinette's, "let them eat cake," for its own idiosyncratic "let them read Hölderlin."[25]

In light of these dialectical problems, we are in a better position to consider a paradox that thrives in Heidegger's work, namely how Heidegger can continuously claim he is not moralizing, yet often seems to write in a severely moralizing tone. In *Being and Time*, for instance, Heidegger states repeatedly that he should not be interpreted as commending authenticity over against inauthenticity:

> Our interpretation has a purely ontological intention and is far removed from any moralizing critique of everyday Da-sein, and from the aspirations of a "philosophy of culture."

> The expression "idle talk" is not to be used here in a disparaging sense. It would be a misunderstanding if the explication of these phenomena [curiosity, ambiguity, idle talk] were to seek to be confirmed by the approval of the they.[26]

> [*Verfallenheit*, Fallenness] does not [more literally, *should not*] express any negative value judgment, [but] means that Da-sein is initially and for the most part *together with* the "world" that it takes care of.[27]

---

[24] Adorno, *Minima Moralia*, 1.

[25] For an excellent poem that dramatizes this concern, see Robert Bringhurst, "These Poems, She Said," in *The Beauty of the Weapons: Selected Poems 1972–1982* (Port Townsend: Cooper Canyon Press, 1982).

[26] SZ, 167/ BT, 157.

[27] SZ, 175/ BT, 164.

The ontological-existential structure of falling prey would also be misunderstood if we wanted to attribute to it the meaning of a bad and deplorable ontic quality which could perhaps be removed in the advanced stages of human culture.[28]

The ontological critique of the vulgar interpretation of conscience could be subject to the misunderstanding that by showing the lack of *existential* primordiality of the everyday experience of conscience one wanted to pass judgment upon the *existentiell* "moral quality" of Dasein.[29]

Heidegger maintains a similar resistance to moralistic interpretations of his work in his later writings as well:

When one translates *dike* as "justice," and understands justice in a juridical-moral sense, then the word loses its fundamental metaphysical content. The same holds for the interpretation of *dike* as norm. In all its domains and powers, the overwhelming, as regards its powerfulness, is fittingness. Being, *phusis*, is, as sway, originary gatheredness: *logos*. Being is fittingness that enjoins: *dike*.[30]

Or as he puts it in *Being and Truth*:

If we ask for the *content* of what the highest idea is and what the *good* means, we must free ourselves from every sentimental notion, but also from conceptions that have become run-of-the-mill through Christian morality and then in secularized ethics. *Agathos*, good, originally has no moral meaning[...] The good is what succeeds, stands fast, holds up, what is fit for something [...] It is hopeless to want to comprehend the essence of the good on the basis of the Christian concept—this concept will not take us one step closer to understanding what the good actually means.[31]

Yet despite Heidegger's numerous claims that his thought is not moralistic, it is evident that what he is rejecting are simply metaphysical conceptions of morality, which see "the good" as a ready-made concept waiting

---

[28] SZ, 176/ BT, 165.
[29] SZ, 295/ BT, 271.
[30] *Introduction to Metaphysics*, 171; GA 40, 123.
[31] Heidegger, *Being and Truth*, 147.

to be applied by subjects. As Dennis Schmidt compellingly argues, "the basic task of hermeneutics is to overcome the notion that understanding needs to be applied."[32] Another way that we can understand Heidegger's protestations against the moralistic reading of his work is as a recognition that bringing about a more humane, less exploitative world, cannot simply be effected overnight, but requires an engagement with the current world as it is. As such, the refusal to be moralistic is a refusal to cast our responsibility in the stark and overly simplistic logic of either/ or: either we are for the status quo or against it. Far from throwing normativity to the winds, then, Heidegger's criticisms of morality might be taken as reminders that the terms of our responsibility require nuance and compromise, and cannot simply be formulated in the abstract. Thus, Heidegger says that we should think of our responsibility for Being not in terms of commandedness, but in terms of invitedness: "To call means not so much a command as a letting-reach...[It] has an assonance of helpfulness and complaisance...and means something like 'to invite.'"[33] Or if we are to think of our responsibility in terms of commandedness, then we should appreciate that "to command' basically means, not to give commands and orders, but to commend, entrust, give into safe-keeping, keep safely."[34]

What is crucial about the language of invitation, in contrast to the language of command (in the ordinary sense), I suggest, is that it asks the respondent to take responsibility for *how* she responds, rather than simply for the fact of her responding. Moreover, the language of invitation implies that the terms of our calling are less a matter of "right" or "ought" than a matter of "need" or "please." In the context of our discussion about how we can dwell and think poetically in a metaphysical world, the language of invitation reveals our responsibility as dialectical rather than dichotomous. Thinking and dwelling poetically, in other words, does not involve overturning or obliterating standardization, calculation, ratiocination, conceptualization, and so on, but rather allowing that which is nonstandard, non-calculable, and non-conceptual to come to presence *within* our standardized, metaphysical world. This is an ongoing and elusive challenge, but one that involves

---

[32] Schmidt, "Sources of Ethical Life," 41.
[33] *What Is Called Thinking?*, 117.
[34] Ibid., 118.

an ability to accept the provisional reign of metaphysics while avoiding the extremes of either triumphalistically celebrating it or resentfully condemning it.

Thus, Heidegger writes, in 1955, "We can say "yes" to the unavoidable use of technological objects, and we can at the same time say "no," insofar as we do not permit them to claim us exclusively and thus to warp, confuse, and finally lay waste our essence [*Wesen*].[35] And, "To think in the midst of the sciences means to pass near them without disdaining them."[36] "By no means should our discussions be understood as hostile toward science. In no way is science to be rejected. Merely its claim to absoluteness—that is, as the standard measure for all true properties—is warded off as arrogant presumption."[37] Thus, thinking is best considered as a non-oppositional dance *with* the various apparatuses of metaphysics, and one that subverts them precisely by refusing to play the metaphysical game of oppositional thinking, which treats all that is adverse as something to be corrected:

> To think Being without beings means: to think Being without regard to metaphysics. Yet a regard for metaphysics still prevails even in the intention to overcome metaphysics. Therefore, our task is to cease all overcoming, and leave metaphysics to itself.[38]

> What is unthought in metaphysics is therefore not a defect in metaphysics. Still less may we declare metaphysics to be false, or even reject it as a wrong turn, a mistake, on the grounds that it rests upon [an] unthought matter.

> Every metaphysics of metaphysics, and every logic of philosophy, that in any way whatever attempts to climb beyond metaphysics falls back most surely beneath metaphysics, without knowing where, precisely in so doing, it has fallen.[39]

From these passages, the paradox of Heidegger's attempt to wrestle with metaphysics comes through. On the one hand, metaphysics is

---

[35] *Gelassenheit*, 22–23; *Discourse on Thinking*, 54; I borrow Michael Zimmerman's translation here. See Zimmerman, *Heidegger's Confrontation with Modernity*, 219.

[36] "The Word of Nietzsche," in *The Question Concerning Technology*, 56.

[37] *Zollikon Seminars*, 110; GA 89, 143.

[38] *On Time and Being*, trans. Joan Stambaugh (Chicago: Chicago University Press, 2002), 24; GA 14, 25.

[39] "The Word of Nietzsche," 109.

characterized by a way of being-in-the-world that is unrelentingly strategic, and that treats things primarily in terms of their capacity to be manipulated. Yet in his own subtle and elliptical way, Heidegger himself describes a *strategy* for curtailing such a way of-being-in-the-world, a strategy for opening a nonstrategic relationship to "what is" in a world that is inevitably ordered by strategic thinking. Rather than dismiss this paradox as a simple contradiction, however, I am arguing that it is what gives integrity to ontology an enterprise that is always already and not yet ethical, poetic, and thoughtful.

Having examined the general stakes and challenges of thinking non-metaphysically in a metaphysical world, let us now turn to the medium in which Heidegger claims thinking most basically occurs (or fails to occur): language.

THE DECISIVENESS OF LANGUAGE

"Language," Heidegger writes, "is the primal dimension within which man's essence is first able to correspond at all to Being and its claim, and, in corresponding, to belong to Being."[40] It is "the home of man's essence."[41] And, it facilitates both "the first and most extensive humanizing of beings" as well as "the most original dehumanizing of the human being."[42] It is also, Heidegger says, both "the most innocent of occupations" and "the danger of dangers."[43] And, "not only is it the danger of dangers," but "it necessarily shelters within itself a continual danger to itself." Finally, Heidegger says, somewhat more opaquely, but no less grandiosely, "language is the most delicate and thus the most susceptible vibration holding everything within the suspended structure of the Event of Appropriation" (*Ereignis*).[44] Thus, the stakes of how we understand and "use" language are high, and, most crucially, according to Heidegger, they belong to the nature of language itself.

We saw already in the previous chapter that Heidegger's conception of language is ontological, and should not simply be *conflated*

---

[40] "The Turning," 41.

[41] "Letter on Humanism," 237.

[42] *Contributions to Philosophy*, 401; GA 65, 510.

[43] *Elucidations of Hölderlin's Poetry*, 61.

[44] *Identity and Difference*, 38.

either with ontic human utterances or with ontic grammatical rules. As Heidegger writes, "[w]hat we usually mean by 'language,' namely, a stock of words and rules for combining them, is only an exterior aspect of language."[45] Here, however, we investigate the features and consequences of Heidegger's ontological definition of language in further detail.

Like Heidegger's enigmatic definitions of "being," "truth," and "poetry," Heidegger's definitions of "language" are often framed apophatically and/or tautologically. For example:

> [L]anguage is not a tool. Language is not this and that, is not also something else besides itself. Language is language. Statements of this kind have the property that they say nothing and yet bind thinking to its subject matter with supreme conclusiveness. The boundlessness with which such sentences can be abused corresponds to the infinity into which they direct the task of thinking.[46]

Although Heidegger admits that he is at risk of saying nothing when he says, "language is language," his point is simply that we cannot define language from the outside, because we are always already in it.[47] Or to put it somewhat awkwardly, our being is always already languaged. But if our being is always languaged, if we are always already "in" language, then language, like being, can never simply be represented as an object in our world amongst others. Rather, language, like being, "is" synonymous with the world itself. And that is why, according to Heidegger, "the nature of language does not exhaust itself in signifying, nor is it merely something that has the character of sign or cipher."[48] Rather, what Heidegger calls "language" is rather the condition for the possibility of all signifying in the first place. As he writes, "only where there is language, is there world...only where world holds sway is there history...language is a good in a more primordial sense [than the things

---

[45] *Elucidations of Hölderlin's Poetry*, 56.

[46] Ibid., 55–56.

[47] Heidegger's point here is also succinctly, if mystifyingly, captured in his dictum, "*Das Wesen der Sprache: Die Sprache des Wesens*" (the being of language: The language of being). For by eliding the copula, Heidegger intimates that one can never say what being or language "are" without already being caught up in a relation to being/language. GA 12, 170.

[48] "What Are Poets For?," 129.

which we call 'good']."[49] Or as he puts it more poetically, "language is the precinct (*templum*), that is, the house of Being."[50] And,

> [i]t is because language is the house of Being that we reach what is by constantly going through this house. When we go to the well, when we go through the woods, we are always already going through the word "well," through the word, "woods," even if we do not speak the words and do not think of anything relating to language.[51]

To say that we are always passing through the word, even when we are not thinking or speaking it, is to say that meaning is given to us, and not simply our ad hoc creation. It is to say, in the more quotidian and analytic terms of *Being and Time*, that our access to things is always mediated by an "as-structure," a taking of something *as* something (or, as Heidegger describes it here, a giving of something *as* something). It is also to say, as Heidegger puts the same point more poetically in his later writings that "language itself speaks," i.e., that the meaning of a given situation unfolds not simply according to our plans and expectations, but according to the spontaneous play of meaning itself. As Heidegger puts it, although "[m]an acts as though he were the shaper (*Bildner*) and master (*Meister*) of language," "in fact *language* remains the master of man."[52]

Given the above, we can now ask: why is it so crucial that we come to an authentic understanding of language? What makes language the site of both humanization and dehumanization, and therefore "the danger of dangers"? According to Heidegger, the answer is simple: how we understand language directly impacts how we speak and listen, as well as how we think. When we understand language simply as a set of signifiers whose meaning is more or less fixed, we stunt our critical and creative faculties, and we begin to regard ourselves and others simply as information devices. As Heidegger writes,

> Within Enframing (*Gestell*), speaking turns into information. It informs itself about itself in order to safeguard its own procedures by information

---

[49] *Elucidations of Hölderlin's Poetry*, 55.

[50] "What Are Poets For?," 129.

[51] Ibid.

[52] "Building Dwelling Thinking," 171.

theories. Enframing [...] commandeers for its purposes a formalized language, the kind of communication which "informs" man uniformly, that is, gives him the form in which he is fitted into the technological-calculative universe, and gradually abandons "natural language."[53]

I suspect that Heidegger puts the phrase "natural language" in quotation marks to demonstrate that when he says "natural," he is speaking onto-logically, and not biologically, Still, we might press Heidegger's point, and ask about the kind of language that is lost when we treat language strictly as a means for conveying information. In his essay on "Hölderlin and the Essence of Poetry," Heidegger writes that while "the Being of man is grounded in language," "[language] occurs primarily [and] authentically in conversation" [*im Gespräch*].[54] Thus, if we follow this claim through, the problem with formalized language is that it obstructs our capacity to converse with each other *as Dasein*, that is, as "beings for whom our Being is (singularly) an issue."

Now, obviously, as we have seen above, "the danger" is not with for-malized language as such, since some degree of standardization is also a prerequisite for conversation, but with its tendency to enforce a for-getfulness of that which prompts us to converse in the first place. As Heidegger had already warned in a lecture course on *The History of The Concept of Time* (1924),

Communication must be understood in terms of the structure of Dasein as being with the other. It is not a matter of transporting information and experiences from the interior of one subject to the interior of the other one. It is rather a matter of being-with-one-another becoming manifest in the world.[55]

"[W]e are already together with the other beforehand, with the being which the discourse is about."[56] And, "Discoursing with others about something as a speaking-about is always a *self-articulating*."[57] With these passages, Heidegger indicates that communication is not simply a *means*

---

[53] *On the Way to Language*, 132.
[54] GA 4, 38 (translation mine); *Elucidations of Hölderlin's Poetry*, 61.
[55] *History of the Concept of Time*, 263.
[56] SZ, 166/ BT, 155.
[57] *History of the Concept of Time*, 263.

toward greater knowledge *about* things, but is, more elementally, a way of letting the world itself in its singular and shared inflections come into salience. In particular, Heidegger's claim that "speaking-about is always a *self-articulating*" indicates that communication is as much a matter of *what* we say (and don't say) as it is about *who* we say (and don't say). And, to the extent that our being is always already *with*-others, it indicates that we are always engaged in communication, self-articulation, and self-discovery, "self" here meaning being-in-the-world and not simply ego.

We should note that although our example here has been verbal articulation, the same arguments could be made for any medium, such as music, dance, or architecture, since, on Heidegger's account, these would all fall under his definition of language in the expansive, ontological sense. And so we should consider someone who treats walking in merely functionalist terms as a way to get from place A to place B, in much the same way as we would someone whose conception of language is simply as an instrument for expressing or extracting information. Similarly, we might consider a parallel between a poetic understanding of language—as that which is always already speaking, always already letting the world come to presence in a particular way—and a poetic understanding of walking, in which the steps themselves become a way of letting the world come to presence. Which is all to say that how we understand language bears consequences not just for how we hold and shape linguistic space, but for how we hold and shape sonic, visual, and kinesthetic space as well. Do we regard music as something that only happens in certain venues? Or can we regard music as an essential feature of the world as always already *sounded* and *re-sounding*? Do we regard dance simply as a skill or a profession to be taken up by those who are "good at it"? Or can we regard our every gesture and gait as a way in which we embody our ecstatic existence as both "thrown" and "ahead of itself"? In each of these cases, Heidegger's conception of language as "the house of Being" shows that we make a critical mistake if we think of art simply in aesthetic terms. As Heidegger says explicitly, "in order to understand what the work of art and poetry are as such, philosophy must first break the habit of grasping the problem of art as one of aesthetics."[58]

[58] "The Projection of Being in Science and Art," in *The Heidegger Reader*, 107; GA 34, 63–64.

Thus, we should appreciate that the instrumentalization of truth—the reduction of truth to what is measurable, reproducible, and generally considered valid by calculative-technical reason—is a phenomenon that potentially affects not just how we communicate at a linguistic level, but also how we comport ourselves at an embodied level, as well.[59] In short, if we regard language simply as a means for transmitting information, whether subjective (my feelings) or objective (facts), we strip away the existential singularity of our discourses, dispositions, and practices, as discourses, dispositions, and practices that are always *in-the-world*. In so doing, we reduce the meaning of our encounters either to what can be generalized or to what can be privatized. In so doing, we not only flatten our world, making it difficult for us to question, critique, debate, or revise it, but we alienate ourselves from the kind of care that would make it possible for us to regard the other as "a being for whom its own being is an issue."

Thus, the task of poetic thinking is to guard against the dangers of a flattened world, to preserve and restore the bumps and curves, the tics and creaks, the questions, tensions, and difficulties that give it depth. But as we have noted above, poetic thinking does not demand that we overthrow all standards, or that we repudiate instrumentalist and metaphysical reasoning altogether. Instead, it means making space *within our metaphysical world* for ways of being that can put us in closer contact to the mysterious source of our care. Thus, poetic thinking should not simply be understood as a meta-discourse that stands outside or beyond the "fallen" language of "everydayness." Instead, poetic thinking is best understood, as we will see more fully in the next section, as a practice of listening, one that is attuned to the poetic dimensions concealed even in the thoughtlessness of formalized language of metaphysics. When we listen, we let the ongoing struggle between the said and the unsaid, the sayable and the unsayable, the generic and the singular, itself become manifest.

[59] On the interconnectedness of thinking and embodiment in Heidegger, see David Michael Levin, *The Body's Recollection of Being: Phenomenological Psychology and the Deconstruction of Nihilism* (London: Routledge, 1985) and "Usage and Dispensation: Heidegger's Meditation on the Hand," in *Gestures of Ethical Life: Reading Hölderlin's Question of Measure After Heidegger* (Stanford: Stanford University Press, 2005).

Thinking Is Listening

Heidegger frequently claims explicitly that thinking is most basically a practice of listening. As he writes, "Thinking is of Being inasmuch as thinking, propriated by Being, belongs to Being. At the same time, thinking is of Being insofar as thinking, belonging to Being, listens to Being." [*Das Denken ist des Seins, insofern das Denken, vom Sein ereignet, dem Sein gehört. Das Denken ist zugleich Denken des Seins, insofern das Denken, dem Sein gehörend, auf das Sein hört*].[60] And, "thinking [...] is a listening to the grant" [*das Hören der Zusage*].[61] The connection between thinking, being, and listening is also implicitly thematized in *Being and Time*, insofar as Heidegger there describes the call of conscience—the zero point of authenticity—as something that speaks to us in silence, and which we must therefore abide in "reticence."[62] As he writes, "the discourse of conscience never comes to utterance. Conscience only calls silently, that is, the call comes from the soundlessness of uncanniness and calls Da-sein thus summoned back to the stillness of itself, and calls it to become still."[63] In characterizing the call of conscience as "soundless," Heidegger indicates that listening to it is not a matter of registering information or deciphering a message, but a matter of making room for absence itself to come to presence. Heidegger also comments in a note that when he says "Being' 'is' only in the understanding of [Dasein]," he means "understanding as hearing."[64]

As is evident from these examples, Heidegger's notion of listening, like his notion of language, moves beyond the metaphysical definition, which would see listening simply as a technique or a skill, to a more holistic and expansive definition. Accordingly, Heidegger's claim that listening, thinking, and belonging belong together—a claim that he enacts precisely by listening to language (i.e., to the homophony of *Hören* and *Gehören*)—indicates that listening is not just something we do when we converse with others, but is an essential feature of being-in-the-world.

[60] GA 9, 316.
[61] *On the Way to Language*, 76; GA 12, 165.
[62] SZ, 273/ BT, 296.
[63] Ibid.
[64] SZ, 183/ BT, 172.

As such, it is one of the most powerful and intimate ways that we can embody the kind of non-metaphysical relation to truth for which Heidegger calls.

At the same time, I want to suggest that Heidegger's contention that thinking is listening also gestures toward the possibility of a genuinely dialogical ethics, one that regards the other not as an object standing in opposition to me, a subject, but instead as a partner or fellow traveler in the co-existential struggle for wholeness. In other words, I want to suggest that understanding the essence of thinking to consist in listening (rather than representing or conceptualizing) means understanding that "the other" is not just an incidental character within our screen of vision, but the condition for the possibility of our own authenticity. As Heidegger approximates this point in a letter to Medard Boss, "[r]eal thinking cannot be learned from books. It cannot be taught unless the teacher remains a learner well into old age. Therefore, let us hope for a dialogue."[65] Here, Heidegger indicates that thinking involves learning—not strictly from books—but from engaging in dialogue with the other. A thinker's mastery is here paradoxically described as the capacity to maintain a sense of perpetual humility before the other, a sense that one always has more to learn.[66]

---

[65] Heidegger, "Letter to Medard Boss, June 14, 1948," in *Zollikon Seminars*, 239; GA 89, 301.

[66] This conclusion bears strong resemblances to a variety of wisdom traditions. *Pirkei Avot* (4:1) states that a sage is one who can learn from anyone. In *The Cloud of Unknowing*, trans. A.C. Spearing (London: Penguin, 2001), the spiritual seeker is described as one who can practice continuously clearing his mind of concepts to make way for the non-propositional, non-representational event of divine revelation. In *Orthodoxy*, G.K. Chesterton, describes God's wisdom as the wisdom of a child, explaining that whereas adults tire of routine, children welcome repetition. In this way, Chesterton proposes, God's perfection to consist in his capacity to always be amazed. See G.K. Chesterton, *Orthodoxy* (New York: John Lane Co., 1908), 108. Shunryu Suzuki describes the practice of Zen in similar terms as the practice of maintaining "a beginner's mind." On his view, the difference between an expert and a master craftsman is that the master craftsman does not let his technical knowledge crowd-out his sense of freshness. Common to all of these models is the seemingly paradoxical suggestion that a master is not one who possesses technique or cleverness, but simply an open spirit (although clearly the master also has great technique). In *Echolalias*, Daniel Heller-Roazen recounts a medieval Islamic parable about a poet who is instructed by his teacher to memorize 100,000 lines of verse. After ten years, the poet returns, having successfully accomplished the feat. He is then instructed to forget those 100,000 lines. Roazen notes that whereas the feat of memorization can be tested, there is no objective way to test whether one has genuinely forgotten a line of poetry. Only the poet can himself

Obviously, such a conclusion may be shocking to strict readers of Heidegger, especially for exegetes of *Being and Time*, since that is where Heidegger most notoriously defines "*anticipatory resoluteness*" and "*being-towards-death*" as the condition for the possibility of authenticity. Nevertheless, it would be too simplistic to characterize Heidegger's notion of listening as *merely* metaphorical, having nothing to do with what we ordinarily mean by listening. For how else do we learn how to listen in the expansive sense, if not by listening in the ordinary sense? As Heidegger writes explicitly, it is only from a metaphysical position that one would seek to separate the ontic aspect of a metaphor (the sensible) from the ontological truth behind it (the nonsensible), i.e., to treat metaphors as *merely* metaphors:

> The idea of...metaphor is based upon the distinguishing, if not complete separation, of the sensible and the nonsensible as two realms that subsist on their own[...] Metaphysics loses the rank of the normative mode of thinking when one gains the insight that the above-mentioned partitioning of the sensible and the nonsensible is insufficient.[67]

Thus, we should understand that "listening" in the ontological sense (of listening to language, listening to Being) and listening in the "ontic" senses (of listening to a person, or to one's body, or to the sounds outside one's window) are not two essentially separate kinds of listening, but co-imbricated. When we listen in the expansive, ontological sense, we are always doing so within a concrete, embodied situation. And vice versa: when we listen—truly listen—to what is occurring (around us, within us, between us), we are always also listening to being, to language.[68]

---

know if he has truly forgotten, but, paradoxically, if he has truly forgotten, then it is also questionable whether he can know he has forgotten. In any event, what is striking about this parable, Heller-Roazen shows, is that true learning also involves unlearning. See Daniel Heller-Roazen, *Echolalias: On the Forgetting of Language* (New York: Zone, 2005), 191–194.

[67] Heidegger, *The Principle of Reason*, trans. Reginald Lilly (Bloomington: Indiana University Press, 1996), 48; GA 10, 88–89.

[68] For an article that extends this point even further, by showing that there is an essential connection between regarding "the truth of being" and coming to authentic "friendship" with the other, see Krzysztof Ziarek, "Semiosis of Listening: The Other in Heidegger's Writings on Hölderlin and Celan's 'The Meridian,'" *Research in Phenomenology* 24, no. 1 (1994): 113–132, 127.

Still, we should ask, what is it about listening specifically, and not say, seeing or touching, that makes it the operative posture for thinking? First, listening, in the ordinary sense, is a posture of passivity, receptivity, and openness. It distinctively involves not doing something, i.e., not talking. At the same time, however, listening is also a profoundly active comportment requiring us "to be present," and to keep ourselves from "drifting off" or "spacing out." Thus, listening is an embodiment of activity in passivity and passivity in activity. It involves a non-egocentric mode of world-openness, and yet it is also only possible on the basis of a sense of mineness (*jemeinigkeit*). In other words, listening offers a way to embody the very paradox of *Gelassenheit* that we have referred to above and in the previous chapters, namely, that is a non-oppositional, non-willing way of being-in-the-world that nevertheless requires an acute degree of vigilance and restraint.[69]

Another reason why listening is a helpful way to enact the task of thinking is that listening involves an acute sense of meaning as *temporal*, i.e., as something that is always unfolding in the interplay between projection and recollection, anticipation and retrieve. When we listen, we never just hear something, but always hear it in its arriving and vanishing. As such, the practice of listening enables us to trace the occurrence of unconcealment as a play between presence and absence, echo and intimation, proximity and distance. In listening, we discover that the meaning of a situation is never simply fixed or innate, but always undergoing transformation. Thus, listening enables us to regard the present not simply as what is actual, but just as profoundly, if not more essentially, as what is possible. This, anyways, would be one way to parse Heidegger's claim that "[t]hinking [is] a coming-into-nearness to the far."[70]

Another reason why listening is critical to our capacity to think non-metaphysically has to do with the fact that words alone cannot be trusted to do the work for us. As Heidegger writes,

---

[69] The paradox of *Gelassenheit* is perhaps most acutely captured in the "Serenity Prayer" or "Alcoholic's Anonymous Prayer," attributed to the theologian Reinhold Niebuhr: "Lord, grant me the serenity to accept the things I cannot change/ The courage to change the things I can change/ And the wisdom to know the difference." Notably, the German version is called the *Gelassenheitsgebet*, and translates "serenity" as *Gelassenheit*.

[70] *Country Path Conversations*, 75; GA 77, 116.

Words fail us; they do so originally and not merely occasionally, whereby some discourse or assertion could indeed be carried out but is left unuttered, i.e., where the saying of something sayable or the re-saying of something already said is simply not carried through…[71]

How do words *essentially* fail us? One answer may have to do with the fact that our words, no matter how original and poetic at their inception, lose their force and urgency almost as soon as they are uttered, hardening inevitably into objects to be analyzed and consumed by calculative reason. As such, only listening protects discourse from becoming what Heidegger calls "idle chatter." Thus, Heidegger writes, "[A] transformation of language is needed which we can neither compel nor invent. This transformation does not result from the procurement of newly formed words and phrases. [Rather], it touches on our *relation* to language" (my emphasis).[72]

Heidegger's conclusion that we transform our language most basically not through linguistic innovation, but instead through a different way of hearing language may come as a surprise given that Heidegger is also, famously, a strong proponent of the power of words, and a major linguistic innovator himself. How, if at all might we reconcile Heidegger's suggestion that it is our relation to language, and not our use of language, that is decisive with his claims that:

> Essential words are not artificially invented signs and marks which are pasted on things merely to identify them. Essential words are deeds which happen in those moments where the lightning flash of a great enlightenment goes through the universe.[73]

And, "words and language are not just shells into which things are packed for spoken and written intercourse. In the word, in language, things first come to be and are[?]".[74]

---

[71] *Contributions*, 30; GA 65, 36.

[72] *On the Way to Language*, 135. Bernard Stiegler offers a similar point when he writes, "But if the instrumentalization of language is possible, this is because its instrumentality is inherent to it […] It is a question not of struggling against instrumentalization of language but of resisting the very reduction of an instrument to the rank of means." Stiegler, *Technics and Time 1: The Fault of Epimetheus*, trans. Richard Beardsworth and George Colllins (Stanford: Stanford University Press, 1998), 205–206.

[73] *Schelling*, 25.

[74] *Introduction to Metaphysics*, 15.

The answer, I contend, has to do with the fact that for Heidegger, listening is not only or reducibly refraining from speech, but also, somewhat paradoxically, a way of speaking authentically. To be sure, Heidegger keenly differentiates between the meaningless speech of blabbermouths and the generative and inceptional silence of good listeners. As he writes, "To say [*Sagen*] and to speak [*Sprechen*] are not identical. A man may speak, speak endlessly, and all the time say nothing. Another man may remain silent, not speak at all, and yet, without speaking, say a great deal."[75] Or as he writes in *Being and Time*,

> [T]he person who is silent can 'let something be understood,' that is, he can develop an understanding more authentically than the person who never runs out of words. Speaking a lot about something does not in the least guarantee that understanding is thus furthered. On the contrary, talking at great length about something covers over and gives a false impression of clarity to what is understood, that is, the unintelligibility of the trivial.[76]

Yet Heidegger also claims that we needn't oppose speaking and keeping silent:

> [S]peaking is at the same time also listening. It is the custom to put speaking and listening in opposition: one man speaks, the other listens. But listening accompanies and surrounds not only speaking, but as such, also takes place in conversation. The simultaneousness of speaking and listening has a larger meaning. Speaking is of itself a listening. Speaking is listening to the language which we speak.[77]

In breaking down the dichotomy between listening and speaking, that is, by showing that speaking is always already a mode of listening and listening a mode of speaking, Heidegger indicates that both linguistic innovation and silence have their importance. We need to make room for and attend to silence if we are to find the right words, but we also need the right words to attune ourselves to that silence and to give shape to it.

---

[75] *On the Way to Language*, 122.

[76] SZ, 164/ BT, 154.

[77] *On the Way to Language*, 123.

Thus, Heidegger writes, "*Die Stille [...] ist keineswegs nur das Lautlose.*"
"Silence is in no way only the soundless." With this distinction between
Stille and *Lautlose*—Heidegger indicates that ontological silence (*Stille*)
and ontic silence (*Lautlose*), though related, should not be conflated.
Thus, Heidegger writes, "He who never says anything is [...] unable to
keep silent at a given moment. Authentic silence is possible only in genuine discourse. In order to be silent, Da-sein must have something to
say..."[78]

The question raised by Heidegger's ontological definitions of language and listening, is therefore not simply whether we should speak or
remain silent (in the ontic sense), but how we can speak in such a way
that our words address and authentically respond to what is not being
said. How can we hold silence in such a way that we give support and
nourishment to what could be said? Here again, Heidegger shows that
the task of thinking, as a poetic task, is not a matter of doing *vs.* not
doing, but of doing *and* not doing, a point that he concretizes when he
writes,

[T]he phonetic-acoustic-physiological explanation of the sounds of language does not know the experience of their origin in ringing stillness
(*Geläut der Stille*), and knows even less how sound is given voice and is
defined by that stillness.[79]

In defining the origin of human speech as a "ringing stillness" Heidegger
indicates yet again the paradox of human being as a being that is both
always already what it is (still) and not yet what it is (ringing). As such,
the task of human thought, whether embodied in verbal articulation or
in verbal reticence, is to give voice to—and to let voice be given to—
this paradox. Rather than oppose "ringing" and "stillness," we should
understand them as belonging together. While such an understanding
may seem obscure and irrelevant to everyday life, in the next sections we
will see how it can help us discourse authentically with others, including,
possibly, with the divine.

---

[78] SZ, 165/ BT, 154.
[79] *On the Way to Language*, 122; GA 12, 241. See also GA 12, 27, where Heidegger
writes, "*die Sprache spricht als die Geläut der Stille*" ("language speaks as the peal of silence
[the ringing of stillness]").

A POETIC UNDERSTANDING OF DISCOURSE

We have so far seen that thinking, poetry, and listening are overlapping ways that we can authentically embody a noninstrumental relation to truth. And we have also seen that, precisely because poetic thinking and listening embody a non-calculative and nonrepresentational way of being-in-the-world, it is a mistake to define them simply as aesthetic techniques, as if authenticity were simply a matter of following its own avant-garde formula. This latter point matters, as it frees us from having to cast poetic thinking simply in opposition to metaphysical thinking, replacing one hegemony with another. David Wood elegantly states the consequences of this point for how one can practice poetic thinking in writing:

> It may be wise [...] not to try to mirror in one's writing some pure coincidence between the *what* and the *how*, but rather to deploy a whole range of styles and strategies, accepting at each point, both opportunities and liabilities. We cannot, for example, think or write without making propositional claims, comparative judgments, critical remarks—in other words, we cannot just allow language to speak itself. Whichever way we may turn, we take risks, we enter territory in which we are not entirely in control, and it is through risking failure that we may find success. This is not only unavoidable, but it is something we could celebrate.[80]

Wood argues that understanding the task of thinking requires what he calls a "second-order performativity," which is to say, a style of communication that is open to using both enigmatic and direct language, and does not simply privilege the former over the latter.[81] For it remains just as metaphysical to insist that one must resist declarative, propositional speech as it is to insist that nonpropositional speech is less meaningful than propositional speech. Wood's suggestion that poetic thinking involves a "second-order performativity" shows that poetic thinking is not a pure discourse or a meta-discourse, so much as what I would like to call a "trans-discourse," a way of moving between discourses that can acknowledge both their unique importance and their unique limitations. Understanding poetic thinking as a trans-discourse, we will see, can help

---

[80] David Wood, *Time After Time*, 113.
[81] Ibid., 112.

us speak and listen with greater sensitivity to what our words simultaneously reveal and conceal. And this matters, because by acknowledging and accepting the tension between revealing and concealing, we free ourselves and others from the impossible burden of having to say only those things that are factually valid or metaphysically correct, and we become more sensitive to the holistic concerns from which our speech-acts arise and to which they are directed. In a sense, the discovery of oneself and others as Dasein and the discovery of language as the play of revealing and concealing, say the same. As Karl Jaspers helpfully puts it, giving his own important definition of Dasein, "[w]e are fundamentally more than [either of us] can know about [ourselves]."

To begin our discussion of what it means to engage in conversation (or to read) with a poetic understanding, let us look at one of Heidegger's favorite metaphors for describing the enigma of language: "Language is the language of being as clouds are the clouds of the sky." What is the relationship between clouds and sky? On the one hand, clouds cover up or conceal the sky. When it is cloudy, or "overcast," the sky, we say, is invisible. Yet clouds also give character and texture to the sky, and, in some sense, allow the sky to manifest *as* sky. Without clouds, the sky—and our position under it—would not be placeable. Yet there is a further feature of clouds that makes it a good metaphor for thinking about language, and that is that clouds both block the sun and are lit up by it. As such, clouds allow us access to a light that would otherwise be too powerful to look at directly. Thus, language is to being as clouds are to sky, because language also offers indirect access to being, simultaneously blocking it and portioning it into something manageable, identifiable, and safe. In addition, language is cloud-like, in that, while it is distinctive in its particular moment—it can be large or small, heavy or light, fast-moving or stationary—it is essentially ethereal, transient. One could also note that some clouds hold the possibility of rain, and therefore, like some modes of language, offer premonitions of nourishment and replenishment (or gloom).

Now understanding language in this way is important, I am arguing, for a variety of reasons. First, it helps us consider that no discourse can be pure, i.e., above question. The fact that language offers only indirect access to *die Sache selbst* (the matter itself), and yet is itself the only way for the matter to come to presence, and thereby, to matter *to us*, means that we may regard all discourses with a sense of generosity, doing our best to locate the points of tension and inconsistency in the words of others not as faults, but as questions. Moreover, understanding language as a play of revealing and concealing, can help us appreciate the extent to which our discourses are often structured by a conflict between desire to be averagely understood, and on the other, a desire to say something original and uniquely pertinent. And such appreciation, I am arguing, can go a long way toward helping us tend to the needs and calls of others as they articulate them, for it allows us to approach the needs of the other not in fixed, objective terms only, but as needs that are entrenched in the drama of Dasein itself.

In addition, Heidegger's expansive conception of language holds significant consequences for how we approach the task of theology, and, by extension, interfaith (and extra-faith) dialogue. By showing that our relationship to language is decisive for how the world itself comes to presence, Heidegger helps us consider that the task of theology cannot only be to draft correct propositions about God—even supposing such a thing could be done—but must also be engaged in poetic listening. Accordingly, the theologian who takes seriously the task of thinking must seek to preserve in her words (and to hear in the words of others) the tension between God's concealment and revealment. Moreover, the theologian cannot simply treat her inherited sources as texts whose meanings are fixed, but must appreciate them, instead, as texts that, qua arrangements of language, bear witness to open questions.

Such a view may seem woefully "postmodern," and yet, if it is, it is also consistent with a number of Biblical themes and passages. Consider, for instance, the Biblical figure of the burning bush, which is aflame and yet not consumed. Does this image not encapsulate the paradox we bear witness to in poetic thinking and poetic listening, namely, that each occurrence of meaningfulness is both iridescent and opaque? Might we not think of the burning bush as a visual corollary to Heidegger's notion of language as a "ringing stillness"? And might we not consider the miracle of the burning bush, moreover, to consist not simply in the fact that such a bush could exist (as an object "out there"), but rather that it could pass unnoticed in broad daylight, and yet address Moses as a sign about his life's mission as a servant of God and a liberator of the Israelite people? (Exodus 3:1–3:22).

Or consider the Biblical story of Job, in which God reprimands Job's friends for speaking falsely, while insisting that Job's words, which they had denounced as blasphemous, were, in fact, true (Job 42:7).

We might read this moment as an indictment of the view that truth is strictly propositional. In other words, what was false (*lo n'chona*) about the friends' words was not that they were necessarily incorrect in the logical sense, but that they were generic—they failed to engage with Job as a *singular* case, and instead tried to apply a top-down *explanation* of his suffering. Likewise, when God says that Job spoke truly, we needn't take this as evidence that Job's words were correct according to a correspondence theory of truth—in fact, most parts of the text would indicate otherwise—but simply that they gave authentic voice to his circumstances. In other words, perhaps what is true about Job's words and false about the words of his friends consists not in their *what*, but in their *how*. On this reading, theological truth would have to be considered not in terms of whether we say correct things about God—however that might be determined—but rather in terms of whether we are capable of listening to the voice that speaks "out of the whirlwind" (Job 38:1).[82]

Another example where the Hebrew Bible overlaps with Heidegger's conception of truth as unconcealment, is the episode in Kings 19:11–12, where Elijah encounters God "not in the wind," "not in the earthquake," and "not in the fire," but as and in "the still small voice" (*kol d'mama daka*). Here, the presence of God is figured not as noise, or commotion, or force, i.e., with something "positive," but as the stillness and emptiness that resounds in the trace of what remains after they have passed. I offer these passages not as "proof-texts" that would either confirm the Hebrew Bible as Heideggerian or else confirm Heidegger as somehow crypto-Biblical, but only to show that strong parallels can be made between Heidegger's expansive conception of Being and the Hebrew Bible's descriptions of God.[83] In both cases, transcendence

---

[82] This conclusion would be in deep accord with Heidegger's claim that "[t]he *being true* (*truth*) of the statement must be understood as *discovering*. Being-true as *discovering* is in turn ontologically possible only on the basis of being-in-the-world." SZ, 218/ BT, 201.

[83] For a book that does try to argue this, however, see Marlene Zarader, *The Unthought Debt: Heidegger and the Hebraic Heritage*, trans. Bettina Bergo (Stanford: Stanford University Press, 2006). For a similar argument, but one that more plausibly situates him within anti-Greek, anti-philosophical Christian lineage, see John Van Buren, *The Young Heidegger: Rumor of the Hidden King* (Bloomington: University of Indiana Press, 1994), 151.

(Being/God) is figured as coming to presence only indirectly, and, bracketing the first two chapters of Genesis, primarily for Dasein.[84] And, in both cases, Dasein is thematized as needing special signs/markers/ metaphors that can make the paradox of presence/absence palpable. Appreciating these parallels, however, does grant us some insight into the ways that ontology and faith can potentially overlap in their capacity to open us to a non-graspable, non-calculable dimension.

That theology thematizes this dimension in terms of "God," whereas ontology thematizes this dimension in terms of "Being," does yield some crucial differences.[85] The language of "God," for instance, offers a certain degree of consolation that the more impersonal language of Being cannot. Moreover, the language of "God" enables us to understand ourselves more readily in terms of a "calling" and a "covenant" than the language of "Being," which, despite Heidegger's later descriptions of Being as gift [es gibt] and need [es braucht], does not literally care about us. The Biblical God commands, judges, punishes, loves, rewards, weeps, and laughs. Being, however, simply "presences" [Anwest]. The Biblical God charges humanity to care for the widow, the stranger, and the orphan. Being, however, simply "unfolds."[86] Hence, Levinas's polemical claim that

---

[84] Levinas goes so far as to argue that even the creation story can only be understood as a prelude to the revelation story. Quoting a midrash in which God tells the non-human beings he has just created that "If Israel accepts the Torah, you will continue to exist; if not, I will bring you back to chaos," Levinas writes, "Being has a meaning. The meaning of being, the meaning of creation, is to realize the Torah. The world is here so that the ethical order has the possibility of being fulfilled. The act by which the Israelites accept the Torah is the act which gives meaning to reality. To refuse the Torah is to bring being back to nothingness." Levinas, *Nine Talmudic Readings*, trans. Annette Aronowicz (Bloomington: Indiana University Press, 1994), 41.

[85] For an important and original investigation of the way that different thinkers have sought to grapple with the relationship between "God" and "Being," see George Pattison, *God and Being: An Enquiry* (Oxford: Oxford University Press, 2011).

[86] Note that this tension is not simply a tension between Biblical faith and Greek philosophy, as if these could be neatly separated, but one that divides theologians themselves. Arguably, the most central figure in the history of Jewish theology, Maimonides, taking up the influence of Aristotle insists, in his *Guide for the Perplexed* that none of the Bible's anthropomorphic descriptions of God are to be taken literally. Properly speaking, from a Maimonidean perspective, God does not feel anything or want anything. Abraham Joshua Heschel, meanwhile, taking up the influence of Neoplatonic, Kabbalistic, and Midrashic sources, wants to insist that God, as it were, is not perfect, but precisely "in need of man."

Being receives a challenge from the Torah, which jeapordizes its pretension of keeping itself above or beyond good and evil. In challenging the absurd, 'that's the way it is' claimed by the Power of the powerful, the man of the Torah transforms being into human history.[87]

And yet, for all these differences in inflection, we needn't oppose ontology and theology as Levinas suggests. For as Heidegger shows, there is an essential connection between "God" and "the holy" and between "the holy" and "Being."
As he writes,

How can man at the present stage of world history ask at all seriously and rigorously whether the god nears or withdraws, when he has above all neglected to think into the dimension in which alone that question can be asked? But this is the dimension of the holy, which indeed remains closed as a dimension if the open region of Being is not cleared and in its clearing [...] near [...]"

Here, I take Heidegger to be saying that theistic language will fall flat in the modern age if it does not take up the challenge of articulating the circumstances in which we might not just talk *about* God, but encounter "him." But such an encounter is made possible only if we are capable of treating things in a non-calculable, nonconceptual, and non-objectifying way. Therefore, if we are going to encounter God, we need to be able first to encounter the holy (*das Heilige*), that is, a "dimension" that cannot be fathomed by the subjectivist and objectivist gaze. And this is where, Heidegger indicates, ontology can help. For by opening up our understanding of Being as not simply a concept, an idea, or a being, but instead as the paradoxical way in which things simultaneously give themselves to us and hold themselves in reserve, we can come into a greater sense of the essential depth, mystery, and singularity of our being-in-the-world. In doing so, we can encounter ourselves, too, as ecstatic beings marked by the paradoxical unity of integrity and alienation, possession and dispossession. And all of this, Heidegger intimates, is requisite if the God or gods named by ancient theological traditions are to appear. And note that the connection Heidegger draws between being and holiness and between holiness and God is not simply arbitrary, but is also

---

[87] Levinas, *Nine Talmudic Readings*, 39.

central to the Hebrew Bible, and in particular, to Leviticus, where God commands the Israelites, "be holy, for I the Lord your God am holy" (Leviticus 19:12). The question, then, for theological discourse, must be, how can it open up "the holy," that is, how can our speech about God, and invocation of God, bring us into greater intimacy with the non-graspable and non-objectifiable dimension of our existence? In a word, the task of theology is to think God poetically. As we have seen above, there is no single path to or formula for poetic thinking. Perhaps thinking God poetically may involve keeping silent about God, following Heidegger's claim that "a sober, observant openness for the holy is at the same time an attunement to quietness..."[88] Or perhaps thinking God poetically will involve holding onto the word "God," not as a philosophical term signifying a known object, but as a placeholder for our most basic questions, hopes, and aspirations, as John Caputo does, when he writes, "The name of God is auto-deconstructing, a self-displacing name that keeps making way for the event, effacing its own trace, which is what I love about it." And, "The greatest strength of a weak theology is to keep us on our knees before the unknown God."[89] But regardless of which path or combination of paths theologians take, what is clear, from a Heideggerian perspective, is that their words must be guided by the task of thinking, which is to say, the task of holding open a space for the incalculable and ungraspable dimensions of our existence to come to presence as incalculable and ungraspable.

The need for theology to *think*, in the expansive sense, is made palpable in Heidegger's commentary on Nietzsche's *Thus Spoke Zarathustra*. There, Heidegger writes that the "unbelievers...have given up the possibility of belief" not "because God has to them become unworthy of belief," but because "they are no longer able to *seek* God" (emphasis added).[90] Meanwhile, "they can no longer seek [God]" says Heidegger, "because they no longer think."[91] This inability to think, Heidegger argues, is in turn owed to the fact that "those standing about in the

---

[88] *Elucidations of Hölderlin's Poetry*, 141.

[89] Caputo, *The Weakness of God*, 297. Elliot Wolfson offers a similar argument in "*Gottwesen* and the De-Divinization of the Last God: Heidegger's Meditation on the Strange and Incalculable."

[90] "The Word of Nietzsche," 112.

[91] Ibid.

market place have…[not only] replaced [thinking] with idle babble," but have made a habit crying "nihilism" whenever they "suppose [their] own opinion to be endangered."[92]

If we take this passage seriously, then the task of theology cannot simply be to supply us with words about God, which, even if correct, may amount to nothing but "idle babble," but instead to help us engage at an existential level with the challenges of encountering God's presence *in the world*. And this task, in turn, as we have already seen, involves expanding our conception of language as simply a system of signs and signifiers, to a more basic, yet more mysterious play of unconcealment.

At the same time, however, Heidegger's challenge to theologians (as I have educed it) needn't be cast as a critique of theology as such. Instead, it can be read as an invitation for theology to be *performative*, that is, to attest to, rather than simply describe, God and the holy. In addition, it can also be positively understood as an invitation for theologians to recognize the theological kernel in poetry and art (in the ontic sense), even if, or even when, such poems or works of art are not overtly "religious" or religious in a way that a theist might recognize. As Heidegger writes, "The essential standing of the poet is grounded not in the conception of God, but in the embrace of the holy."[93]

More serious in Heidegger's critique of metaphysics than its challenge to theology is the challenge it poses to secular reason, which would regard religious language as having nothing more to say now that it has been replaced by "science."[94] For by reminding us that language is the house of being, Heidegger shows that not even the sciences can leave this house behind.

The consequences of Heidegger's critique of metaphysical thinking, therefore, challenge a variety of belief-systems, and they do so not by proving these belief-systems false, but by asking us to consider the terms in which we conduct, interpret, and enact them. Do we use our beliefs to insulate ourselves from mystery, and to ward off or stigmatize or condescend to those who do not share our beliefs? Or do we let the terms of our belief emerge and evolve in conversation with

---

[92] Ibid.

[93] "Der Wessenstand des Dichters gründet nicht in der Empfängnis des Gottes, sondern in der Umfängnis durch das Heilige." GA 4, 67 (translation mine).

[94] I am thinking here of the "New Atheist," Richard Dawkins. See Richard Dawkins, *The God Delusion* (London: Bantam Press, 2006).

our being-in-the-world? Epistemology asks us, "How do you know?" Ontology asks: "Are you listening?"

How does one answer the question "are you listening?" This, indeed, would be as difficult as answering the question, "are you authentic?" Listening, like authenticity, is something that, by definition, we are always only on the way toward. And yet, it is also a question that, when asked and listened to, can wake us up and help us on our way. Perhaps listening begins with the question, "am I listening?" And perhaps the simple admission that one is not listening or not yet listening, that one is always already not hearing something, is what enables us to begin listening.

Heidegger's claim that thinking is most basically a posture of listening means that no discourse can be a meta-discourse standing as the herme-neutic "key" to other discourses. Instead, all discourse, all occurrences of language, must be understood as always already in need of translation. As such, translation must, like listening, not simply be understood in the narrow sense as a skill or operation that we perform, but must be under-stood most basically as an element of being-in-the-world and being-with. As Heidegger writes, "The difficulty of a translation is never merely a technical issue, but concerns the relation of human beings to the essence of the word and to the worthiness of language."[95] And, "[T]here is... translating [even] within one and the same language."[96] If we take seri-ously Heidegger's claim that translation occurs even in the same lan-guage, then it is clear that translation does not just mean the exchanging of like terms, but the elemental way in which we come to communicate and understand anything at all. In asserting the primacy of translation, moreover, Heidegger shows that communication is always filled with tensions, always mediated by a dialectic of sameness and difference, and by demands for fidelity that, at least ontically speaking, can only be par-tially fulfilled. Nevertheless, the recognition that these tensions belong to language itself, we have seen, can be immensely freeing, as it can allow us to focus our attention less on speaking and listening simply along an axis of correctness/incorrectness or agreement/disagreement, and instead to consider our words and the words of others as both opening up and cov-ering up "the world." When we orient ourselves in this way, we open ourselves to the poetry of language itself, and in doing so, we allow for

[95] *Der Ister*, 63.
[96] Ibid., 62.

our discourses to be not just information delivery systems, or war by other means, but ways of collaborating in the difficult, but always needed and welcome task of thinking.

CONCLUSION

A major question which modern human beings face is how we can care for each other in ways that are guided not just by statistical considerations—whose basic premise is the reduction of the living human being to a replaceable object, and whose criteria for success and failure are primarily behavioristic—but also by a readiness to listen and attend to the needs of others as they are singularly disclosed *to us*. For no matter how good we may be at statistical differentiation, and isolating the needs of "niche populations," if we cannot *be with* others—if we cannot share in and make space for the articulation of the denser problems of (co) existence that elude scientific measurement—we turn our world into a grid.

It is the task of disciplines such as political economy and political geography to interrogate the ways in which the life-conditions in this grid reproduce themselves, and it is the task of politicians, political activists, and entrepreneurs to strive to make life in this grid fairer and less intolerable for the powerless. But it is the task of "poetic thinking" to illuminate and inspire ways of being-in-the-world that preserve the world as something other than a grid. While "poetic thinking" can be accused of naiveté and even complacency to the extent that its rhetorical focus is directed less at circumstances within the grid and more at how we might let the world emerge as something other than a grid (a charge that we examined in Chapter 2), this is no reason to reject it out of hand. Instead, as we have seen, a more dialectical approach is called for, one that considers the critique of poetic thinking as belonging to poetic thinking itself. The gap between what poetic thinking inspires and what it effects, in other words, should not be construed as a count against it, but instead as something that poetic thinking itself can help us confront. Paradoxically, then, the need for poetic thinking is both a true and an untrue need. It is true in that it enables us to face our individual and social problems as ontological issues, but it is untrue in that while it can cast *some* light on the complex, structural conditions in which it unfolds, it is also embroiled in those conditions. Thus, to believe in the need for poetic thinking is to believe at the same time that it is necessarily insufficient, yet to believe that it is necessarily insufficient is also to preserve its critical relevance.

CHAPTER 5

Being Needed by Being, Being Needed by Others

The calling calls thinking to the crossroads of way, no way, and wrong way. But the way of thinking is of such a kind that this cross-roads can never be crossed by a once-for-all decision and choice of way, and the way can never be put behind as once-for-all behind us. Where does this strange triple way lead? Where else but into what is always problematical, always worthy of questioning?[1]

In the preceding chapters we have seen that while we can never over-come the structural obstacles to authenticity, acknowledging these obsta-cles as essential to who we are is itself one of the most radical ways that we can begin to respond to them. We have seen, in particular, that by regarding the questions and challenges of daily life not simply along an axis of correct/incorrect or right/wrong, but instead as questions posed to us in the singular, we can come to accept existential responsibility for the essential questionability of our (co)existence. Questioning, thinking, and listening, were thereby shown to be not just techniques for com-ing to answers, but as the most basic ways that we might live responsibly as "beings for whom our being is an issue." Finally, we have also seen that, to the extent that the basic assumptions of metaphysical thinking inhibit our capacity to relate to ourselves and others in non-objectifying and noninstrumentalizing ways, poetic thinking serves a critical, and

---

[1] *What Is Called Thinking?*, 175.

© The Author(s) 2018
Z. Atkins, *An Ethical and Theological Appropriation of Heidegger's Critique of Modernity*,
https://doi.org/10.1007/978-3-319-96917-6_5

ur-ethical role in that it can move us to attend to the dimensions of our being here (as both singular and social) that metaphysical thinking represses, stigmatizes, belittles, or simply fails to acknowledge. In the previous chapter, we saw that one such dimension can be called "the holy."

Yet, we have also grappled with a tension. For all our promising talk of mystery, awe, openness, and humility—important categories to be sure—we have not fully answered the concern that the questions, challenges, and insights raised by ontology have any *direct relevance* to the questions, challenges, and insights raised by ontic disciplines such as ethics, politics, sociology, economics, law, or theology. Is ontology simply agnostic—seeing silence as the most authentic stance one should take on ontic questions—we have wondered, or is ontology a way of asking the same questions that the ontic disciplines ask, but in a different, "more penetrating" way (to borrow Heidegger's idiom)? We have seen that this question is one that numerous commentators, most especially Levinas, have posed as a major challenge to ontology. But we have also seen that it is a question implicit in Heidegger's thought as well, which walks a fine, if inconsistent line, between claiming, on the one hand, to be a merely neutral and descriptive account of "what is," and claiming, on the other hand, to be an important corrective to what it diagnoses as a global condition of "injurious neglect."[2]

This chapter seeks to examine these questions in greater detail, elucidating them as questions that spring from a fundamental phenomenon of "being needed." In doing so, I hope to offer a constructive reading, rather than an exegetical account, of Heidegger's numerous claims that human existence can be most basically characterized by the phenomenon of being needed, and in particular, by the phenomenon of being needed by Being. As Heidegger writes, "Man, in his very being, is in demand, is needed," and "belongs within a needfulness which claims him."[3] Or again, "Man's essence belongs to the essence of Being and is needed by Being to keep safe the coming to presence of Being into its truth."[4] "Being...for its opening, needs man as the there of its manifestation."[5]

---

[2] "The Turning," 48.
[3] Heidegger, *On the Way to Language*, 32; GA 12, 119.
[4] "The Turning," 40.
[5] *Four Seminars*, 63; GA 15, 109.

"Being cannot be Being without needing humans for its revelation, preservation, and formation."[6] Heidegger also repeats the theme of being needed in a commentary on Hölderlin, writing gnomically that "the poet's saying is needed [...] to allow the appearance of the advent of the gods, who need the poet's words for their appearance, because only in their appearing are they themselves."[7] Even more strangely, Heidegger writes, in his *Contributions to Philosophy*, "[B]eings are brought into their constancy [*Beständigkeit*] through the *downgoing* [*der Untergang*] of those who ground the truth of beyng. Being itself requires this [*Solches fordert das Seyn selbst*]. It needs those who go down and has already *appropriated* [*er-eignet*] them, assigned them to itself, wherever beings appear."[8] And again, "The relation of Da-sein *to* beyng pertains intrinsically to the essential occurrence of beyng itself, which could be conveyed by saying that beyng needs Da-sein and does not at all essentially occur without this appropriation."[9]

Given Heidegger's dramatic insistence that Dasein is characterized by ontological neededness, and given his suggestion that Being/truth itself might be characterized as essentially needy or needful, the question we ask is: What is the relationship between being needed by Being and being needed concretely by the various others we encounter (or fail to encounter, but perhaps hear about on "the news") in daily life? And what relation, if any, exists between being needed by Being for the task of revealing, preserving, and forming "it" (as stated above by Heidegger) and being needed by the hosts of others, near and far, known and unknown, living and nonliving, human and nonhuman, who call on us for a wide variety of assistance? Does being needed by Being have anything to do with being needed by the most vulnerable? And why, finally, must the human being be characterized as fundamentally need*ed* rather than, say, fundamentally *needy*? Even going along with Heidegger's high-flown idiom, why should we not say that to exist is to be fundamentally *in need of* Being?

In attempting to answer these questions, this chapter will show that Heidegger's claim that we are fundamentally needed by Being can be

---

[6] "Der Spiegel Interview," in *The Heidegger Reader*, 326.

[7] *Elucidations of Hölderlin's Poetry*, 218.

[8] *Contributions to Philosophy*, 8; GA 65, 6–7.

[9] Ibid., 200.

taken in two ways: first, as a suggestion that our ontological responsibility *exceeds*, but does not *exclude*, our ontic responsibility, and second, as a suggestion that our responsibility to others can never be disentangled from our more general responsibility to reveal the world itself as a site of meaningfulness. Thus, ontological sensitivity and onto-ethical responsibility are interlinked: the more capable we are of appreciating the inexhaustible claims that Being itself makes upon us, I argue, the better capable we will be of responding to the claims of others with existential integrity. In the second part of this chapter, I respond to a potential line of criticism that one could make against the concept of ontological responsibility and the language of "being needed by Being," and that is the apocalyptic concern, coming out of Adorno and Fredric Jameson that it is simply too late to talk about ontology. Perhaps the language of ontological need might have mattered in the past, so their argument goes, but now that the perils of modernity have already run their course, ontology is at best an empty gesture, and at worst, a discourse that willfully denies the irreversibility and irredeemability of modernity's catastrophic logic. This line of criticism fails to undermine ontology *in toto*, I argue, because even if the perils of modernity are irredeemable—which it is impossible to prove one way or the other—ontology would still be capable of offering a compelling call to dialectical responsibility. This becomes particularly evident once we understand that Heidegger's evocative descriptions of Being are not anthropomorphisms of an ethereal, impersonal substance, but as phenomenological descriptions about how meaningfulness—always earthly, always human, always *with*-others—works.[10]

In the Clearing of the "Ontological Difference"

As we have seen in the previous chapters, language is always at risk of concealing precisely when it seeks to reveal. In the case of this chapter, that risk is most apparent in that, while seeking to articulate a conception of responsibility that is nondual, i.e., that is neither subjectivist nor objectivist, I will nevertheless have to make recourse to a discussion of "self" and "other" as if these were two separate entities standing in opposition to each other. In fact, however, part of the reason

---

[10] As Matthew King writes, "Being [...] is the happening of meaning *to us*." King, *Heidegger and Happiness: Dwelling on Fitting and Being* (London: Continuum, 2009), 6.

why it may be helpful to describe our responsibility in terms of "being needed by *Being*" and not (or not only) "being needed by *beings*" is that the language of Being reminds us that the origin of our care and responsibility is not to be located either in subjectivity or in objectivity, but instead in being-in-the-world, or in what Heidegger also calls "the clearing." (Heidegger writes, in 1973, "Dasein must be understood as being-the-clearing.")[11] Moreover, it reminds us that the needs of others are always also ontological needs. Nevertheless, the fact also remains that we *do* experience ourselves and others "initially and for the most part" (to use Heidegger's phrase) in dualistic terms. Thus, our language falters no matter which way we attempt to describe the phenomena of need and responsibility. Too much emphasis on *Being* and we turn Being into a super-object, or super-subject, standing beyond anything concrete (Platonism), something Heidegger explicitly rejects: "Beyng 'is' neither round about humans nor does it merely vibrate right through them as through beings. Instead, being appropriates Dasein and only thus essentially occurs as *event (Ereignis)*."[12] But too much emphasis on *beings*, and we lose sight of "the clearing" wherein the needs of others—and our capacity to respond to them—come to presence (or fail to come to presence). In short, my discussion must wrestle in metaphysical language— for all propositional language is metaphysical—with the difficulty that Heidegger names "the ontological difference."

In *Identity and Difference*, Heidegger explains the problem thus:

> We think of Being rigorously only when we think of it in its difference with beings, and of beings in their difference with Being. The difference thus comes specifically into view. [Yet] [i]f we try to form a representational idea of it, we will at once be misled into conceiving of difference as a relation which our representing has added to Being and to beings. Thus the difference is reduced to a distinction, something made up by our understanding (*Verstand*).[13]

Here, Heidegger insists that Being is both inseparable from beings and yet other than beings, and yet he also claims that the difference between Being and beings cannot simply be grasped as a simple relation or

[11] *Four Seminars*, 69.
[12] *Contributions to Philosophy*, 201; GA 65, 255–256.
[13] *Identity and Difference*, 62.

distinction, as if Being and beings were two kinds of entities that had to later be conjoined as an afterthought.

In the *Contributions to Philosophy*, Heidegger explains why it is a metaphysical pitfall to regard the difference between Being and beings as one of relation:

> To speak of the relation of the human being to beyng and, conversely of the relation of beyng to the human being makes it seem as if beyng essentially occurred, with regard to the human being, as something *over and against* it, as an object.[14]

Or as he puts it again, in his essay, "Language,"

> The dif-ference (*Unter-schied*) [between world and thing, or between Being and beings] is neither distinction nor relation. The dif-ference is, at most, a dimension for world and thing [Being and beings]. But in this case "dimension" also no longer means a precinct already present independently in which this or that comes to settle. The dif-ference is the dimension, insofar as it measures out, apportions, world and thing, each to its own.[15]

These are dense statements, but essentially what Heidegger is struggling to articulate is that the categorical distinction between "Being" and "beings" made by metaphysical ontology (i.e., by ontology conducted as ousiology) must be understood not as a fixed distinction that exists somewhere "out there" in logical space, but instead, as something that is dynamic and always already immanent to being-in-the-world. That is to say, the difference between "Being" and "beings" is, as Heidegger spells it, a "dif-ference," an ongoing playing out of difference, and not a categorical difference that can be conceptually identified. Thus, rather than understand Being as the ground of beings, i.e., as a zone that lies behind or beneath beings, we must understand Being (meaningfulness) and beings as co-emergent and do-dependent: Things are meaningful because they move within a realm of meaningfulness; yet meaningfulness is in turn, only operative when there are beings, and in particular, when there is Da-sein, the being characterized by openness to meaning. All of

---

[14] *Contributions to Philosophy*, 201; GA 65, 255–256.
[15] "Language," 200.

this may be succinctly said in the very word "Da-sein" itself, which, especially when hyphenated, reveals the occurrence of meaningfulness (*Sein*) as something that is always already mediated by a particular position or "there" (*Da*), and which is in turn always already mediated by meaningfulness (*Sein*). In this circular flow, Dasein and Being are tethered to each other, not as two distinct units forming a third, but as the very play of transcendence in immanence and immanence in transcendence itself. Meaning is always *here*, yet the *here* in which it occurs is itself always already beyond itself, *there*. (In German, *Da* can mean both "here" and "there.") And this incessant fracturing of here and there is not something that is secondary to Dasein, but what Dasein is. Thus, meaning is always the meaning that is given to and for Dasein, but Dasein is in turn a being whose awareness of Being (or openness to Being) is always already divided, non-congruous, ecstatic. Thus, Heidegger's emphasis on the *difference* or *dif-ference* between Being and beings, as both constitutive of, and, at the same time, emergent with Being and beings, is but another way of saying that who we are and what Being "is" are essentially open. Thus, in a manner of speaking, we might poetically render the psalmist's "Deep calleth unto deep" (Psalms 42:7) in Heideggerian terms as "Open calleth unto open."

To make this difficult and essentially elusive matter more tangible, however, let us turn to Heidegger's metaphorics of the bridge, which he describes at length in "Building Dwelling Thinking." Although, in that essay, Heidegger is describing a physical bridge, his example is helpful for unpacking the "relation" between Being and Dasein. Moreover, Heidegger elsewhere explicitly refers to Dasein as a kind of bridge, writing "Man [...] is a passage, a transition; he is a bridge [...]".[16] Here, then, is Heidegger's description of the bridge:

[The bridge] does not just connect banks that are already there. *The banks emerge as banks only as the bridge crosses the stream* (emphasis added). The bridge designedly causes them to lie across from each other. One side is set off against the other by the bridge. Nor do the banks stretch along the stream as indifferent border strips of the dry land. With the banks, the bridge brings to the stream the one and the other expanse of the landscape lying behind them. It brings stream and bank and land into each

---

[16] *What Is Called Thinking?*, 160. Heidegger likely takes this metaphor from Nietzsche. See *Thus Spoke Zarathustra*, Book 1, paragraph 4.

other's neighborhood. The bridge *gathers* the earth as landscape around the stream. Thus it guides and attends the stream through the meadows. Resting upright in the stream's bed, the bridge-piers bear the swing of the arches that leave the stream's waters to run their course [...] Even where the bridge covers the stream, it holds its flow up to the sky by taking it for a moment under the vaulted gateway and then setting it free once more.[17]

What is crucial about this passage for our purposes is Heidegger's suggestion that we think of the bridge not simply as an object in space, surrounded by other objects, but as a being that is both called for by that space and transformative of it. The bridge exists for a purpose: to make the stream crossable. This purpose is both essential to what the bridge is, and, at the same time, only made possible by something which the bridge itself is not: the stream. Similarly, while a stream always cuts through land, a relation between the land on one side of the stream and the land on the other side only comes to presence if a bridge exists to connect them. And without that connection they are not "banks," but only strips of land. Thus, in Heidegger's telling, bridge, banks, and stream, each need each other to be what they are, and in co-presencing they form what he calls a "neighborhood" (*Nachbarschaft*). (A skeptic might here ask if the stream really *needs* a bridge to be a stream. Answer: yes, to be a *stream* in the ontological sense, rather than simply an ontic body of liquid, some human action/institution must be involved.) In addition, Heidegger notes that the presence of the stream does not dissipate simply where the bridge obstructs its visibility. Instead, the covering up of the stream's visibility by the bridge offers something positive, namely, the possibility of redirecting our gaze elsewhere, in Heidegger's example, to the sky. In so doing, we come to see that stream, bridge, and banks, open out into an even larger world. But wherever we fix our gaze, this much is clear: the relationship between the different "things" we might see or come into contact with is not one of the atomic units existing side by side, but instead one of co-emergence. To stand on the bridge above the stream, between the banks, and beneath the sky, is not just an incidental matter—a circumstance that happens to apply to a subject—but a distinct configuration of Dasein as the being that it is.[18]

---

[17] "Building Dwelling Thinking," 150; GA 7, 154.

[18] A version of this insight is poetically articulated by the Heidegger-influenced poet, George Oppen, who writes, "There are things/ We live among, 'and to see them/ Is to know ourselves.'" See George Oppen, *Of Being Numerous* (New York: New Directions,

Now to elucidate this metaphor: just as we should understand stream, bridge, and banks, as belonging together, and interdependent, so much so that, although recognizing them as distinct, we might nevertheless describe them as simply different aspects of the same situation, so we should understand Being, Dasein, and beings (things and other Dasein), as integral to each other. Of course, this metaphor is imperfect, precisely because Being and Dasein are not to be thought of simply as entities, and yet the idea that it is only in the presence of a bridge that banks can be banks assists us in thinking about Dasein. Consider, for instance, that the hyphen in Da-sein is quite literally the bridge that gathers two banks: *Da* and *Sein*. In this analogy, *Da* and *Sein* are both distinct and paired. Meanwhile the hyphen conjoining them—the difference itself—is what remains most decisive, and yet most enigmatic.

And here, Heidegger's critique of metaphysics becomes palpable. Where metaphysics goes astray is in privileging one being as the ground of all the others beings. And while it maintains that there is an ontological difference between them, it fails to see that the difference between them is co-emergent with, and co-constituted by their interplay, rather than absolute. As Heidegger writes, "Since metaphysics thinks of beings as such as a whole, it represents beings in respect of what differs in [their] difference [from Being], [but] without heeding the difference as difference."[19] "The origin of the difference [itself]," however, Heidegger writes, "can no longer be thought of within the scope of metaphysics."[20]

Another way to describe where metaphysics goes astray is surprisingly articulated by Levinas, who, favorably credits Heidegger with showing that "[p]hilosophy [...] even when it [is] not aware of it" is "an attempt to answer the question of the signification of being, as a verb."[21] As Levinas here reminds us, The German "*Sein*" is an infinitive verb, literally meaning "to be," and therefore should not be understood as a noun, as metaphysics (or ontology conducted as ousiology) typically treats it.

1968). On Oppen's Heideggerian influence, see Peter Nicholls, *George Oppen and the Fate of Modernism* (Oxford: Oxford University Press, 2007). For a work that describes this same point as a matter of *embodied* knowledge, see Alphonso Lingis, *The Imperative* (Bloomington: Indiana University Press, 1998), 59.

[19] *Identity and Difference*, 70.
[20] Ibid., 71.
[21] Levinas, *Ethics and Infinity*, 38.

We might also consider Heidegger's critique of metaphysics (as a failure to think the ontological difference *as* difference) by looking at the crucial distinction he draws between the "same" and the "equal" or "the same" and "the identical." As he writes,

> The same (*Das selbe*) never coincides with the equal (*mit dem gleichen*), not even in the empty indifferent oneness of what is merely identical (*leeren Einerlei des bloß Identischen*). The equal or identical always moves toward the absence of difference (*Unterschiedlose*), so that everything may be reduced to a common denominator. The same, by contrast, is the belonging together of what differs, through a gathering by way of the difference (*Zusammengehören des Verschiedenen aus der Versammlung durch den Unterschied*). We can only say "the same" if we think difference. It is in the carrying out and settling of differences that the gathering nature of sameness comes to light. The same banishes all zeal always to level what is different into the equal or identical. The same gathers what is distinct into an original being-at-one (*Ursprüngliche Einigkeit*).[22]

Here, Heidegger indicates that there is a fundamental difference between saying things are equal or identical, which always involves comparing them by way of a third term or holding them up to some common standard, and saying that things are "the same," which requires no such categorical comparison—and thus no attempt to bridge their difference—but instead precisely a recognition of their sameness in their unbreachable difference. As Heidegger writes, using one of his favorite examples, "Poetry and thinking meet each other in one and the same only when, and only as long as, they remain distinctly in the distinctness of their nature" (*entschieden in der Verschiedenheit ihres Wesens bleiben*).[23] With these comments, Heidegger seems to be arguing that true concord is not based on "having something in common," but on sharing the difference itself.[24]

---

[22] "...Poetically Man Dwells...," 216; GA 7, 196–197.

[23] Ibid.

[24] Heidegger's insight—that our capacity to think non-metaphysically is dependent upon whether we can think difference as difference, i.e., as singular and irreducible—is also shared by some thinkers in the Jewish mystical tradition. As Hans Blumenberg tells it, "Rabbi Israel of Rischin [1796-1850] taught that the messianic world would be a world without likenesses, because in it the comparison and what is compared could no longer be related to one another. But that would mean, Gershom Scholem comments, 'that a new

Thus, to summarize and distill, metaphysics fails to appreciate that the phenomenon of "difference" cannot be represented or conceptually grasped or objectified without implicitly turning it into a fixed gradient or tissue that separates Being and beings. Non-metaphysical thinking, by contrast, understands that the difference between Being and beings is co-emergent with them, and therefore cannot be represented, since Being and beings are themselves always in an ecstatic process of re- and co-constitution.

A number of other passages strengthen this conclusion. First, Heidegger writes,

> If we now fail to recognize the strangeness and *uniqueness* (incomparability) of *beyng* and, in unity with that, the essence of Da-sein, then we will all-too-easily lapse into the opinion that that [the] "relation" [between them] corresponds to—or is even identical with—the one between subject and object. Da-sein, however, has overcome all subjectivity, and beyng is never an object, something we set over and against ourselves, something representable.[25]

Second, Heidegger writes,

> To speak of the relation of Da-sein makes beyng ambiguous; it makes beyng into something over and against, which it is not—inasmuch as it itself first appropriates precisely *that which* it is supposed to be over and against. Therefore this relation is also utterly incomparable to the subject-object relation.[26]

Third, Heidegger writes, "[W]hat we casually call a relationship is one of the trickiest of all matters, all the more so since we are bewitched by one-sided notions about what we call a relationship."[27] From these passages, we can see that, although he often referred to a "relationship" between

---

mode of being will emerge which cannot be pictorially represented.'" Blumenberg, *Work on Myth*, 226.

[25] *Contributions*, 199; GA 65, 252.

[26] *Contributions*, 200; GA 65, 253.

[27] *The Principle of Reason*, 42; GA 10, 78–79.

Being and Da-sein, Heidegger emphatically did not want us to think this relationship in dualistic terms.

All of this matters, we will see, because now we can understand that when Heidegger says "Man, in his very being, is in demand, is needed," and "belongs within a needfulness which claims him," we can insist that parsing this does not require us to *oppose* being needed by *Being* with being needed by *beings*, yet nor does it require us to conflate being needed by Being and being needed by beings.[28] Instead, we can claim that the phenomenon of being needed by Being testifies not to an objective, identifiable need, but to the meta-need of having to contend with the irreducibility of difference itself.

Thus, being needed by Being is not a phenomenon that occurs prior to being needed by concrete beings for concrete things, but is coterminous with it. At the same time, the needs of others (as well as our own needs) always already present themselves to us in a "clearing" and are therefore never simply detachable from the ontological context in which they address us. If we take this point seriously, then Levinas and Heidegger are closer to each other than Levinas and Levinasians typically acknowledge. For one of the primary objections that Levinas poses to Heidegger is that he privileges Being *over and against* existents. And yet, as we have just seen, this is far from the case. Levinas's critique of Heidegger is, at least in part, precisely Heidegger's critique of metaphysics.

My conclusion that Heidegger can be taken in a Levinasian direction (and that Levinas, in turn, can be read as a Heideggerian) finds further support in Derrida's acknowledgment that Levinas is just as difficult to squeeze into a normative box as Heidegger. As he writes,

> Levinas does not seek to propose laws or moral rules, does not seek to determine *a* morality, but rather [seeks] the essence of the ethical relation in general. But as this determination does not offer itself as a *theory* of Ethics, in question then, is an Ethics of Ethics. In this case, it is perhaps serious that this Ethics of Ethics can occasion neither a determined ethics nor determined laws without negating and forgetting itself.[29]

---

[28] Heidegger, *On the Way to Language*, 32; GA 12, 119.

[29] Jacques Derrida, "Violence and Metaphysics," in *Writing and Difference*, trans. Alan Bass (Chicago: University of Chicago Press, 1980), 111.

Nevertheless, the conclusion that neededness by Being and neededness by others are imbricated is still only a formal conclusion. It shows that a meeting of the ways between Heidegger and Levinas is *possible*, but it does not answer the larger question of this chapter, which is whether recognizing the fundamentality of ontological need necessarily entails—or at least, strongly commends—a responsibility to clothe the naked, visit the sick, shelter the homeless, and so on. To put it most basically: what is cleared in "the clearing"? What sort of stance does authenticity (defined here as an embodied understanding of oneself as Dasein) entail for how Dasein interacts with the ontic others it encounters?

Here, for the sake of analytic clarity, it is important to remember that for Heidegger an "understanding of others already lies in Dasein's understanding of being because its being is being-with."[30] "[T]his understanding is not a knowledge derived from cognition, but a primordially existential kind of being which first makes knowledge and cognition possible. Knowing oneself is grounded in primordially understanding being-with."[31] Yet the sheer fact that Dasein's awareness is shared with other Dasein does not tell us much about the quality of this awareness and the possible actions that it might encourage or discourage.

To answer our question I suggest that we go not to *Being and Time*, but to a passage in Heidegger's "Letter on Humanism":

> Thinking is—this says: Being has fatefully embraced its essence. To embrace a "thing" or a "person" in its essence means to love it, to favor it. Thought in a more original way such favoring means to bestow essence as a gift. Such favoring is the proper sense of enabling, which not only can achieve this or that but also can let something unfold in its provenance, that is, let it be.[32]

Although the pretext for Heidegger's discussion is the "relation" between Being and Dasein, his comments are acutely relevant to how we

---

[30] SZ, 123/ BT, 116.

[31] SZ, 124/ BT, 116.

[32] "Letter on Humanism," 219. "Das Denken ist—dies sagt: das Sein hat sich je geschicklich seines Wesens angenommen. Sich einer 'Sache' oder einer 'Person' in ihrem Wesen annehmen, das heißt: sie lieben: sie mögen. Dieses Mögen bedeutet, ursprünglicher gedacht: das Wesen schenken. Solches Mögen ist das eigentliche Wesen des Vermögens, das nicht nur dieses oder jenes leisten, sondern etwas in seiner Her-kunft 'wesen,' das heißt sein lassen kann." GA 9, 316.

think of Dasein's "relation" to others, be they other persons or other things. Moreover, as we have already seen, because Being and Dasein are not to be taken as distinct entities, Heidegger's descriptions of Being as "embracing" its essence must be taken phenomenologically (and not ousiologically). In this passage, Heidegger moves quickly through a series of evocative identifications: embracing something means loving it, loving it means favoring it, favoring it means bestowing it with essence, bestowing it with essence means enabling it to unfold into its provenance, enabling it to unfold into its provenance means letting it be.

Although Dasein is initially figured in the above passage in the passive role, as the one who is embraced, we have already seen that we make a metaphysical error if we assume that Being is an entity standing over and above Dasein literally doing things to Dasein. Thus, we parse the passage most rigorously if we regard it as a poetic description of what happens to Dasein *when Dasein thinks*. In other words, we are dealing here not with a matter of cause or effect, but of Dasein in a mode of active passivity or engaged receptivity. Remember from our previous chapter that "thinking" for Heidegger is most critically embodied as a posture of listening.

Thus, the above passage offers some important clues as to a possible ethical content that we discover when we "think," i.e., when we find ourselves standing in "the clearing." In particular, what we discover is that authentic care involves assisting and supporting the other in her ownmost struggle to become who she is, rather than simply removing her existential difficulties from her. In other words, "letting [the other] be" involves—at least at an ontological level—neither negligence nor paternalism, but rather an assistance that is guided by the ownmost needs of the other as they present themselves singularly to me in the mode of being-with-them. Heidegger makes a version of this point in *Being and Time* with his distinction between "leaping-in for" and "leaping-in-ahead for," yet there the emphasis is on helping the other accept "being-towards-death" as the basis for her care, but not necessarily on helping her in any ontic way. That account, therefore, seems insufficient for describing what it would mean to authentically care for a homeless person in need of shelter or an ex-convict in need of a job. The passage in the "Letter on Humanism" by contrast, seems to be more directive. For it indicates that "loving" others means "bestowing them with essence," that is, affirming them not simply in terms of what they have done, but more primordially, in terms of who they might become.

While Heidegger himself does not indicate that regarding the other in terms of their possibilities for being necessarily leads to a posture of compassion, forgiveness, or hope—perhaps because understanding the other in terms of possibility might just as basically mean understanding them as a potentiality for failure, error, or "acting out"—I nevertheless want to claim, drawing on Heidegger's language of "favoring," that caring authentically for the other is inflected with generosity. Ontically, of course, matters are trickier. And perhaps in a given social context, "letting be" might involve imprisonment or even capital punishment. Yet, ontologically, at least, letting be involves "bestowal" and is therefore oriented by an ethics of rehabilitation and repair rather than vindictiveness or punishment. We should also note that, ontically speaking, determining the point at which "letting be" requires aggressive intervention and the point at which it requires quiet surrender will always be contentious. If we think about what "letting be" means, for instance, in the context of end-of-life care, it is an open question whether "letting be" means not treating a terminal illness or aggressively seeking to beat it. In both cases, the language of "letting be" carries force, precisely since what is at issue is what kind of possibilities one seeks to unfold. Does "bestowing essence" mean helping the person live longer (though perhaps in a state of significantly weakened faculties and health) or does "bestowing essence" mean helping the person take account of their life, say goodbye to their children, and leave this world peacefully? Finally, we might ask who, in circumstances where Dasein is unconscious or in a coma, should be the one to decide on that Da-sein's fate? These questions are well beyond the purview of Heidegger's own explicit concerns and are even brought to language in ways that might offend Martin Heidegger, the historical person. And yet they raise questions for which ontology may be importantly suited, if not to solve, then to think through.

In particular, one of the significant contributions that ontology offers to such difficult topics is the recognition that Dasein is not simply the same as the conscious, rational ego, but a being whose being is an issue for it, and for whom this "issue" is itself always riven by tensions between a sense of mineness and a sense of commonness, or between a sense of ownmostness and a sense of belonging to others. Authenticity cannot patch this rift, but it can help us move within it with both heightened sensitivity to the challenges that it poses and heightened commitment to accept responsibility for those challenges. Moreover, insofar as "the clearing" reveals us and others to be neither simply subjects nor simply objects, but rather beings whose being is constituted by an originary openness to meaningfulness, it can help us consider that caring for ourselves and others can never be exhausted by short-term solutions or answers, but instead always involves, helping ourselves and others take responsibility for the essential questionability of existence.

Here, we might conclude, that authenticity—or being receptive to the clearing—evokes certain aspects of Hegelian ethics, but without the teleology. In particular, authenticity might be regarded as a practice of recognition—of recognizing oneself in the other and the other in oneself, and of recognizing the other as other and the self as self—but in which the recognition, rather than ever being concluded or conclusive, is always the recognition of the essential questionability of being and being-with. And here, once again, this may be why ontology cannot simply be reduced to a theoretical or cognitive project, but must be understood as an embodied practice and commitment to live out that questionability.

As should now be evident, "the clearing" does not directly require us to commit certain deeds and not others, but it does enjoin us—when we find ourselves held within its dynamic embrace—to let beings be. How we can let beings be, how we can enable them to be and become what they are, and how we can do this, in particular, when there is strong disagreement about what things are and should be, is far from simple or self-evident. And yet the fact that our enjoinment is difficult hardly means that it is ontically irrelevant or that it is a matter of indifference.

Instead, as can now be appreciated, Heidegger's claim that we are needed by Being can be interpreted as saying that we are needed not only for this and for that particular task or challenge, but that we are always already also needed for the task and challenge of authentic world-disclosure, that is, of coming to an understanding of ourselves and our world that is marked by integrity and sensitivity. If we focus only on the needs of others, but forget our ontological responsibility to acknowledge the world itself as the site where those needs and our capacity to respond to them come to presence, we are at risk of both self- and other-objectification. Moreover, we are at risk of failing to respond to them in a way that is sensitive to what is truly needed, and instead in danger of responding to them simply according to an unquestioned set of assumptions that we project through calculative reasoning.[33]

---

[33] For a popular article on this point, see Paul Bloom, "The Baby in the Well: The Failure of Empathy," in *The New Yorker*, May 20, 2013. http://www.newyorker.com/arts/

Another way to say much of the above is that the needs of others do not simply stand neutrally and nakedly before us, but present themselves to us only because we are always already *thrown* into a world in which those needs can make a claim on us. It is why, typically, the needs of friends and loved ones are easier to answer—and to know how to respond to—than the needs of political prisoners thousands of miles away. And this is so not simply for epistemological reasons, but for existential reasons. When friends confront us for something, they do so not only for the sake of bringing about a certain result, but also as a way of renewing, strengthening, preserving, or testing an already extant relationship. Even in a trivial case, where, say, a friend asks me to take out the trash, what she is asking is not simply that I take out the *trash*, but also that *I* take out the trash. Moreover, implicit in her question is a demand that I demonstrate my care for her in caring for our shared "with-world" (*Mit-welt*).[34] In contrast, there are many people who need blood transfusions and kidneys in this very moment who might address me if they could, yet because they do not—because I only know of their need as a fact that floats peripherally in the ambit of my more immediate concerns—their needs do not make a strong claim on me. Is this right? Would a righteous person be "thinking" in each moment—or, at the very least, in many more moments—of all the ways she might alleviate the suffering of what Frantz Fanon calls "the wretched of the earth"?[35]

First, we should point out that even our theoretical saint who spends each waking moment in a state of constant giving, and constant openness to the needs of the near and the far, is limited—limited by bodily faculties, limited by monetary resources, limited by linguistic ability, limited by mental faculties (one can't be an expert in everything), limited by geographic location, and so on. As such, even she must prioritize what needs are most salient to her. Does she rank these needs solely according to the extremity of the need? Does she rank them solely according to the feasibility of responding to them in a way that is rehabilitative? Does

critics/atlarge/2013/05/20/130520crat_atlarge_bloom?currentPage=all (accessed May 4, 2014).

[34] Here, I am drawing on Heidegger's claim that "[t]he world of Da-sein is a *with-world*." SZ, 118/ BT, 112.

[35] Frantz Fanon, *The Wretched of the Earth*, trans. Richard Philcox (New York: Grove Press, 2004).

she rank them according to her own capacity to have the most "impact"? And how is "impact" to be measured? Ontology reveals that authenticity is not achieved when these questions are answered once and for all, but instead, when we appreciate that the questions and the limitations that inspire them are part and parcel of living ethically. In addition, as we have already shown indirectly in previous chapters, the operation of ranking is a representational enterprise that can only be derivative of a more originary understanding of one's being-in-the-world. As such, if one holds by rankings alone, one may lose touch with the very circumstances that gave rise to those rankings in the first place. To the extent that ontology reminds us that our understanding is always hermeneutic, it helps us appreciate that our responsibility is never simply an objective state of affairs, but is always mediated by our own understanding of the world and our place in it. In claiming that we are "needed by Being," Heidegger allows for the conclusion that clarifying (and revising) our understanding of who we are is just as critical as responding to the ontic needs of the needy. At the same time, we have seen that understanding who we are and responding to the needs of others are not simply two distinct modes of human being, but are essentially interlinked. We clarify who we are by responding to others, and we respond to others most significantly and sensitively when we do so out of a clarified sense of who we are. Finally, as we have seen above, appreciating the irreducibility of ontological difference, and in particular, realizing that the difference between Being and beings is not fixed, but rather a dif-ference of Being and beings in their interplay, is directly relevant to our capacity to treat ourselves and others in non-objectifying ways.

Granted the above, however, we may still ask: why "being needed" and not "being *needy*"? The answer, I suggest, is more a matter of rhetoric than substance. As readily as we are fundamentally needed, we are also fundamentally needy. Nevertheless, in emphasizing that we are needed, rather than *needy*, Heidegger is able to bolster his point that human existence is constituted by receptivity rather than simply "the will," as is typically assumed in rationalist thinking. As such, emphasizing the primacy of *neededness* rather than *neediness* indicates that our own egoic capacity to need emerges only out of (or within) the a priori givenness of understanding. In addition, Heidegger seems to indicate that self-understanding, when authentic, is not concerned with what it *lacks*, but is instead simply affirmative of who it is. In other words, part of what it means to discover oneself authentically as Dasein is to discover that one's incompleteness or neediness is not a detriment to being oneself, but an essential aspect of being the self that one is. As Ben Vedder elucidates this point:

> Th[e] difference between the inauthentic desire of curiosity and the [authentic] desire of the possible gives us the following suggestions. Can we not say that inauthentic fallenness is an inherent consequence of desire-as-lack, where the force of such an experience spawns a hyperbolic attachment to actuality in order to "fill" the lack? This means that authentic engagement with the world stems from being educated in the "negativity" of desire-as-withdrawal, of its inevitable surplus of possibility. Authentic desire, then, follows from being educated in the essential finitude of being, where we learn to overcome the "addiction" to presence and actuality that compels us to flit about in search of perpetual fixes of surface stimulation—which not only alienates us from the meaning of being in general but also from a deeper appreciation of specific phenomena in the world.[36]

Vedder's point is also obliquely corroborated by the fact that when Heidegger does refer to human beings as fundamentally needy, he suggests, as we saw in previous chapters, that our "greatest need is our lack of our sense of need."[37] With this claim, Heidegger indicates that the most basic need of Dasein is not the result of its lacking something positive, but is, on the contrary, borne from the fact that it fails to yearn for an intimate understanding of Being. And yet, were we to come to an intimate understanding of Being, as we have now seen, it would involve appreciating the irreducibility of our being needed.

Is "Thinking" Too Little Too Late?

In the previous section, we saw that the language of "being needed" offers a potential bridge between ontological and ethical concerns, and that ontological responsibility and onto-ethical sensitivity are best regarded as complements rather than as mutually exclusive alternatives. Yet we have also noted in previous chapters that authenticity is an enigma, and therefore rarely, if ever, enacted. As such, the above

---

[36] Ben Vedder, "Heidegger and Desire," *Continental Philosophy Review* 31, no. 4 (1998): 353–368, 365.

[37] "Overcoming Metaphysics," 102; GA 7, 89; *Contributions to Philosophy*, 11; and "Building Dwelling Thinking," 159.

discussion is best read as a description of how to live aspirationally rather than as a program for how to avoid conflicts or mistakes. In this section, we focus on the concern—raised by Fredric Jameson and Adorno—that such an aspirational project is doomed from the onset, either because the challenges of modernity are already so entrenched in our world as to make all aspiration futile, or else because the historical calamities on which modernity has been predicated reveal its essential monstrosity. As such, the aspiration to enact a life lived with sensitivity to "the clearing" is "too little too late." In answering this line of objection, my argument will seek not to appeal to Heidegger's thought directly—since this is what is under challenge—but instead to a short and enigmatic passage in *Pirkei Avot*, an ancient Jewish text, that seems to be grappling with a similar set of ontological difficulties, albeit in an entirely different context.[38] In doing so, my aim is not to refute the fatalist-Marxist critique of ontology—though it should be noted that this critique would apply to Levinas as well—so much as to show that this critique can be accommodated within ontology itself. Although the language of being needed by Being is at risk of becoming a theodicy that might justify indifference to the larger, structural problems of modernity (such as ecological pollution, the ghettoization and criminalization of the poor, or the destruction of indigenous traditions and communities), this is no reason, I argue, to reject it out of hand.[39] Instead, we need an ontology that can affirm the structural challenges of modernity while nevertheless affirming the importance of "good deeds." Such a conclusion is not one that Heidegger directly affirms, although he does conclude his essay "... Poetically Man Dwells..." by describing "Kindness" (*Freundlichkeit*, *charis*) as the locus where poetic dwelling comes to pass.[40] Yet it is a conclusion that can be supported by Heidegger's claim that poetry and works of art open up possibilities whose fecundity cannot be discerned simply in terms of present calculation. As he writes, "What art founds can [never] be compensated and made up for by what is already at hand

---

[38] The reason that this ancient text is relevant to our discussion is twofold. First, it shows that the tension between affirmation and despair is not uniquely modern. Second, it shows that dialectical thinking, as a response to this tension, is also not uniquely modern.

[39] For a sociological examination of modernity's discontents, see Zygmunt Bauman, *Globalization: The Human Consequences* (Cambridge: Polity, 1998); Bauman, *Liquid Modernity*, 53–129.

[40] "...Poetically Man Dwells...," 227.

and available. Founding is an overflow, a bestowal."[41] And since, as we have seen, art and poetry, in the essential sense, are not reducible to aesthetic judgments or to what museum galleries and poetry anthologies call "art" and "poetry," it is possible to consider that daily acts of kindness can also be, in their own way, poetic.

In *Postmodernism: Or the Cultural Logic of Late Capitalism*, the Marxist literary critic Fredric Jameson declares Heidegger's projects too modernist to be contemporarily relevant. As he writes,

> Heidegger's "field path" [has been] irredeemably and irrevocably destroyed by late capital, by the green revolution, by neocolonialism and the megalopolis, which runs its superhighways over the older fields and vacant lots and turns Heidegger's "house of being" into condominiums, if not the most miserable unheated, rat-infested tenement buildings.[42]

The key words in Jameson's dirge—"irredeemably" and "irrevocably"— are not easily answered. Their austerity forbids simply countering them by appealing to serious texts, since what is at issue is the very status of those texts, and of text itself, in a postmodern age. Jameson's concern is that the very gestures of critique and impulses toward redemption that once held a genuine dialectical efficacy have themselves become fetishized, and are now merely bywords that reinforce, rather than contest, what he describes as the irresistible hegemony of late capitalism.[43] As

---

[41] "Origin of the Work of Art," 200.

[42] Fredric Jameson, *Postmodernism: Or, the Cultural Logic of Late Capitalism* (London: Verso, 1991), 35. For a similar concern that Heidegger's thought, specifically his understanding of the work of art, is outdated see Peter Sloterdjik, *You Must Change Your Life: On Anthropotechnics*, trans. Wieland Hoba (Cambridge, MA: Polity Press, 2013), 434. For a more generally articulated concern regarding the purpose of an education in a "discredited civilization" see Allen Grossman, *True-Love: Essays on Poetry and Valuing* (Chicago: University of Chicago Press, 2009), 163–173.

[43] Here, Jameson seems to repeat Heidegger's notion of the double plight, only he replaces the forgetting of Being with something like the forgetting of socialism. Jameson's plaint can be substantiated by a variety of examples. Here, let us take two: Just think of Mastercard's compelling tag-line, which exploits self-deprecation, irony, and nostalgia to beatify itself as the perfect ersatz for and compliment to what eludes market-value: "Some things are priceless, but for everything else there's Mastercard." This kind of advertisement is a perfect example of how easily the very desire for authenticity and purity can become a selling point for an empty product. The existential understanding of freedom as a potentiality-for-being has been subtly reworked as a potentiality-for-buying. More recently, it has been shown that the take-away food chain, Pret A Manger, uses a system of financial

Jameson uneasily discerns, even the critique of postmodernism may be just another trick by which postmodernism perpetuates its dead-endedness. With this, Jameson repeats Adorno's self-undermining lament, "All post-Auschwitz culture, including its urgent critique, is garbage," as well as his claim that

> [I]f one were drafting an ontology in accordance with the basic state of facts, of the facts whose repetition makes their state invariant, such an ontology would be pure horror. An ontology of culture, above all, would have to include where culture as such went wrong; a philosophically legitimate ontology would have more of a place in construing the culture industry than in construing Being. Good would be nothing but what has escaped from ontology.[44]

Or as Adorno also puts it, somewhat dizzyingly, "If ontology were possible at all, it would be possible [only] in an ironic sense, as the epitome of negativity."[45]

Strangely, though, neither Jameson's nor Adorno's exasperated cries are as new as they might want us to believe. Their plaint, in fact, is at least as old as the opening of Ecclesiastes (*Qohelet*), whose pseudonymous author, King Solomon, is described elsewhere in the Bible as both a sagacious architect and as an idolatrous glutton: "Vanity of vanities. All is vanity" (Ecclesiastes 1:1). Here, as in Jameson's and Adorno's formulations, the dilemma is not simply that *all* is vanity, but that even the analysis of vanity is vain—that it's vanity *all the way down*. While the official Hegelian position might be to dismiss these formulations as examples of "bad infinity," or else to suggest that we read these plaints, against themselves, as double-negations whose net result remains positive and reconciliatory, their pathos consists precisely in contesting *the justice*

incentives and disincentives to ensure that its workers always appear to be genuinely cheerful. One of the job requirements for selling sandwiches at near minimum wage is that one can't be doing it—or seem to be doing it—"just for the money." In other words, authenticity itself (or the convincing affect of it) has become a selling point, just another item in the marketplace of "goods and services." See Paul Myerscough, "Short Cuts," *London Review of Books Online.* http://www.lrb.co.uk/v35/n01/paul-myerscough/short-cuts (accessed April 24, 2013).

[44] Theodor W. Adorno, *Negative Dialectics*, 367, 122.

[45] Ibid., 121.

of such an appropriative move. Our plight, however named, they would protest, is too great simply to be, in Hegel's terminology, *aufgehoben*, that is, reconciled, elevated, brought to accord.[46] To imagine that humpty-dumpty can be put back together again—to hope for the day in which humpty-dumpy is restored—is to collaborate with the same powers that shattered humpty-dumpty in the first place, they seem to argue.

Yet however precarious the ontological enterprise might be, Adorno nevertheless insists that it is still possible—and indeed incumbent upon us—to be hopeful, and to hold ourselves answerable for the bearing of a redeemed world no matter what:

> The only philosophy which can be responsibly practiced in the face of despair is the attempt to contemplate all things as they would present themselves from the standpoint of redemption. Knowledge has no light but that shed on the world by redemption: all else is reconstruction, mere technique. Perspectives must be fashioned that displace and estrange the world, reveal it to be, with its rifts and crevices, as indigent and distorted as it will appear one day in the messianic light [...] But beside the demand thus placed on thought, the question of the reality or the unreality of redemption itself hardly matters.[47]

Jameson, likewise, does not give up hope altogether. As he writes,

> It would be best, perhaps, to think of [Utopia] as an alternate world—better to say the alternate world, our alternate world—as one contiguous with ours but without any connection or access to it. Then, from time to time, like a diseased eyeball in which disturbing flashes of light are perceived or like those baroque sunbursts in which rays from another world suddenly break into this one, we are reminded that Utopia exists and that other systems, other spaces, are still possible.[48]

---

[46] For powerful articulations of how Hegel's thought is paradoxically both impossible to agree with and impossible not to agree with—impossible to read correctly and impossible not read correctly—see Maurice Blanchot, *The Writing of the Disaster*, trans. Ann Smock (Lincoln: University of Nebraska Press, 1986), 46–47; Theodor Adorno, *Hegel: Three Studies*, trans. Shierry Weber Nicholsen (Cambridge: MIT Press, 1994), 145–148.

[47] Adorno, *Minima Moralia*, 247.

[48] Jameson, *Valences of the Dialectic* (London: Verso, 2010), 612.

Formally, Adorno's and Jameson's arguments here pursue a Kantian strategy: that the light of redemption cannot be deduced by *pure reason* does not mean that it cannot be—or should not be—presupposed as a necessary hypobook for *practical reason*. To the extent that we are incapable of being stirred by a desire for redemption, Adorno suggests, we will be nothing more than lifeless bureaucrats. To the extent that we cannot but be haunted by such desire, however, the dim light of redemption is sustained. Jacques Rancière makes a similar argument in a commentary on Walter Benjamin's "Theses on the Philosophy of History":

> The unlikelihood of the coming of the Messiah does not prevent us from keeping a narrow passage open. That narrow passage through which no Messiah is likely to come is also the vanishing point of that meaning which we can from time to time wrest from the mad rationalizations of the world's course, that little bit of reason Nietzsche spoke about, scattered from star to star in the madness of the rationalized world.[49]

Yet if these articulations bear a formal resemblance to Kant, their pathos suggests a far more ambivalent text, namely, a short passage in an ancient compilation of rabbinic aphorisms known as *Pirkei Avot* (c. 200 B.C.E.–200 C.E.) There, we read two mutually contradictory claims uttered by the same sage, Rabbi Yaakov: "A single hour of repentance and good deeds in this world (*olam hazeh*) is more beautiful than an entire lifetime in the world to come (*olam habah*)," and "A single hour of enlightenment or satisfaction (*korat ruach*) in the world to come is more beautiful than an entire lifetime in this world."[50] Here, asceticism and worldliness are not opposed, but collaged. On the one hand, "this world" is recognized as unsatisfactory in comparison to an imagined alternative world, but on the other hand, "this world" is affirmed as the sole locus where striving for an alternative world can take place. The brokenness of this world, the text enjoins, is not an excuse for condemning it as an illusion. Not only that, but we must entertain, even more ludicrously, that participation in the broken world is preferable to obtaining Paradise itself. Struggle, not

---

[49] Jacques Rancière, "The Archaemodern Turn," in *Walter Benjamin and the Demands of History*, ed. Michael P. Steinberg (Ithaca: Cornell University Press, 1996), 40.

[50] *Pirkei Avot* 4:17, translation mine. The literal meaning of *korat ruach* is something like "A Cooling Spirit," implying a sense of calm.

accomplishment, is here advocated as the mark of a beautiful life. Or as Adorno put it, "Suffering, not positivity, is the humane content of art."[51]

Yet what exactly does it mean to carry out "good deeds" (*ma'asim tovim*) and "repentance" (*teshuvah*)? If a single hour of doing them is better than a lifetime in Paradise, then why doesn't this passage say more about what to do and how to do it? No sooner are we given the assurance that the struggle to live well is enough—no, *better* than enough—than we are told that it is not enough. What are we to make of this reversal?

As I understand it, the second half of the text bears a challenge, though not a refutation, of the first half. The challenge is this: How is it possible to perform good deeds or engage in repentance in a world that is structurally flawed?[52] Is this not the reason that, against the world-affirming, and hence, conservative position of the first half of the text, the second half of the text maintains an antinomian rejection of the sufficiency of repentance and good deeds? After all, an ethics of repentance and good deeds might help privileged individuals be better neighbors, but it will not necessarily empower them to address the structural injustices on which their very neighborhood is based, for instance, an economy based on slave labor, war, and patriarchal rule. For in this case, what might be needed are not simply repentance and good deeds, but a radical investigation of how repentance and good deeds are being defined in the first place.

Thus, individual heroism is never enough. Not only that, but to the extent that one promotes the individual hero as an ethical ideal, one also usually comes to judge adversely those who are unable, for whatever reason, to rise to hero status. The second half of the passage thus protests against a world in which virtue is so glorified that those who are deemed less virtuous are made to feel ashamed simply because their deeds do not register as such. It protests, moreover, against the pretension that heroes are not also and more significantly human beings, people whose existence would be impossible without the support and labor

---

[51] Adorno, *Aesthetic Theory*, trans. Christian Lenhardt (London: Routledge, 1986), 369.

[52] This is another way of articulating Hegel's challenge to Kant in his famous analysis of "The Beautiful Soul." As Hegel writes, "The 'beautiful soul', lacking an *actual* existence [is] entangled in the contradiction between its pure self and the necessity to externalize itself and change itself into an actual existence." Hegel, *The Phenomenology of Spirit*, 406–407.

of others. As Hegel writes, "No man is a hero to his valet; not, however, because the man is not a hero, but because the valet—is a valet, whose dealings are with the man, not as a hero, but as one who eats, drinks, and wears clothes […] with his individual wants and fancies."[53] With this, Hegel insists that heroism is an existential mode of being and *not* a character trait exclusive to the gifted and talented. He insists, moreover, that while heroism is an exceptional mode of being, it should not be understood apart from the social context that motivates and supports it. Thus, to extol a heroic ethics without considering the material and existential conditions both of the valets and of their masters when they are not behaving like heroes is to idealize a world that celebrates the strong and punishes the weak.

One might object, of course, that such a world would actually be great. "If only the malicious or the lazy were more ashamed of themselves," one might say. But we are not necessarily talking here about malice or laziness. We are talking primarily about those who are thrown into a state of disenfranchisement, marginalization, and stigmatization through no fault of their own: those who are "left-handed" (*sinister*), "queer," and "heretical," in the broadest sense, and who are identified as lesser beings because they are not "right," "correct," "straight," and "orthodox." Thus, an hour in a different world, a coming world, is more beautiful than a lifetime in this one, not because it is in fact more beautiful, but because an encounter with such an alternative world allows us to recognize the (potential) complicity of our current ideals in maintaining a world where creditors alone are considered magnanimous, while debtors are deemed lazy and worthless.[54]

What are we to make of this tension? How can we embrace an ethics of good deeds and repentance without relinquishing our desire for a world where a more radically democratic ethic reigns? How can we affirm a this-worldly ethics of process without forswearing our hope for—and commitment to—a coming world that is more welcoming of those that this world renders refugees? Can we avoid the temptation to decorate the world instead of fixing it while at the same time avoiding the temptation to denounce our decorative impulses as degenerate?[55]

[53] Hegel, *The Phenomenology of Spirit*, 404.

[54] I mean this in the broad sense, and not simply in the material-economic sense.

[55] These questions are inspired by Gillian Rose's essay, "Walter Benjamin: Out of the Sources of Modern Judaism," in *The Actuality of Walter Benjamin*, ed. Laura Marcus and Lynda Nead (London: Lawrence & Wishart, 1998).

Without denying the force of these difficult questions, I would like to suggest a preliminarily positive answer to them. For while Rabbi Yaakov's words highlight a variety of tensions—between reform and revolution, tradition and eschatology, effort and contentment—they also entreat us to live with these tensions, rather than to resolve them. Good deeds and repentance, taken on an individual basis, will not be able to address such large-scale problems as global warming or refugee resettlement, but at the same time a world where we individuals do not aspire to good deeds and repentance will surely be an inhospitable one. To insist on the importance of good deeds and repentance in spite of their structural limitations is to insist, therefore, that each of us is *needed*. It is to insist, albeit in different terms, that onto-ethical and ontological responsibility are not ancillary to the standing of the world, but decisive for the kind of world that comes to presence. (Here, I am parsing "good deeds" as onto-ethical occurrences, and "repentance" as something akin to authenticity: the perpetual "turning" and "re-turning" to the questionability of who one is.) Thus, even if the policies of multinational corporations, banks, nation-states, courts, and organized religious institutions are more efficacious, in scientifically measurable terms, than the way you and I *are* in the world, an hour of existing *as Dasein*, with all of its intractable difficulties, this text suggests, remains more beautiful than a lifetime in a future where there are "apps" to make sure we never have to care for Being again. Thus, although Rabbi Yaakov's words do not completely allay Jameson's and Adorno's suggestion that thinking is in a stalemate, they at least allow us to regard it as a challenge to, rather than as a wholesale refutation of, thinking. Ultimately, this conclusion is not far from Adorno's own admission that "[ontology's] effect would be unintelligible if it did not meet an emphatic need, a sign of something missed, a longing that Kant's verdict on a knowledge of the Absolute should not be the end of the matter."[56]

CONCLUSION

As this chapter has shown, Heidegger's enigmatic language of "being needed by Being," though seemingly abstract, or else, crudely anthropomorphic, is more generously read as a phenomenological way of saying

---

[56]Adorno, *Negative Dialectics*, 61.

that ontological sensitivity and onto-ethical responsibility are interlinked. Being needed by Being and being needed by others are not mutually exclusive modes of being needed, but two ways to describe the same fundamental condition. To say that we are needed by Being, however, is to emphasize that the needs of others (as well as our own needs) are never simply objective or neutral, but always hermeneutically and phenomenologically situated. As such, we respond to the needs of others most authentically (and therefore most helpfully and most sustainably), when we do so as Dasein, meeting others in the clearing of a "with-world." This chapter has also built on the previous chapters in showing that "thinking" is not simply a cogitative or solipsistic enterprise, but is instead, as Heidegger describes it in his "Letter on Humanism," a way of being held within the embrace of Being (meaningfulness). In allowing ourselves to be so embraced, we come to understand that loving or favoring another does not simply mean satisfying their ontic needs, but much more crucially, "bestowing them with essence," however difficult and questionable such an enterprise might be. This chapter has also shown that the task of thinking is to affirm our responsibility for the present world, even though, in doing so, we are at risk of justifying things as they are. "Good deeds" and "repentance" are, from one perspective, never enough. Yet from another perspective, they name important ways that we can respond to our fundamental condition of being needed.

CHAPTER 6

"Thinking Is Thinking": From Anxiety to Gratitude

More endowing than poetizing/More founding than thinking/ Remains gratitude.
(*Stiftender als Dichten/ gründender als Denken,/ bleibe der Dank.*)[1]

All reflective thinking is poetic, and all poetry in turn is a kind of thinking. The two belong together by virtue of that Saying which has already bespoken itself to what is unspoken because it is thought as thanks.[2]

So far, we have seen that Heidegger's critique of subjectivism and objectivism must be taken not simply as a *philosophical* critique of metaphysics, but, much more crucially, as an existential injunction to enact and embody a non-metaphysical way of being *in the world*. We saw that Heidegger's own terms for such a non-metaphysical way of being include "dwelling," "poetizing," "thinking," and "listening," and that these all belong together. And finally, we have seen that while Heidegger himself framed his concerns as ontological, and not as ontic, the notion that the ontological and the ontic are wholly distinct domains is itself a metaphysical presumption. Therefore, the practice of ontology, or thinking (in the expansive sense), is most generously understood not as a retreat from the ethical challenges of everydayness, but as a posture in which we

---

[1] GA 16, 741.
[2] *On the Way to Language*, 136.

© The Author(s) 2018
Z. Atkins, *An Ethical and Theological Appropriation of Heidegger's Critique of Modernity*,
https://doi.org/10.1007/978-3-319-96917-6_6

affirm and accept responsibility for these tensions. As such, authenticity was shown to consist not in indifference to others, but as a clarification and an intensification of our ontico-ontological responsibilities to them qua *thrown*.

At the same time, we have also wrestled with the concern that, given the essential elusiveness and paradoxical nature of terms like "authenticity," "releasement," "letting be," and "openness to the clearing" ontology's aspirations are either vapid or irrelevant. As Adorno writes, "[Ontology's very] consistency takes it to a no-man's land," since it cannot make "a [positive] move without fearing the loss of what it claims."[3] And this means that, ultimately, for Adorno, the truth of ontology is solely negative: "the truth of philosophy falling silent."[4]

Adorno's Trappist conclusion is consistent with Heidegger's claims that "Language is grounded in silence," and that "silence is the most concealed holding to the measure," and yet, as this chapter will show, ontology can also yield some positive and constructive truths besides the truth of silence.[5] In particular, it will show that gratitude offers one of the most critical and transformative ways that we can authentically respond to the modern condition.

Drawing on Heidegger's reading of Hölderlin's lines—"Full of merit, yet poetically, man/Dwells on this earth,"—this chapter will show that it is only by saying "yes" to the ineradicable "yet" at the basis of our being that we can come to a peaceful and free relation to Being and beings. It will also show that genuine gratitude is oriented toward Being as such, and not only selectively at those things that we deem worthy of merit. When we show gratitude for Being as such, we come into a non-instrumental relation to truth as our attention shifts from seeing things in terms of their relative value to encountering them and our being there with them in the simplicity of their unconcealment. Moreover, a gratitude that is extended for Being itself, this chapter argues, offers a direct way to access "the clearing," insofar as, refusing to take anything simply as an object, it also holds subjectivity in suspense. Gratitude, in other words, constitutes an authentic occurrence of Dasein—a point Heidegger does not make in *Being and Time*—yet which this chapter will show is the complement of what he there calls *Angst*.

---

[3] Ibid.
[4] Ibid.
[5] *Contributions*, 401; GA 65, 510.

If one were only to read *Being and Time*, the conclusion that ontology leads to gratitude would be strange. After all, Heidegger famously argues in that text that *Angst* is the most "fundamental attunement" of Dasein, insofar as Dasein is always being-toward-death.[6] As Heidegger writes, "*Angst* as a mode of attunement first discloses the *world as world*."[7] Of course, Heidegger does not simply mean that we are always ontically (i.e., psychologically or physiologically) anxious. Rather, as he puts it, "The physiological triggering of *Angst* is possible only because Da-sein is anxious in the very ground of its being."[8] Heidegger also argues that *Angst* offers Dasein the most basic path toward self-understanding, because "*[t]hat about which one has Angst is being-in-the-world as such.*"[9] And, "What *Angst* is about is not an innerworldly being," but rather "Da-sein as *being-possible*."[10] Or again, "The fact that Da-sein is entrusted to itself shows itself primordially and concretely in *Angst*."[11]

Heidegger's privileging of *Angst* is also one of the central themes in his essay "What Is Metaphysics?" There, Heidegger writes, "Anxiety (*Angst*) reveals the nothing."[12] And, "If Dasein can relate itself to beings only by holding itself out into the nothing and can exist only thus; and if the nothing is originally disclosed only in anxiety; then must we not hover in this anxiety (*Angst*) constantly in order to be able to exist at all?"[13]

And yet, as this chapter will show, gratitude is best regarded not as the dissolution of our constitutive *Angst*, but as the alchemical result of affirming it. This conclusion is supported by a variety of passages in Heidegger. Even in *Being and Time*, for instance, Heidegger writes, "Together with the sober *Angst* that brings us before our individualized potentiality-of-being, goes the unshakeable joy in this possibility."[14] Heidegger is here quick to note that elaborating further would take him "beyond the limits drawn for our present inquiry [whose aim is] fundamental ontology," and yet

---

[6] SZ, 190, 251/ BT, 178, 232.

[7] SZ, 187/ BT, 175.

[8] SZ, 190/ BT, 177.

[9] SZ, 186/ BT, 174.

[10] SZ, 186, 188/ BT, 174, 176.

[11] SZ, 192/ BT, 179.

[12] "What Is Metaphysics?," 101.

[13] Ibid., 104.

[14] SZ, 310/ BT, 286.

elsewhere, where Heidegger's concerns are not strictly "fundamental," he indicates that Anxiety is hardly the only comportment in which an authentic understanding of Being/truth comes to pass.[15] In his *Elucidations of Hölderlin's Poetry*, for instance, he writes of "the joy whose essence it is to shelter what is true, and to entrust it over for a free use," and of "the gaiety that allows everything to be at home."[16]

Heidegger's most famous remarks on gratitude appear in his lecture course *What Is Called Thinking?* Picking up on the etymological connection between "thinking" (*Denken*) and "thanking" (*Danken*), Heidegger suggests that "the Old English noun for thought is *thanc* or *thonc*," and can mean "a thought (*Gedachtes*), a grateful thought (*Gedanke*), and the expression of such a thought (*Dank*)." Commenting on this connection, Heidegger writes, "the '*thanc*,' that which is thought, the thought, implies the thanks."[17] Heidegger then goes on to ask a series of questions, whose euphony helps him perform his argument that the assonance between "thinking," "thanking" and "remembering/memorializing" (*Gedenken*) testifies to a deeper, ontological connection between them. As he writes, "Is thinking a giving of thanks? (*Ist das Denken ein Danken*)? What do thanks mean here (*Was meint hier Danken*)? Or do thanks consist in thinking? (*Oder beruht der Dank im Denken*)? Is memory no more than a container for the thoughts of thinking, or does thinking itself reside in memory (*Ist das Gedächtnis nur ein Behälter für das Gedachte des Denkens, oder beruht das Denken selber im Gedächtnis*)?"[18] Heidegger's eventual conclusion is circular. As he writes,

What gives us food for thought ever and again is the most thought-provoking. We take the gift it gives by giving thought to what is most thought-provoking. In doing so, we keep thinking what is most thought-provoking. We recall it in thought. Thus we recall in thought that to which we owe thanks for the endowment of our nature—thinking. As we give thought to what is most thought-provoking, we give thanks.[19]

---

[15] Ibid.

[16] *Elucidations of Hölderlin's Poetry*, 118, 36.

[17] *What Is Called Thinking?*, 139; GA 8, 142.

[18] Ibid.

[19] Ibid., 146. "Das, was uns je und je zu denken gibt, ist das Bedenklichste. Was es gibt, seine Gabe, übernehmen wir dadurch, daß wir das Bedenklichste bedenken. Hierbei halten wir uns denken an das Bedenklichste. Wir denken es an. So gedenken wir dessen, dem wir

Yet what is significant for us in Heidegger's circular reasoning is that thinking can be understood as a devotional practice and not simply as a skill, technique, or hobby. As he says explicitly, the "thanks" embodied in thinking "is not a recompense (*kein Abgelten*); but [an] offering (*Entgegentragen*); and only by this offering do we allow (*belassen*) that which properly gives food for thought to remain what it is in its essential nature."[20] Here, Heidegger indicates that what is thought-provoking (what gives thought) and our capacity to think are interdependent. Without the a priori givenness of that which provokes thought, we would not be capable of thinking. At the same time, without our own capacity to respond to this givenness and gratefully acknowledge it as that which enables us to think at all, it would not be "thought provoking." In other words, our own receptivity to what gives thought, embodied in thankfulness, is here figured as essential to its very nature. Although what Heidegger here describes may seem dizzying from a conceptual or representational perspective, if the whole point of thinking/thanking is to come into a non-conceptual and non-representational understanding of Being, then this dizziness simply testifies to the metaphysician's failure to embody gratitude.

It is important to note that the devotion that Heidegger speaks of here is not directed at (or at least, needn't be directed at) God—understood as a creator or a first cause—but instead at the essential mystery of "what gives thought," and remains ever "to be thought." And it is also important to note that the thanksgiving that Heidegger describes here is not to be conflated with the thanks that we might express when we receive an ontic gift, such as a new bicycle, or a sunny day, or even a "miraculous" cure for a life-threatening disease. Instead, as Heidegger expressly puts it, "Thinking [...] does not need to repay, nor be deserved, in order to give thanks."[21] Or again, "Real thanks [...] never consists in that we ourselves come bearing gifts, and merely repay gift with gift. Pure thanks is rather that we simply think—think what is really and solely given, what is there to be thought."[22] In his *Country*

die Mitgift unseres Wesens, das Denken, verdanken. Insofern wir das Bedenklichste denken, danken wir." GA 8, 151.

[20] Ibid.

[21] Ibid.

[22] Ibid., 143.

Path Conversations, Heidegger's "Guide" puts this point even more strongly, suggesting that "forbearing noble-mindedness" (*der langmü- tige Edelmut*) is characterized by the kind of thinking "which does not first express gratitude *for something*, but rather simply thanks for being allowed to thank" (my emphasis).[23]

Heidegger's claim that true thanking is marked not by thankfulness *for* an object, but instead by "being allowed to thank," is crucial, we will see, for both tracing its connection to *Angst* (which likewise has no direct object) as well as for appreciating what is so potentially radical about it. But before we can pursue that argument, we need to emphasize that Heidegger's suggestive remarks on the connections between thinking (*Denken*), thanking (*Danken*), and recollective or meditative thinking (*Andenken*) are not quite argued for by Heidegger so much as they are rhetorically performed. As such, my interpretation of Heidegger's remarks constitutes a constructive, rather than an exegetical account of what they give us to think. Consequently, I will be placing a different emphasis on Heidegger's words than Heidegger himself did. In particular, I seek to emphasize that thinking is most powerfully enacted as a posture of *thanking*. By contrast, Heidegger himself, in the above passages, seems to place the emphasis differently, arguing that thanking is most basically enacted as *thinking*, and in particular, thinking what is "there to be thought." Ultimately, this difference in inflection needn't matter. In thinking (in the expansive sense) we come to be thankful, and in giving thanks (in the expansive sense), we come to be thoughtful. And yet, by emphasizing that thinking is *thanking*, rather than that thanking is *thinking*, the larger argument of this book is more forcefully expressed, namely that thinking is most authentically embodied in a non-objectivist, non-subjectivist posture of engaged receptivity to what cannot be conceptualized, because it is both congruous with and non-congruous with Dasein. Moreover, in emphasizing that thinking is *thanking*, just as we emphasized in Chapter 4 that thinking is *listening*, we indicate that the stakes of ontology are not idiosyncratic to those who are called "thinkers," but directly relevant to the challenges of everyday life that confront each and every Dasein as the being whose being is both singularly and socially charged. Understanding that thinking is *thanking*, we will see, means understanding that Heidegger's critique of metaphysics is aimed

---

[23] *Country Path Conversations*, 97; GA 77, 148.

not simply at *what* metaphysics fails to think, but more crucially, at *how* it defines thinking itself. To say that thinking is thanking, in other words, is to say that, when we take the critique of metaphysics to heart, we don't simply internalize a different theory about what "Being" signifies, but we come to live differently, and in particular, come to live with an abiding sense of gratitude. As Heidegger writes, "[T]here are matters concerning thought [*Sachen im Denken*] not only where a concept fails, but where it does not belong at all."[24] And, "We may have a correct idea of what is being talked about [in a text], and yet may not have let ourselves become involved in what is being said."[25] With passages such as these, Heidegger suggests that thinking cannot simply be conflated with conceptual comprehension, but is more robustly and essentially understood as an embodied posture of non-conceptual openness to what gives thought, i.e., to the singular occurrence of meaningfulness as it unfolds in each moment.

Heidegger does not argue in a sustained or systematic way that gratitude is an authentic way that we can respond to the modern metaphysical condition for a variety of reasons that we have already examined in previous chapters. First, to do so would be to risk sounding metaphysically prescriptive, treating gratitude as if it were a categorical imperative whose "value" stood above time and place and whose meaning could be generically defined. Second, to do so would risk sounding subjectivist, turning gratitude into something that *we* as individual subjects must perfect on our own. Third, to do so might risk being misinterpreted as a theological claim that gratitude is "owed" to a transcendental giver, personified as God. Fourth, to do so might risk being misinterpreted as a servile acceptance of the status quo and a forfeiture of all judgment and discernment. And yet despite these reasons that might have prevented Heidegger from developing his brief suggestions that thinking and thanking belong together, he did write in 1974 that "[m]ore endowing than poetizing/More founding than thinking/ Remains gratitude."[26] To understand why this might be the case, we now turn to Heidegger's essay on Hölderlin, "...Poetically Man Dwells..."

[24] *Zollikon Seminars*, 97; GA 89, 126.
[25] *What Is Called Thinking?*, 85.
[26] GA 16, 741.

"Full of Merit, Yet..."

Commenting on Hölderlin's lines, "Full of merit, yet, poetically man/ Dwells on this earth" (*Voll Verdienst, doch dichterisch, wohnet/ Der Mensch auf dieser Erde*), Heidegger suggests that although the word "*yet*" (*doch*) seems to "introduce a restriction on the profitable, meritorious dwelling of man," in fact, "it is just the reverse."[27] Instead, Heidegger wants us to read the opening phrase, "Full of merit," diminutively, and the "yet, poetically" as its redemptive turn. In this way, Heidegger indicates that what warrants our deepest attention and appreciation is not our ontic accomplishments (merits), but rather our ontological condition itself—the fact that we dwell poetically "on this earth." Thus, Heidegger writes, "Merits due to [human] building [...] can never fill out the nature of dwelling. On the contrary, they even deny dwelling its own nature when they are pursued and acquired purely for their own sake."[28] Here, Heidegger indicates that too much obsession with merit in the ontic sense—too much pursuit of "success"—obscures our ability to recognize and affirm the source of our projects as what is most worthy of thought and as what gives meaning to our projects. And what is this source, according to Heidegger? None other than the fact that we dwell "on this earth," that is, that we are "mortals," beings whose being is essentially constituted by finitude. As Heidegger later explains, "Man exists as a mortal. He is called mortal because he can die. To be able to die means to be capable of death as death. Only man dies—and indeed continually, so long as he stays on this earth, so long as he dwells."[29] Thus, what Heidegger seems to be saying, if we read him closely, is that our ontic merits can never take away or diminish our essential mortality. If anything, they simply testify to our mortality as the basis for our capacity to formulate and pursue our projects in the first place. Heidegger's reading of the "yet," or the *doch*, in other words, repeats his claim in *Being and Time*, that the essence of who we are is most basically grasped not by appealing to some "innerworldly" definition of what we have done or can do, but instead as "care." "Care," in turn, however, Heidegger writes, "is being-toward-death."[30]

[27] "...Poetically Man Dwells...," 214.
[28] Ibid., 215
[29] Ibid.
[30] SZ, 329/ BT, 303.

And note that by "being-toward-death," Heidegger does not simply mean the vague awareness that some day in the future we will cease
breathing, but instead, a fundamental structure of being-in-the-world
that accompanies us in each moment. That is why Heidegger states
above that "we are continually dying." What he means is not that we
are "getting on in years," but rather, that in every moment, we are
always choosing (even when our choosing is not explicit or transparent)
to enact certain possibilities of being and not others. Moreover, we are
always dying, because no matter what possibilities we end up enacting
these will themselves always be susceptible to further revision and repetition. Thus, the ineradicable "yet," which both animates and haunts our
projects, is also a marker of our essential incompleteness. All of the above
accords with Heidegger's much-discussed argument that *Angst* is constitutive of Dasein.

And yet, if we consider that Heidegger wants us to read this "yet"
positively, i.e., as showing that *dwelling poetically on this earth* is in fact
more worthy of praise or awe than being "full of [ontic] merit," then
these same lines can also be read an injunction to gratitude. The "yet"
can then be read as saying something like, "Don't just be grateful for
what human will and enterprise can accomplish. Be grateful for the very
mysterious non-ground on which such will and enterprise are made possible and meaningful." Or, "Don't just celebrate human building. Also
celebrate human dwelling." And here, the line "on this earth" gives this
point full force. For if buildings reach up into the sky, giving humans
the sense that they have transcended their earthly condition, Heidegger's
contention is that dwelling poetically precisely means accepting and
acknowledging our condition as earth-bound, which means, as he puts it
in *Being and Time*, "not to be bypassed." As he writes, "As a potentiality
of being, Da-sein is unable to bypass the possibility of death. Death is
the possibility of the absolute impossibility of Da-sein. Thus *death* reveals
itself as the *ownmost nonrelational possibility not to be bypassed.*"[31] Thus,
the "yet," in Hölderlin's poem, as parsed by Heidegger, testifies to a
possible congruence between anxiety and gratitude. On the one hand, it
repeats the claim of *Being and Time* that anxiety is the primary basis for
care. On the other hand, however, it also suggests that anxiety enables us
to "dwell poetically on this earth," which is to say, to care about (our)

---

[31] SZ, 251/ BT, 232.

Being in a way that doesn't just seek to avoid or repress our constitutive finitude, but enables us to embrace it.

In addition, the "yet" speaks to a congruence between anxiety and gratitude insofar as it anticipates what is to come, that is, what is "not yet." This "yet" evokes anxiety, because the ultimate destination of Dasein is "the possibility of its impossibility." Yet it can also elicit gratitude precisely because it reveals the present not as a fixed point, but as an ecstatic site where possibilities are perpetually disclosed, gathered, and transformed.

A final point of intersection between anxiety and gratitude is in the fact that neither one takes a direct object. As Heidegger writes,

> Anxiety is indeed anxiety in the face of..., but not in the face of this or that thing. Anxiety in the face of...is always anxiety for...but not for this or that. The indeterminateness of that in the face of which and for which we become anxious is no mere lack of determination but rather the essential impossibility of determining it.[32]

Likewise, Heidegger writes that gratitude (in the ontological sense) cannot simply be accounted for in terms of the ontic gifts that occasions it:

> We receive many gifts, of many kinds. But the highest and really most lasting gift given to us is always our essential nature, with which we are gifted in such a way that we are only through it. That is why we owe thanks for this endowment, first and unceasingly.[33]

In this latter passage, Heidegger indicates that true gratitude is directed not at this or that particular thing, but rather for the gift of "our essential nature." And what is that essential nature? Dasein. Therefore, as should now be clear, anxiety and gratitude are each authentic ways that Dasein can come to self-understanding. Moreover, because they are ontological, and not simply ontic categories, the difference between them cannot simply be reckoned psychologically. Instead, it is more appropriate to say that Dasein is both essentially anxious and essentially gifted, and that when Dasein says "yes" to its anxiety, it enacts a posture of gratitude. Meanwhile, when Dasein comes to embody gratitude, in the ontological

---

[32] "What Is Metaphysics?," 100–101.
[33] *What Is Called Thinking?*, 142.

sense, Dasein does not simply dissolve its anxiety, but rather it appreciates anxiety as a crucial condition for the possibility of meaning. In short, gratitude and anxiety overlap, precisely because both are capable of recognizing that, as Heidegger writes, "a boundary is not that at which something stops but [...] that from which something *begins its presencing*."[34] Having seen that gratitude and anxiety are not mutually exclusive, we can now elaborate on the ethical and theological ramifications of Heidegger's conception of thinking as a posture of gratitude.

First, to the ethical ramifications. As we have seen in previous chapters, ontological responsibility and onto-ethical sensitivity are interlinked. Therefore, although Heidegger does not indicate explicitly that gratitude is a posture we might display toward others, this does not mean that it has nothing to do with others. Instead, as we saw in the previous chapter, learning to be grateful for Being (meaningfulness) and learning to be grateful for the existence/presence of others are imbricated. Even though gratitude for Being as such is not reducible to gratitude for beings, we come to gratitude for Being only by way of gratitude for beings. As such, ontological gratitude and ontic gratitude needn't be opposed. In fact, ontic gratitude is our best reminder of and pathway toward the basic human capacity for ontological gratitude. Meanwhile, ontological gratitude is not just an abstract gratitude that we "feel" for beings in general, but is a gratitude that emerges precisely in the midst of our particular, thrown situation.

Note, too, that gratitude for Being as such does not mean that we have to "like" or "accept" in the ontic sense, the particulars that constitute our situation. To be grateful for Being (meaningfulness) does not mean that I must be grateful for torture or famine or political corruption. Rather, it more plausibly means that I can be grateful for the conditions that enable me to judge, condemn, and seek to curtail such injustices. In other words, the advantage of defining gratitude as an ontological posture, i.e., as a way of being, is that its truth can never simply be decided on the basis of empirical evidence. Gratitude for Being (meaningfulness), and for being Dasein, does not depend for its justification on the world being good or just or created by God, but is simply the most authentic way that we can recognize, acknowledge, and affirm our constitutive finitude as a positive condition rather than regard it as something to overcome.

[34] "Building Dwelling Thinking," 152.

Obviously, the above stance is not without an implicit theology, and an implicit faith—the suicidal might say, "a prejudice"—that existence is "better" than non-existence. As Raymond Geuss writes,

> Any of us who have survived to become more or less functional adults have done so in part because as infants we lived in a "good enough" world, and so any survivors form a possible audience for a true naturalistic theodicy: For them, at any rate, the world was sufficiently rational and good, and with sufficient empirical knowledge one could tell a true story about how their empirical world provided an environment which allowed them to become the functional agents capable of affirmation and self-affirmation they have become.[35]

Yet Geuss's argument doesn't entail a refutation of gratitude. Of course, we can always refuse gratitude, citing any number of traumatic circumstances as "a reason" not to be grateful, and yet the posture of gratitude that ontology enables, I claim, is not one that denies or justifies these traumas, but rather one that seeks to find in them a "saving power." As Heidegger writes, "The self-refusal of the truth of Beyng" allows itself to be felt not simply as a defeat or a rejection, but instead as "a yet ungranted grace" (*die noch ungewährte Gunst*).[36]

No doubt, there is a delicate line to be walked between trivializing or instrumentalizing suffering, on the one hand, and obsessively refusing to acknowledge anything else as true, on the other. As Charles Scott puts it:

> The question we face with regard to suffering is whether we can care for it without the hope of curing it. Can we work with passion to eliminate torture, to feed and clothe those who suffer deprivation, to recognize and respond to suffering as we find it every day, and yet not domesticate it and thereby proliferate it blindly in a system of meaning and virtue? Can we live in the perpetual mourning that is here prescribed without becoming morbid and ineffectual? These are questions directly related to the question of authenticity in which we face the issue of living properly with

---

[35] Raymond Geuss, "Art and Theodicy," in *Morality, Culture and History: Essays on German Philosophy* (Cambridge: Cambridge University Press, 1999), 109.

[36] GA 79, 73; "The Turning," 43. For an essay that places this quotation within a larger analysis of Heidegger's thinking on grace, see Andrew Mitchell, "The Exposure of Grace: Dimensionality in the Later Heidegger," *Research in Phenomenology* 40, no. 1 (2010): 313, 309–330.

our being in the alien, meaningless, and ungraspable difference that we undergo visa-a-vis our being. Our "most proper" living is found not in the rightness of our values or of our ethos but in a demanding alertness that intensifies our sense of suffering in the absence of its resolution or removal.[37]

Scott's conclusion that authenticity involves "a demanding alertness that intensifies our sense of suffering," is—on the face of it—patently at odds with gratitude, which incites quietude and peacefulness rather than deep suffering.

And yet, as we have seen, gratitude, understood in the ontological sense, is perfectly compatible with Scott's claims, for gratitude, in the essential sense, does not mean gratitude at the expense of dispositions such as melancholy or rage, but a more originary openness that recognizes "the clearing" as the nondual space in which any disclosure can occur. Gratitude, in other words, cannot simply be reckoned as an attitude—this would be to understand it subjectivistically and metaphysically. Instead, gratitude is better understood as a way of being in which we recognize "the clearing" as something that both happens *to* us and happens *through* us, i.e., as something which transcends our egoic, rational will, and yet which could not occur without our singular presence as Dasein. Such "recognition," we have repeatedly seen, is not strictly a mental process, but instead a holistic adjustment of how we embody our understanding of Being.

Thus, the ethical ramifications of embodying a posture of gratitude are palpable and not simply theoretical, just as the ethical ramifications of embodying a posture of listening were also shown in Chapter Three to be palpable and not simply theoretical. Both gratitude and thinking allow the world to emerge as something whose essential worth is not reducible to calculative demands for efficiency and productivity. And both enable us to understand ourselves and others in non-objectivist and non-subjectivist terms. Gratitude, finally, enables us to treat our essential limitations and the limitations of others not as counts against us, but as the unique basis on which we can come to a sense of meaningfulness and responsibility.

---

[37] Scott, *The Question of Ethics*, 119.

What are the theological ramifications of understanding gratitude as an authentic human posture? One is that traditional religious practices of thanksgiving embodied in prayer (even when they are addressed explicitly to God) can be crucial ways that we come to a non-instrumental relation to truth, a positive understanding of finitude, and a non-subjectivist and non-objectivist understanding of who we are. And this is so even when the content of the prayers, if analytically dissected, might reveal metaphysical propositions that would be unacceptable if taken ousiologically, rather than phenomenologically. Since, however, the utterance of a prayer in chant or song or silence, is not the same as the declaration of a philosophical statement, religious prayers can be understood "poetically," that is, as a way of coming into existential proximity to language as "the house of being," and for those given over to the power of the word "God," God. At the same time, understanding that gratitude is an authentic human posture gives "non-believers" the possibility of something akin to a religious life—or to put it even more strongly, reveals the essence of Dasein to be "religious" in an ontological sense. For it shows that gratitude is not simply a matter of paying back a debt, or of uttering the proposition, "the world is fundamentally good," but is most basically a way of being that is its own reward and needs no external justification. Gratitude reveals the self to be something other than just a subject and the world to be something other than just an object, yet it does so, not by arguing this point in propositional language, but by disclosing it in the most immediate, tangible way.

As we have seen above, ontological gratitude is not a posture that undoes our essential negativity and incompleteness but is rather a posture in which this negativity and incompleteness are reconceived as gifts. A metaphysical theologian might insist that these gifts are *evidence* of God's existence, and perhaps such an insistence serves a pedagogic function, reminding us that we *ought* to be more grateful even when we are not. But from an ontological perspective, the gift of being here needn't appeal to a giver to be considered a gift. Instead, Being (meaningfulness) simply becomes a gift when we are thankful.

CHAPTER 7

Conclusion

> Honesty, authenticity, integrity without love may lead to the ruin of others, of oneself, or both. On the other hand, love, fervor, or exaltation alone may seduce us into living in a fool's Paradise—a wise man's Hell.[1]

> The time is destitute because it lacks the unconcealedness of the nature of pain, death, and love.[2]

This book has offered a constructive reading of Heidegger's thought, rather than a presentation of its intentional message, whatever that might have been. Instead of interpreting Heidegger reductively as either a pragmatist or a critical theorist or a mystic or a Western Zen master or a technology theorist or an individualist or a communitarian, it has sought to give each of these versions of Heidegger their respective due. In addition, it has sought to engage a variety of Heidegger's fiercest critics, most especially, Levinas and Adorno, so as to show that their criticisms, though trenchant, needn't be taken as the last word on ontology. Instead, ontology is more charitably read, we saw, as a practice that seeks to hold open a space where truth can be encountered non-instrumentally, where the human being can be encountered as Dasein (and not "the most important raw material"), and where Being (meaningfulness) can be encountered without falling into the metaphysical traps of

---

[1] Abraham Joshua Heschel, *A Passion for Truth* (London: Secker & Warburg, 1974), xv.

[2] Heidegger, "What Are Poets For?," 95.

© The Author(s) 2018   213
Z. Atkins, *An Ethical and Theological Appropriation
of Heidegger's Critique of Modernity*,
https://doi.org/10.1007/978-3-319-96917-6_7

subjectivism and objectivism. As such, this book showed that openness to our essential questionability, poetry, listening, attentiveness to the needs of others, and gratitude, are authentic ways that we can hold such a space open.

In particular, this book has demonstrated that Heidegger's thought needn't be taken as the death-knell of ethics and theology, but instead as an invitation to conduct them in a non-metaphysical way. Whether Heidegger himself saw his project as ethical or theological is another matter, and, as we have seen, one whose answer depends a great deal on what we expect the terms "ethical" and "theological" to signify. My argument, however, has been to show that ontology cannot simply be taken as an analytical project, which takes "Being" (meaningfulness) as an object of detached study, but must be understood instead as an injunction to "become who we are." This conclusion is already succinctly captured in Heidegger's claim in *Being and Time* that ontology, phenomenology, and hermeneutics belong together, as well as in his claim that "we must [...] be careful not to misinterpret [phenomenology] as one movement among other 'movements' and schools of philosophy."[3] Yet my book has sought to focus Heidegger's charge by examining the ways in which the legacy of modern metaphysics has made it especially difficult to "become who we are." In so doing, it has sought to show that ontology can be taken up as both a critical and a constructive project, even though Heidegger himself remained—for reasons consistent with his thought—mostly on the critical side. Ontology cannot offer concrete directives when it comes to everyday questions, yet by framing these questions as questions of meaningfulness, by reminding us that it is our finitude that makes their resolution possible, and by showing us that language is both a site of revelation and concealment, it can help us come to terms with them in ways that honor who we are as beings whose being is both singular and social.

[3] *Zollikon Seminars*, 131–132; GA 89, 172.

BIBLIOGRAPHY

WORKS BY HEIDEGGER (IN GERMAN)

GA 4: *Erlaüterungen zu Hölderlin's Dichtung* (1936–1938). Frankfurt am Main: Vittorio Klostermann, 1981.

GA 5: *Holzwege* (1935–1946). Frankfurt am Main: Vittorio Klostermann, 1977.

GA 6: *Nietzsche II* (1936–1946). Frankfurt am Main: Vittorio Klostermann, 1997.

GA 7: *Vorträge und Aufsätze* (1936–1953). Frankfurt am Main: Vittorio Klostermann, 2000.

GA 8: *Was Heißt Denken?* (1951–1952). Frankfurt am Main: Vittorio Klostermann, 2002.

GA 9: *Wegmarken* (1919–1961). Frankfurt am Main: Vittorio Klostermann, 1976.

GA 10: *Der Satz vom Grund* (1955–1956). Frankfurt am Main: Vittorio Klostermann, 1997.

GA 11: *Identität und Differenz* (1955–1957). Frankfurt am Main: Vittorio Klostermann, 2006.

GA 12: *Unterwegs zur Sprache* (1950–1959). Frankfurt am Main: Vittorio Klostermann, 1983.

GA 13: *Aus der Erfahrung des Denkens* (1910–1976). Frankfurt am Main: Vittorio Klostermann, 1983.

GA 14: *Zur Sache des Denkens* (1962–1964). Frankfurt am Main: Vittorio Klostermann, 2007.

GA 15: *Vier Seminare* (1951–1973). Frankfurt am Main: Vittorio Klostermann, 1986.

© The Editor(s) (if applicable) and The Author(s),
under exclusive license to Springer Nature Switzerland AG 2018
Z. Atkins, *An Ethical and Theological Appropriation
of Heidegger's Critique of Modernity*,
https://doi.org/10.1007/978-3-319-96917-6

GA 16: *Einführung in die Phänomenologische Forschung* (1923–1924). Frankfurt am Main: Vittorio Klostermann, 2000.

GA 26: *Metaphysische Anfangsgründe der Logik im Ausgang von Leibniz*. Frankfurt am Main: Vittorio Klostermann, 1978.

GA 36/37: *Sein und Wahrheit* (1933–1934). *1. Die Grunfrage der Philosophie. 2. Vom Wesen der Wahrheit*. Frankfurt am Main: Vittorio Klostermann, 2001.

GA 39: *Hölderlin's Hymnen "Germanien" und "Der Rhein"* (1934–1935). Frankfurt am Main: Vittorio Klostermann, 1980.

GA 40: *Einführung in die Metaphysik* (1935). Frankfurt am Main: Vittorio Klostermann, 1983.

GA 42: *Schelling: Vom Wesen der Menschlichen Freiheit* (1936). Frankfurt am Main: Vittorio Klostermann, 1988.

GA 53: *Der Ister* (1942). Frankfurt am Main: Vittorio Klostermann, 1984.

GA 54: *Parmenides* (1942–1943). Frankfurt am Main: Vittorio Klostermann, 1982.

GA 55: *Heraklit* (1943–1944). Frankfurt am Main: Vittorio Klostermann, 1979.

GA 59: *Phänomenologie Religiosen Lebens* (1920–1921). Frankfurt am Main: Vittorio Klostermann, 2011.

GA 64: *Der Begriff der Zeit* (1924). Frankfurt am Main: Vittorio Klostermann, 2004.

GA 65: *Beiträge zur Philosophie (Vom Ereignis)* (1936–1938). Frankfurt am Main: Vittorio Klostermann, 1989.

GA 66: *Besinnung* (1938–1939). Frankfurt am Main: Vittorio Klostermann, 1997.

GA 71: *Das Ereignis* (1941–1942). Frankfurt am Main: Vittorio Klostermann, 2009.

GA 77: *Feldweg-Gespräche* (1944–1945). Frankfurt am Main: Vittorio Klostermann, 1995.

GA 81: *Gedachtes* (1910–1975). Frankfurt am Main: Vittorio Klostermann, 2007.

GA 89: *Zollikoner Seminare—Zwiegespräche—Briefe* (1959–1971). Frankfurt am Main: Vittorio Klostermann, 1987.

SZ: *Sein und Zeit* (1927). Tübingen: Max Niemayer Verlag. 2006.

Works by Heidegger (in English)

"The Age of the World Picture." In *The Question Concerning Technology and Other Essays*, 115–154. Translated by William Lovitt. New York: 1977, Harper & Row.

Basic Concepts of Aristotelian Philosophy. Translated by Robert D. Metcalf and Mark B. Tanzer. Bloomington and Indianapolis: Indiana University Press, 2009.

The Basic Problems of Phenomenology. Translated by Albert Hofstadter. Bloomington: Indiana University Press, 1982.

Becoming Heidegger: On the Trail of His Early Occasional Writings, 1910–1927. Edited by Theodore Kisiel and Thomas Sheehan. Evanston: Northwestern University Press, 2007.

Being and Time. Translated by Joan Stambaugh. Albany: State University of New York, 1996.

Being and Truth. Translated by Gregory Fried and Richard Polt. Bloomington: Indiana University Press, 2010.

"Building Dwelling Thinking." In *Poetry, Language, Thought*, 141–161. Translated by Albert Hofstadter. New York: Harper & Row, 1971.

Contributions to Philosophy (Of the Event). Translated by Richard Rojcewicz and Daniela Vallega-Neu. Bloomington: Indiana University Press, 2012.

Discourse on Thinking. Translated by John M. Anderson and E. Hans Freund. Harper & Row: New York, 1969.

Elucidations of Hölderlin's Poetry. Translated Keith Hoeller. Amherst, NY: Humanity Books, 2000.

"The End of Philosophy and the Task of Thinking" (television interview). http://www.youtube.com/watch?v=qouZC17_Vsg. Accessed March 18, 2013.

The Essence of Truth: On Plato's Cave Allegory and Theaetetus. Translated by Ted Sadler. London: Continuum, 2009.

Four Seminars. Translated by Andrew Mitchell and F. Raffoul. Bloomington: Indiana University Press, 2003.

The Fundamental Concepts of Metaphysics: World, Finitude, Solitude. Translated by Wiliam McNeill and Nicholas Walker. Bloomington and Indianapolis: Indiana University Press, 1995.

History of the Concept of Time: Prolegomena. Translated by Theodore Kisiel. Bloomington and Indianapolis: Indiana University Press, 1992.

Hölderlin's Hymn "Der Ister." Translated by William McNeill and Julia Davis. Bloomington: Indiana University Press, 1996.

Identity and Difference. Translated by Joan Stambaugh. Chicago: University of Chicago Press, 2002.

Introduction to Metaphysics. Translated by Gregory Fried and Richard Polt. New Haven and London: Yale University Press, 2000.

Kant and the Problem of Metaphysics, 5th ed. Edited and translated by Richard Taft. Bloomington and Indianapolis: Indiana University Press, 1997.

"Language." In *Poetry, Language, and Thought*, 185–208. Translated by Albert Hofstadter. New York: Harper & Row, 1971.

"Letter on Humanism." In *Basic Writings*, 213–267. Edited and translated by David Farrell Krell. New York: HarperCollins, 1993.

Logic: The Question of Truth. Translated by Thomas Sheehan. Bloomington and Indianapolis: Indiana University Press, 2010.

"Martin Heidegger Critiques Karl Marx—1969" (public television recording). https://www.youtube.com/watch?v=jQsQOqa0UVc. Accessed August 12, 2013.

The Metaphysical Foundations of Logic. Translated by Michael Heim. Bloomington: Indiana University Press, 1984.

Mindfulness. Translated by Parvis Emad and Thomas Kalary. London: Continuum, 2006.

Nietzsche: Volumes III and IV. Edited and translated by David Farrell Krell. HarperOne: San Francisco, 1991.

On Time and Being. Translated by Joan Stambaugh. Chicago: Chicago University Press, 2002.

On the Way to Language. Translated by Peter D. Herz. San Francisco: Harper & Row, 1982.

Ontology: The Hermeneutics of Facticity. Translated by John van Buren. Bloomington and Indianapolis: Indiana University Press, 2008.

"The Origin of the Work of Art." In *Basic Writings,* 139–213. Edited and translated by David Farrell Krell. New York: HarperCollins, 1993.

"Overcoming Metaphysics." In *The End of Philosophy.* Translated by Joan Stambaugh. New York: Harper & Row, 1973.

Parmenides. Translated by André Schuwer and Richard Rojcewicz. Bloomington: Indiana University Press, 1998.

"...Poetically Man Dwells..." *Poetry, Language, Thought,* 209–227. Translated by Albert Hofstadter. New York: Harper & Row, 1971.

The Phenomenology of Religious Life. Translated by Matthias Fritsch and Jennifer Anna Gosetti Ferencei. Bloomington and Indianapolis: Indiana University Press, 2010.

The Principle of Reason. Translated by Reginald Lilly. Bloomington: Indiana University Press, 1996.

"The Question Concerning Technology." In *The Question Concerning Technology and Other Essays,* 3–35. Translated by William Lovitt. New York: Harper & Row, 1977.

Schelling's Treatise: On the Essence of Human Freedom. Translated by Joan Stambaugh. Athens: Ohio University Press, 1985.

"Science and Reflection." In *The Question Concerning Technology and Other Essays,* 155–182. Translated by William Lovitt. New York: Harper & Row, 1977.

"The Thing." *Poetry, Language, Thought,* 161–184. Translated by Albert Hofstadter. New York: Harper & Row, 1971.

"The Turning." In *The Question Concerning Technology and Other Essays,* 36–49. Translated by William Lovitt. New York: Harper & Row, 1977.

"What Are Poets For?" *Poetry, Language, Thought,* 87–140. Translated by Albert Hofstadter. New York: Harper & Row, 1971.

What Is Called Thinking? Translated by Glenn J. Gray. New York: Harper & Row, 1968.

"What Is Metaphysics?" In *Existence and Being.* Translated by R.F.C. Hull and Alan Crick. Chicago: Henry Regnery and Co., 1988.

"What Is Metaphysics?" In *Basic Writings,* 89–111. Edited and translated by David Farrell Krell. New York: HarperCollins, 1993.

"The Word of Nietzsche: 'God Is Dead.'" In *The Question Concerning Technology and Other Essays,* 53–112. Translated by William Lovitt. New York: Harper & Row, 1977.

Zollikon Seminars: Protocols—Conversations—Letters. Edited by Medard Boss. Translated by Franz K. Mayr and Richard K. Askay. Evanston: Northwestern University Press, 2000.

OTHER SOURCES

Adorno, Theodor W. *Aesthetic Theory.* Translated by Christian Lenhardt. London: Routledge, 1986.

———. "Difficulties*." In *Essays on Music.* Edited by Richard Leppert. Translated by Susan H. Gillespie. Berkeley: University of California Press, 2002.

———. *Hegel: Three Studies.* Translated by Shierry Weber Nicholsen. Cambridge: MIT Press, 1994.

———. *Minima Moralia: Reflections from a Damaged Life.* Translated by E.F.N. Jephcott. London: Verso, 2006.

———. *Negative Dialectics.* Translated by E.B. Ashton. London. Routledge. 1973.

Anonymous. *The Cloud of Unknowing and Other Writings.* Translated by A.C. Spearing. London: Penguin, 2001.

———. *The Illuminated Pirkei Avot: Ethics of the Fathers.* Edited and translated by Rabbi Yonah Weinrib. Brooklyn: Mesorah Publications, 2002.

———. *Tanakh.* 2nd ed. Philadelphia: Jewish Publication Society, 1999.

Arendt, Hannah. *The Life of the Mind.* New York: Harcourt Brace, 1978.

———. "Tradition and The Modern Age." In *Between Past and Future,* 17–40. New York: Penguin, 2006.

Balakrishnan, Gopal. *The Enemy: An Intellectual Portrait of Carl Schmitt.* London: Verso, 2002.

Barrett, William. "Zen for the West." In *Zen Buddhism: Selected Writings of D.T. Suzuki.* Edited by William Barrett. New York: Image Books, 1996.

Bauman, Zygmunt. "Ethics of Individuals." *The Canadian Journal of Sociology* 25, no. 1 (2000): 83–96.

———. *Globalization: The Human Consequences.* Cambridge: Polity, 1998.

———. *Liquid Modernity.* Cambridge: Polity, 2000.

Benjamin, Walter. *Illuminations.* Translated by Harry Zohn. New York: Schocken, 1969.

Bernstein, Richard J. "Heidegger's Silence? Ethos and Technology." In *The New Constellation: The Ethical-Political Horizons of Modernity/Postmodernity*, 79–141. Cambridge: MIT Press, 1991.

———. *Violence: Thinking Without Banisters.* Cambridge: Polity, 2013.

Blanchot, Maurice. *The Writing of the Disaster.* Translated by Ann Smock. Lincoln: University of Nebraska Press, 1986.

Bloom, Allan. *The Closing of the American Mind.* New York: Simon & Schuster, 1987.

Bloom, Paul. "The Baby in the Well: The Failure of Empathy." In *The New Yorker*, May 20, 2013. http://www.newyorker.com/arts/critics/atlarge/2013/05/20/130520crat_atlarge_bloom?currentPage=all. Accessed May 4, 2014.

Blumenberg, Hans. *Work on Myth.* Translated by Robert M. Wallace. Cambridge: MIT Press, 1990.

Bourdieu, Pierre. *The Political Ontology of Martin Heidegger.* Translated by Peter Collier. Cambridge: Polity, 1991.

Bringhurst, Robert. "These Poems, She Said." In *The Beauty of the Weapons: Selected Poems 1972–1982.* Port Townsend: Cooper Canyon Press: 1982.

Buber, Martin. *I and Thou.* Translated by Ronald Gregor Smith. New York: Schocken, 1958.

———. *Tales of the Hasidim: The Late Masters.* Translated by Olga Marx. New York: Schocken, 1961.

Caputo, John D. *Against Ethics: Contributions to a Poetics of Obligation with Constant Reference to Deconstruction.* Bloomington: Indiana University Press, 1993.

———. *Demythologizing Heidegger.* Bloomington: Indiana University Press, 1993.

———. "Heidegger's Scandal: Thinking and the Essence of the Victim." In *The Heidegger Case: On Philosophy and Politics*, 265–281. Edited by Tom Rockmore and Joseph Margolis. Philadelphia: Temple University Press, 1992.

———. "Meister Eckhart and the Later Heidegger: The Mystical Element in Heidegger's Thought Part Two." *Journal of the History of Philosophy* 13, no. 1 (1975): 61–80.

———. *The Weakness of God: A Theology of the Event.* Bloomington: Indiana University Press, 2006.

Cavell, Stanley. "Aversive Thinking: Emersonian Representations in Heidegger and Nietzsche." In *Emerson's Transcendental Etudes*, 110–141. Stanford: Stanford University Press, 2003.

———. "Politics—As Opposed to What?" In *The Politics of Interpretation.* Edited by W.J.T. Mitchell. Chicago: University of Chicago Press, 1983.

Chesterton, G.K. *Orthodoxy.* New York: John Lane Co., 1908.

Connolly, William E. *Identity/Difference: Democratic Negotiations of Political Paradox.* Ithaca: Cornell University Press, 1991.

Dallmayr, Fred C. *The Other Heidegger.* Ithaca: Cornell University Press, 1993.

Dastur, François. "The Call of Conscience." In *Heidegger and Practical Philosophy,* 87–99. Edited by François Raffoul and David Pettigrew. Albany: SUNY Press, 2000.

DeBoer, Theodore. "An Ethical Transcendental Philosophy." In *Face to Face with Levinas,* 83–116. Edited by Richard A. Cohen. Albany: SUNY Press, 1986.

Derrida, Jacques. "Violence and Metaphysics: An Essay on the Thought of Emmanuel Levinas." In *Writing and Difference.* Translated by Alan Bass. Chicago: University of Chicago Press, 1980.

Dreyfus, Hubert. *Being-In-The-World: A Commentary on Heidegger's Being and Time, Division I.* Cambridge: MIT Press, 1991.

Dungey, Nicholas. "The Ethics and Politics of Dwelling." *Polity* 39, no. 2 (2007): 234–258.

Dussel, Enrique. *Philosophy of Liberation.* Translated by Aquilina Martinez. New York: Orbis Books, 1985.

Esposito, Roberto. *Communitas: The Origin and Destiny of Community.* Translated by Timothy Campbell. Stanford: Stanford University Press, 2010.

Fanon, Frantz. *The Wretched of the Earth.* Translated by Richard Philcox. New York: Grove Press, 2004.

Farías, Victor. *Heidegger and Nazism.* Edited by Joseph Margolis and Tom Rockmore. Translated by Paul Burrell. Philadelphia: Temple University Press, 1989.

Faye, Emmanuel. *Heidegger: The Introduction of Nazism into Philosophy in Light of the Unpublished Seminars of 1933–1935.* Translated by Tom Rockmore. New Haven: Yale University Press, 2011.

Feenberg, Andrew. *Questioning Technology.* London: Routledge, 1999.

Fiorenza, Elisabeth Schüssler. "G*d—The Many-Named—Without Place or Proper Name." In *Beyond Transcendence,* 109–128. Edited by John D. Caputo and Michael Scanlon. Bloomington: Indiana University Press, 2007.

Foti, Veronique M. "*Aletheia* and Oblivion's Field: On Heidegger's Parmenides Lectures." In *Ethics and Danger: Essays on Heidegger and Continental Thought,* 71–82. Edited by Arlene Dallery and Charles E. Scott. Albany: SUNY Press, 1992.

Freire, Paulo. *Pedagogy of the Oppressed.* Edited and Translated by Myra Bergman Ramos. New York: Continuum, 2005.

Freud, Sigmund. *Jokes and Their Relation to the Unconscious.* Translated by James Strachey. New York: Norton, 1989.

Fried, Gregory. *Heidegger's Polemos: From Being to Politics.* New Haven: Yale University Press, 2000.

Geertz, Clifford. "Deep Play: Notes on the Balinese Cockfight." In *The Interpretation of Cultures: Selected Essays*, 412–453. New York: Basic Books, 1973.

Gendlin, Eugene T. "*Befindlichkeit:* Heidegger and the Philosophy of Psychology." *Review of Existential Psychology & Psychiatry* 16, no. 1–3 (1978–79): 43–71. http://www.focusing.org/gendlin_befindlichkeit.html. Accessed March 20, 2013.

Geuss, Raymond. "Art and Theodicy." In *Morality, Culture and History: Essays on German Philosophy*, 78–116. Cambridge: Cambridge University Press, 1999.

Gordon, Peter Eli. "Heidegger in Black." *New York Review of Books*, October 9, 2014.

Grene, Marjorie. "Authenticity: An Existential Virtue." *Ethics* 62, no. 4 (1952): 266–274.

Grossman, Allen. *True-Love: Essays on Poetry and Valuing*. Chicago: University of Chicago Press, 2009.

Guignon, Charles. "Philosophy and Authenticity: Heidegger's Search for a Ground for Philosophizing." In *Heidegger, Authenticity, and Modernity: Essays in Honor of Hubert Dreyfus, Volume 1*. Edited by Mark Wrathall and Jeff Malpas, 79–103. Cambridge: MIT Press, 2000.

Habermas, Jürgen. *Moral Consciousness and Communicative Action*. Translated by Christian Lenhardt and Shierry Weber Nicholsen. Cambridge: MIT Press, 1995.

———. *The Theory of Communicative Action: Reason and the Rationalization of Society*. Translated by Thomas McCarthy. Cambridge: Polity Press, 1991.

———. "The Undermining of Western Rationalism Through the Critique of Modern Metaphysics: Martin Heidegger," 138–152. In *The Philosophical Discourse of Modernity. Twelve Lectures*. Translated by Frederick Lawrence. Cambridge: MIT Press, 1990.

Harman, Graham. *Guerilla Metaphysics: Phenomenology and the Carpentry of Things*. Peru, IL.: Open Court, 2005.

———. *Tool-Being: Heidegger and The Metaphysics of Objects*. Peru, IL: Open Court, 2002.

Harries, Karsten. "Heidegger as a Political Thinker." *The Review of Metaphysics* 29, no. 4 (1976): 642–669.

Hatab, Lawrence J. *Ethics and Finitude: Heideggerian Contributions to Moral Philosophy*. Oxford: Rowman & Littlefield, 2000.

Hegel, G.W.F. *Lectures on the Philosophy of Religion: Volume 1*. Translated by R.F. Brown, P.C. Hodgson, and J.M. Stewart. Berkeley: University of California Press, 1984.

———. *The Phenomenology of Spirit*. Translated by A.V. Miller. Oxford: Oxford University Press, 1977.

Heller-Roazen, Daniel. *Echolalias: On the Forgetting of Language.* New York: Zone, 2005.

Hemming, Lawrence Paul. *Heidegger's Atheism: The Refusal of a Theological Voice.* Notre Dame: Notre Dame University Press, 2002.

———. "Nihilism: Heidegger and the Grounds of Redemption." In *Radical Orthodoxy: A New Theology.* Edited by John Milbank, Catherine Pickstock, and Graham Ward. London: Routledge, 1999.

Heschel, Abraham Joshua. *God in Search of Man: A Philosophy of Judaism.* New York: JPS, 1959.

———. *A Passion for Truth.* London: Secker & Warburg, 1974.

Hodge, Joanna. *Heidegger and Ethics.* London: Routledge, 1995.

Huntington, Patricia. "Stealing the Fire of Creativity: Heidegger's Challenge to Intellectuals." In *Feminist Interpretations of Martin Heidegger,* 351–376. Edited by Nancy J. Holland and Patricia Huntington. University Park: Penn State University Press, 2001.

Ihde, Don. *Heidegger's Technologies: Postphenomenoloigcal Perspectives.* New York: Fordham University Press, 2010.

Irwin, Ruth. *Heidegger, Politics, and Climate Change: Risking It All.* London: Continuum, 2008.

James, P.D. *The Children of Men.* London: Penguin, 1994.

Jameson, Fredric. *Postmodernism, Or, The Cultural Logic of Late Capitalism.* London: Verso, 1991.

———. *Valences of the Dialectic.* London: Verso, 2010.

Jonas, Hans. *The Phenomenon of Life: Towards a Philosophical Biology.* Evanston: Northwestern University Press, 2001.

Kafka, Franz. *Franz Kafka: The Complete Stories.* Edited by Nachum Glatzer. New York: Schocken Books, 1971.

Kearney, Richard. *The God Who May Be: A Hermeneutics of Religion.* Bloomington: Indiana University Press, 2001.

King, Matthew. *Heidegger and Happiness: Dwelling on Fitting and Being.* London: Continuum, 2009.

Kleinberg-Levin, David Michael. "Usage and Dispensation: Heidegger's Meditation on the Hand." In *Gestures of Ethical Life: Reading Hölderlin's Question of Measure After Heidegger,* 204–274. Stanford: Stanford University Press, 2005.

Lacoue-Labarthe, Phillippe. *Heidegger, Art, and Politics: The Fiction of the Political.* Translated by Chris Turner. Hoboken: Wiley-Blackwell, 1990.

———. "Neither an Accident Nor a Mistake." Translated by Paula Wissing. *Critical Inquiry* 15, no. 2 (1989): 481–484.

Lasch, Christopher. *The Culture of Narcissism: American Life in an Age of Diminished Expectations.* New York: Norton, 1978.

Lazier, Benjamin. *God Interrupted: Heresy and the European Imagination Between the Wars.* Princeton: Princeton University Press, 2008.

Levin, David Michael. *The Body's Recollection of Being: Phenomenological Psychology and the Deconstruction of Nihilism.* London: Routledge, 1985.

Levinas, Emmanuel. *Difficult Freedom: Essays on Judaism.* Translated by Seán Hand. Baltimore: Johns Hopkins University Press, 1997.

———. *Entre Nous: Thinking-Of-The-Other.* Translated by Michael B. Smith and Barbara Harshav. New York: Columbia University Press, 1998.

———. *Ethics and Infinity: Conversations with Philippe Nemo.* Translated by Richard A. Cohen. Pittsburgh: Duquesne University Press 1982.

———. *Nine Talmudic Readings.* Translated by Annette Aronowicz. Bloomington: Indiana University Press, 1994.

———. *Otherwise than Being: Or Beyond Essence.* Translated by Alphonso Lingis. Duquesne University Press, 1998.

———. *Outside the Subject.* Translated by Michael B. Smith. London: Continuum, 2008.

———. "Peace and Proximity." In *Basic Philosophical Writings,* 161–170. Edited by Aadrian T. Peperzak, Simon Critchley, and Robert Bernasconi. Bloomington: University of Indiana Press, 1996.

———. "Reflections on the Philosophy of Hitlerism." Translated by Seán Hand. *Critical Inquiry* 17, no. 1 (1990): 63–71.

———. *Time and the Other.* Translated by Richard A. Cohen. Pittsburgh: Dusquesne University Press, 1987.

———. *Totality and Infinity: An Essay on Exteriority.* Translated by Alphonso Lingis. Pittsburgh: Duquesne University Press, 1969.

Lewis, Michael. *Heidegger and the Place of Ethics.* London: Continuum, 2005.

Lingis, Alphonso. *The Imperative.* Bloomington: Indiana University Press, 1998.

Macquarrie, John. *Principles of Christian Theology.* London: SCM Press, 1966.

Malpas, Jeffrey. *Heidegger's Topology: Being, Place, World.* Cambridge: MIT Press, 2007.

Marion, Jean-Luc. *God Without Being,* Translated by Thomas A Carlson. Chicago: University of Chicago Press, 1990.

Marx, Karl. *Capital, Volume One: A Critique of Political Economy.* Translated by Ben Fowkes. London: Penguin, 1976.

———. *The German Ideology.* Amherst, NY: Prometheus Books, 1998.

Marx, Werner. *Heidegger and The Tradition.* Translated by Theodore Kisiel. Evanston: Northwestern University Press, 1971.

———. *Is There a Measure on Earth? Foundations for a Nonmetaphysical Ethics.* Translated by Thomas J. Nenon and Reginald Lilly. Chicago: University of Chicago Press, 1987.

McCumber, John. *Poetic Interaction: Language, Reason, and Freedom.* Chicago: University of Chicago Press, 1989.

McNeill, William. *The Time of Life: Heidegger and Ethos.* Albany: SUNY Press, 2006.

Milbank, John. "The End of Dialogue." In *The Future of Love: Essays in Political Theology*. London: SCM Press, 2009.

———. *Theology and Social Theory: Beyond Secular Reason*. 2nd ed. Oxford: Blackwell, 2006.

Mitchell, Andrew. "The Exposure of Grace: Dimensionality in the Later Heidegger." *Research in Phenomenology* 40, no. 1 (2010): 309–330.

Mouffe, Chantal. *The Democratic Paradox*. London: Verso, 2005.

Moyn, Samuel. *The Origins of the Other: Emmanuel Levinas Between Revelation and Ethics*. Ithaca: Cornell University Press, 2005.

Mulhall, Stephen. *Wittgenstein and Heidegger: On Seeing Aspects*. London: Routledge, 1990.

Myerscough, Paul. "Short Cuts." *London Review of Books Online* 35, no. 1 (2013): 25. http://www.lrb.co.uk/v35/n01/paul-myerscough/short-cuts. Accessed April 24, 2013.

Nagel, Mecthild. "Thrownness, Playing-in-the-World, and the Question of Authenticity." In *Feminist Interpretations of Martin Heidegger*, 289–308. Edited by Nancy J. Holland and Patricia Huntington. University Park: Penn State University Press, 2001.

Nancy, Jean-Luc. *Being Singular Plural*. Translated by Robert Richardson and Anne O'Byrne. Palo Alto: Stanford University Press, 2000.

Nicholls, Peter. *George Oppen and the Fate of Modernism*. Oxford: Oxford University Press, 2007.

Nietzsche, Friedrich. *On the Advantage and Disadvantage of History for Life*. Translated by Peter Preuss. Indianapolis: Hackett, 1980.

Nishitani, Keiji. *Religion and Nothingness*. Translated by Jan van Bragt. Berkeley: University of California Press, 1982.

Olafson, Frederick A. *Heidegger and the Ground of Ethics: A Study of Mitsein*. Cambridge: Cambridge University Press, 1998.

Oppen, George. *Of Being Numerous*. New York: New Directions, 1968.

Pattison, George. *God and Being: An Enquiry*. Oxford: Oxford University Press, 2011.

———. *Heidegger and Death: A Critical Theological Essay*. Aldershot: Ashgate, 2013.

———. *The Routledge Philosophy Guidebook to The Later Heidegger*. London: Routledge, 2000.

Perez-Gomez, Alberto. *Built Upon Love: Architectural Longing After Ethics and Aesthetics*. Cambridge: MIT Press, 2006.

Philipse, Herman. "Heidegger and Ethics." *Inquiry* 42, nos. 3–4 (1999): 439–474.

Rancière, Jacques. "The Archaemodern Turn." In *Walter Benjamin and the Demands of History*. Edited by Michael P. Steinberg. Ithaca: Cornell University Press, 1996.

Raffoul, François. *The Origins of Responsibility*. Bloomington: Indiana University Press, 2010.

Richardson, William J. *Heidegger: From Phenomenology to Thought*. 4th ed. New York: Fordham University Press, 2003.

Richter, Gerhard. *Afterness: Figures of Following in Modern Thought and Aesthetics*. New York: Columbia University Press, 2011.

Ricouer, Paul. *Oneself as Another*. Translated by Kathleen Blamey. Chicago: University of Chicago Press, 1992.

Rockmore, Tom. *On Heidegger's Nazism and Philosophy*. Berkeley: University of California Press, 1992.

Rorty, Richard. *Contingency, Irony, and Solidarity*. Cambridge: Cambridge University Press, 1989.

———. "Heidegger, Contingency, and Pragmatism." In *Essays on Heidegger and Others: Philosophical Papers Volume 2*. Cambridge: Cambridge University, 1996.

Rose, Gillian. "Walter Benjamin: Out of the Sources of Modern Judaism." In *The Actuality of Walter Benjamin*. Edited by Laura Marcus and Lynda Nead. London: Lawrene & Wishart, 1998.

Rosenzweig, Franz. "Revelation and Law." In *On Jewish Learning*. Edited by Nachum Glatzer. Madison: University of Wisconsin Press, 2002.

———. *The Star of Redemption*. Translated by William W. Hallo. New York: Holt Rhineheart & Winston, 1970 (Reprint. University of Notre Dame Press, 1985).

Rosiek, Jan. *Maintaining the Sublime: Heidegger and Adorno*. Bern: Peter Lang, 2000.

Rubenstein, Mary-Jane. *Strange Wonder: The Closure of Metaphysics and The Opening of Awe*. New York: Columbia University Press, 2009.

———. "Thinking Otherwise." *The Immanent Frame*. December 3, 2010. http://blogs.ssrc.org/tif/2010/12/03/thinking-otherwise/. Accessed June 7, 2013.

Rubenstein, Richard. "The Philosopher and the Jews: The Case of Martin Heidegger." *Modern Judaism* 9, no. 2 (1989): 179–196.

Safranski, Rüdiger. *Martin Heidegger: Between Good and Evil*. Translated by Edwald Osers. Cambridge: Harvard University Press, 2002.

Sallis, John. *Phenomenology and the Return to Beginnings*. Pittsburgh: Dusquesne University Press, 1973.

Sartre, Jean-Paul. *The Problem of Method*. Translated by Hazel E. Barnes. London: Methuen & Co., 1963.

Schelling, F.W.J. *Philosophical Enquiries into the Nature of Human Freedom*. Translated by James Gutmann. La Salle: Open Court, 1992.

Schmidt, Dennis. "On the Sources of Ethical Life." *Research in Phenomenology* 42, no. 1 (2012): 35–48.

Schürmann,   Reiner.   *Broken   Hegemonies.*   Translated   by   Reginald   Lilly.
   Bloomington: Indiana University Press, 2003.
———. *Heidegger   on   Being   and   Acting: From   Principles   to   Anarchy.*
   Bloomington: Indiana University Press, 2003.
———. "Ultimate Double Binds." In *Heidegger Towards the Turn*, 243–268.
   Edited by James Risser. Albany: SUNY Press, 1999.
Scott, Charles E. "Heidegger and the Question of Ethics." *Research in
   Phenomenology* 18, no. 1 (1988): 23–40.
———. *The   Question   of   Ethics: Nietzsche,   Foucault,   Heidegger.*   Bloomington:
   Indiana University Press, 1990.
Sennett, Richard. *The Fall of Public Man.* Cambridge: Cambridge University
   Press, 1977.
Sheehan,   Thomas.   "Astonishing!   Things   Make   Sense!"   *Gatherings: The
   Heidegger Circle Annual* 1 (2011): 1–25.
———. "Dasein." In *A Companion to Heidegger*, 193–214. Edited by Hubert
   Dreyfus and Mark A. Wrathall. Blackwell: Oxford, 2007.
———. "A   New   Paradigm   in   Heidegger   Research."   *Continental   Philosophy
   Review* 34 (2002): 183–202.
———. "The Turn." In *Martin Heidegger: Key Concepts*, 82–97. Edited by Bret
   Davis. Durham: Acumen, 2010.
———. "The   Turn: All   Three   of   Them."   In   *The   Bloomsbury   Companion
   to Heidegger.* Edited by François Raffoul and Eric S. Nelson. London:
   Bloomsbury, 2013.
Sloterdjik,   Peter.   *Critique   of   Cynical   Reason.*   Translated   by   Michael   Eldridge.
   London: Verso, 1998.
———. *You Must Change Your Life: On Anthropotechnics.* Translated by Wieland
   Hoba. Cambridge: Polity Press, 2013.
Sluga, Hans. *Heidegger's Crisis: Philosophy and Politics in Nazi Germany.*
   Cambridge: Harvard University Press, 1993.
Stambaugh, Joan. "An Inquiry into Authenticity and Inauthenticity in *Being and
   Time.*" *Research in Phenomenology* 7, no. 1 (1977): 153–161.
Steiner, George. *Martin Heidegger.* Chicago: Chicago University Press, 1989.
Stern,   Günther.   "On   the   Pseudo-Concreteness   of   Heidegger's   Philosophy."
   Philosophy and Phenomenological Research 8, no. 3 (1948): 337–371.
Stiegler, Bernard. *Technics and Time 1: The Fault of Epimetheus.* Translated by Richard
   Beardsworth and George Colllins. Stanford: Stanford University Press, 1998.
Suzuki, Shunruyi. *Zen Mind: Beginner's Mind: Informal Talks on Zen Meditation
   and Practice.* Boston: Shambhala, 2011.
Taminaux, Jacques. "Heidegger on Values." In *Heidegger Towards the Turn*,
   225–242. Edited by James Risser. Albany: SUNY Press, 1999.
Taylor, Mark C. *Erring: A Post-modern A/Theology.* Chicago. University of
   Chicago Press, 1987.

Thomson, Iain. *Heidegger on Ontotheology: Technology and the Politics of Education*. Cambridge: Cambridge University Press, 2005.

———. "Heidegger on Ontological Education: Or How We Become What We Are." *Inquiry* 44 no. 3 (2001): 243–268.

———. "Understanding Technology Ontotheologically, or the Danger and the Promise of Heidegger, an American perspective." In *New Waves in Philosophy of Technology*, 147–166. Edited by Jan Kyrre Berg Olsen Friis, Evan Selinger and Søren Riis. London: Palgrave Macmillan, 2009.

Trungpa, Chögyam. *Cutting Through Spiritual Materialism*. Boston: Shambhala Press, 2002.

Van Buren, John. *The Young Heidegger: Rumor of the Hidden King*. Bloomington: University of Indiana Press, 1994.

Vedder, Ben. "Heidegger and Desire." *Continental Philosophy Review* 31, no. 4 (1998): 353–368.

———. *Heidegger's Philosophy of Religion: From God to the Gods*. Pittsburgh: Duquesne University Press, 2006.

Vogel, Lawrence. *The Fragile We: Ethical Implications of "Being and Time"*. Evanston: Northwestern University Press, 1994.

Wallace, David Foster. "E Unibus Pluram: Television and U.S. Fiction." *Review of Contemporary Fiction* 13, no. 2 (1993): 151–194.

Westphal, Merold. *Overcoming Onto-Theology: Towards a Postmodern Christian Faith*. New York: Fordham University Press, 2001.

White, Stephen K. "Heidegger and the Difficulties of a Postmodern Ethics and Politics." *Political Theory* 18, no. 1 (1990): 80–103.

Woessner, Martin. *Heidegger in America*. Cambridge: Cambridge University Press, 2010.

Wolfson, Elliot R. *The Duplicity of Philosophy's Shadow: Heidegger, Nazism and the Jewish Other*. New York: Columbia University Press, 2018.

———. "Gottwesen and the De-Divinization of the Last God: Heidegger's Meditation on the Strange and Incalculable." In *Heidegger's Black Notebooks and the Future of Theology*. Edited by Marten Björk and Jane Svenungsson. New York: Palgrave Macmillan, 2017.

Wolin, Richard. "Introduction: What Is Heideggerian Marxism?" In *Heideggerian Marxism: Herbert Marcuse*, ix–xxx. Edited by Richard Wolin and John Abromeit. Lincoln: University of Nebraska Press, 2005.

———. *Heidegger and the Politics of Being: the Political Thought of Martin Heidegger*. Cambridge: MIT Press, 1993.

———. "Kant at Ground Zero: Philosophers Respond to September 11." In *The Frankfurt School Revisited: And Other Essays on Politics and Society*. London: Routledge, 2006.

———. "National Socialism, World Jewry, and the History of Being: Heidegger's Black Notebooks." *Jewish Review of Books*. Summer, 2014.

Wood, David. *Time After Time*. Bloomington: Indiana University Press, 2007.

Wyschogrod, Edith. *The Spirit in Ashes: Hegel, Heidegger, and Man-Made Mass Death*. New Haven: Yale University Press, 1985.

Yerushalmi, Yosef Hayim. *Zakhor: Jewish History and Jewish Memory*. New York: Schocken, 1989.

Young, Julian. *Heidegger's Later Philosophy*. Cambridge: Cambridge University Press, 2002.

Zarader, Marlene. *The Unthought Debt: Heidegger and the Hebraic Heritage*. Translated by Bettina Bergo. Stanford: Stanford University Press, 2006.

Ziarek, Krzysztof. "Beyond Critique? Art and Power." In *Adorno and Heidegger: Philosophical Questions*, 105–123. Edited by Iain Macdonald and Krzysztof Ziarek. Stanford: Stanford University Press, 2008.

———. "Semiosis of Listening: The Other in Heidegger's Writings on Hölderlin and Celan's 'The Meridian.'" *Research in Phenomenology* 24, no. 1 (1994): 113–132.

Zimmerman, Michael. *Eclipse of the Self: Developments of Heidegger's Concept of Authenticity*. Athens: Ohio University Press, 1981.

———. *Heidegger's Confrontation with Modernity: Technology, Politics, Art*. Bloomington: Indiana University Press, 1991.

INDEX

Made in the USA
Coppell, TX
11 February 2021

50195826R00138